QUEUE

Reading Comprehension Long Passages

5

by Jonathan D. Kantrowitz
Edited by Patricia F. Braccio

Student Book ISBN: 978-0-7827-1220-9 • Class Pack ISBN: 978-0-7827-1221-6
Item Code QWK1522 • Copyright © 2005 Queue, Inc.

Queue, Inc. • 80 Hathaway Drive • Stratford, CT • 06615
(800) 232-2224 • Fax (800) 775-2729 • www.qworkbooks.com

Table of Contents

TO THE STUDENTS

In this reading comprehension workbook, you will read many fiction and nonfiction passages.   You will then answer multiple-choice and open-ended questions about what you have read.

As you read and answer the questions, please remember:

- You may refer back to the text as often as you like.

- Read each question very carefully and choose the **best** answer.

- Indicate the correct multiple-choice answers directly in this workbook. Circle or underline the correct answer.

- Write your open-ended responses directly on the lines provided. If you need more space to complete your answer, use a separate piece of paper.

Here are some guidelines to remember when writing your open-ended answers:

- Organize your ideas and express them clearly.

- Correctly organize and separate your paragraphs.

- Support your ideas with examples when necessary.

- Make your writing interesting and enjoyable to read.

- Check your spelling and use of grammar and punctuation.

- Your answers should be accurate and complete.

THE HAUGHTY PRINCESS

There was once a very worthy king whose daughter was the greatest beauty that could be seen far or near. She was very proud, however, and would agree to marry no king or prince. Her father was tired out at last. He invited every king, and prince, and duke, and earl that he knew or didn't know to come to his court to give her one trial more. They all came.

The next day after breakfast they stood in a row in the lawn. The princess walked along in the front of them to make her choice. One was fat. She said, "I won't have you, Beer-barrel!" One was tall and thin, and to him she said, "I won't have you, Ram-rod." To a white-faced man she said, "I won't have you, Pale Death," and to a red-cheeked man she said, "I won't have you, Cockscomb!"

She stopped a little before the last of all. He was a fine man in face and form. She wanted to find some defect in him, but he had nothing remarkable but a ring of brown curling hair under his chin. She admired him a little and then carried it off with, "I won't have you, Whiskers!"

So they all went away. The king was so vexed, he said to her, "Now to punish your impudence, I'll give you to the first beggarman or singing troubadour that calls." As sure as his shoulders, a fellow covered by rags, with hair that came to his shoulders and a bushy red beard all over his face, came next morning and began to sing before the parlor window.

When the song was over, the hall-door was opened, the singer asked in, the priest brought, and the princess married to Beardy. She roared and she bawled, but her father didn't mind her. "There," says he to the bridegroom, "is five guineas for you. Take your wife out of my sight, and never let me lay eyes on you or her again."

Off he led her and dismal enough she was. The only things that gave her relief were the tones of her husband's voice and his genteel manners. "Whose wood is this?" said she, as they were going through one. "It belongs to the king you called Whiskers yesterday." He gave her the same answer about meadows and cornfields, and at last a fine city.

"Ah, what a fool I was!" said she to herself. "He was a fine man, and I might have had him for a husband." At last they were coming up to a poor cabin. "Why are you bringing me here?" says the poor lady.

1

"This is my house," said he, "and now yours." She began to cry, but she was tired and hungry, and she went in with him.

Ovoch! there was neither a table laid out, nor a fire burning. She was obliged to help her husband to light it, and boil their dinner, and clean up the place after. The next day he made her put on a stiff gown and a cotton handkerchief. When she had her house readied up, and no business to keep her employed, he brought home sallies (willows), peeled them, and showed her how to make baskets. But the hard twigs bruised her delicate fingers, and she began to cry.

Well, then he asked her to mend their clothes, but the needle drew blood from her fingers and she cried again. He couldn't bear to see her tears, so he bought a creel of earthenware and sent her to the market to sell it. This was the hardest trial of all, but she looked so handsome and sorrowful, and had such a nice air about her, that all her pans, and jugs, and plates, and dishes were gone before noon. The only mark of her old pride was showed with a slap she gave an oaf across the face when he asked her an impudent question.

Well, her husband was so glad, he sent her with another creel the next day; but, faith! her luck was deserting her. A drunken huntsman came riding up. His beast got in among her ware and broke every mother's son of them. She went home crying. Her husband wasn't at all pleased. "I see," said he, "you're not fit for business. Come along, I'll get you a kitchen-maid's place in the palace. I know the cook."

So the poor thing was obliged to stifle her pride once more. She was kept very busy. The footman and the butler were very impudent about looking for a kiss, but she let a screech out of her when the first attempt was made, and the cook gave the fellow such a lambasting with the broom that he made no second offer. She went home to her husband every night, and she carried broken victuals wrapped in papers in her side pockets.

A week after she got service, there was great bustle in the kitchen. The king was going to be married, but no one knew who the bride was to be. Well, in the evening, the cook filled the princess' pockets with cold meat and pudding, and, says she, "Before you go, let us have a look at the great doings in the big parlor."

So they came near the door to get a peep, and who should come out but the king himself, as handsome as you please, and no other but King Whiskers himself. "Your handsome helper must pay for her peeping," said he to the cook, "and dance a jig with me." Whether she would or not, he held her hand and brought her into the parlor. The fiddlers struck up, and away went him and

2

her. But they hadn't danced two steps when the meat and the pudding flew out of her pockets. Everyone roared out and she flew to the door, crying piteously. However, she was soon caught by the king and taken into the back parlor.

"Don't you know me, my darling?" said he. "I am both King Whiskers, your husband the ballad-singer, and the drunken huntsman. Your father knew me well enough when he gave you to me, and all was to drive your pride out of you." Well, she didn't know how she was, with fright, and shame, and joy. Love was uppermost, anyhow, for she laid her head on her husband's breast and cried like a child.

The maids-of-honor soon had her away and dressed her as fine as hands and pins could do it; and there was her mother and father, too. While the company were wondering what would be the end of the handsome girl and the King, he and his Queen, whom they didn't know in her fine clothes, came in, and such rejoicings and fine doings as there was, none of us will ever see, anyway.

1. The princess called the _____ man "Ram-rod."

   a. fat
   b. thin
   c. white-faced
   d. red-cheeked

2. The princess compared the red-cheeked man to a

   a. beer barrel.
   b. stick.
   c. rooster.
   d. corpse.

3. The husband felt sorry for his wife when she

   a. complained about making dinner.
   b. complained about her clothes.
   c. complained about cleaning the house.
   d. cried out in pain.

4. Based on the context, what does "impudent," as used in the tenth and twelfth paragraphs, probably mean?

    a. offensive.
    b. bossy.
    c. modest.
    d. poor.

5. The only one to help the princess was the

    a. huntsman.
    b. footman.
    c. butler.
    d. cook.

6. Why was the princess embarrassed?

    a. She did not want to dance.
    b. She did not want to know how to dance.
    c. Meat and pudding fell out of her pocket.
    d. She had been caught peeping.

7. What is another way to write the following sentence?

His beast got in among her ware and broke every mother's son of them.

    a. He had been fighting for her pottery, but his mother refused to buy it.
    b. A great beast suddenly burst upon the scene and scared all the mothers and their sons.
    c. His horse managed to get in the middle of things and break all her pottery.
    d. His beast and he broke all the mother's son's wares.

8. Which of the following is probably **true**?

    a. The king did not know who the troubadour was.
    b. Most of the people in the palace found out who the kitchen maid was.
    c. The cook knew who the princess was.
    d. The footman and troubadour knew who the princess was.

9. Do you think the king was right to do what he did? Why or why not?

_____

_____

_____

_____

_____

_____

_____

_____

_____

_____

_____

_____

_____

_____

_____

_____

_____

_____

10. Do you think the princess was trying hard to please her husband? What evidence helps you decide?

_____

_____

_____

_____

_____

_____

_____

11. Did you like this story? Why or why not?

_____

_____

_____

_____

_____

_____

_____

THE VALLEY OF DIAMONDS

from "Voyages of Sinbad the Sailor" in **Arabian Nights**

My father was a rich merchant of Persia. He left me a large fortune, which I quickly spent. I grew weary of an idle life, and put to sea with some merchants that I knew. We went from island to island, buying and selling goods.

One day we landed on an island covered with several sorts of fruit trees, but we could see neither man nor animal. We walked in the meadows and along the streams. While some of the company amused themselves with gathering flowers and fruits, I took my provisions, and sat down near a stream between high trees. I made a good meal, and then fell asleep. I cannot tell how long I slept, but when I awoke, the ship was gone.

Not knowing what to do, I climbed to the top of a lofty tree, to see if I could discover any way of escape. When I gazed toward the sea I could see nothing but sky and water; but looking over toward the land, I saw something white. Coming down, I took what provision I had left, and went toward this object.

When I came near, I thought it to be a white dome of great size. I touched it, and found it to be very smooth. I went round to see if it were open on any side, but saw it was not, and that there was no climbing to the top, as it was so smooth. It was at least fifty paces round.

All of a sudden the sky became as dark as if it had been covered with a thick cloud. I looked up and saw a bird of monstrous size that came flying toward me. I had often heard sailors speak of a wonderful bird called the "roc," and I was now sure that the great dome must be its egg. And in fact, the bird lit and sat over the egg.

As I saw her coming, I crept close to the egg so that I had before me one of the legs of the bird, which was as big as the trunk of a tree. I tied myself strongly to the leg with my turban, hoping that the roc next morning would carry me with her out of this desert island.

The bird flew away as soon as it was daylight, and carried me so high that I could not see the earth. Then she came down so fast that I lost my senses. When I found myself on the ground, I quickly untied the knot. I had scarcely done so, when the roc, taking a great serpent in her bill, flew away.

The spot where the bird had left me was surrounded on all sides by mountains that seemed to reach above the clouds, and so steep that no man could climb them. I found that I had gained nothing by the change.

As I walked through this valley I saw that it was covered with diamonds of great size. I took pleasure in looking upon them. But soon I saw a great number of serpents. They were so monstrous that each of them could easily swallow an elephant. They went in the daytime into their dens, where they hid themselves from the roc, and came out only at night.

I spent the day walking about the valley, trying to discover a way of escape. When night came on, I went into a cave, where I might rest in safety. I closed the entrance with a great stone, to keep away the serpents. I supped on part of my provisions, but the loud hissing of the serpents put me into such fear that I could not sleep.

At daybreak the serpents left, and I came out of the cave trembling. I can truly say that I walked upon diamonds without feeling any desire to touch them. At last I sat down and after having eaten a little more of my provisions, I fell asleep, for I had not closed my eyes during the night.

But I had scarcely shut my eyes when something fell by me with a great noise, and awoke me. This was a large piece of raw meat; and at the same time I saw several others fall down from the rocks in different places.

I had heard sailors and others tell of the valley of diamonds, and of the means used by merchants to secure the jewels. The merchants come to the upper rim of the valley when the eagles have young ones, and throw great pieces of meat into the valley.

The diamonds, upon whose points they fall, stick to them. The eagles, seizing the meat in their claws, carry the jewels thus to their nests on the rocks. The merchants then run to the nests, drive off the eagles by their shouts, and take away the diamonds that stick to the meat.

I now saw the means of my escape. I gathered together the largest diamonds I could find. I put them into the leather bag in which I used to carry provisions. This I made fast to my girdle. I then took the largest of the pieces of meat, tied it close around me with my turban, and laid myself upon the ground.

Immediately one of the eagles picked me up with the piece of meat to which I was fastened, and carried me to its nest on the top of the mountain.

The merchants at once began their shouting to frighten the eagles. When they had forced them to quit their prey, one of them came to the nest where I was. He was amazed when he saw me, and began to quarrel with me, asking why I had stolen his goods.

"You will treat me with more kindness," said I, "when you know me better. Do not be uneasy. I have diamonds enough for you and myself too, more indeed than all the other merchants together. Whatever they have they owe to chance; but I chose for myself, in the bottom of the valley, those which you now see."

While I was speaking, the other merchants came crowding about us, much surprised to see me. They were even more amazed when I told them my story.

They took me to their camp, and when they opened my bag, they were indeed surprised at the size of my diamonds. They said that they had never seen any of such beauty. I asked the merchant who owned the nest to which I had been carried, to take as many for his share as he pleased. He took only one, and that, too, the smallest of them all. When I urged him to take more he said, "No, I am very well pleased with this. It will bring me as great a fortune as I desire."

I stayed with the merchants until they were ready to go home. Then we traveled many days across high mountains until we came to the sea, where we set sail. At last we reached Persia, and I settled down to enjoy my riches.

1. How was going out "to sea with some merchants" a way to solve the problem of being "weary of an idle life"?

   a. Sinbad was tired and he thought that the sea air would cure his fatigue.
   b. Sinbad needed more money, so he thought becoming a merchant would help him find it.
   c. Sinbad had been searching for something to do and he just happened to know some merchants.
   d. Sinbad's growing boredom made him think he might try traveling with some merchants.

2. What happened immediately after Sinbad ate his meal?

   a. He sat between some tall trees.
   b. He took a nap.
   c. His ship left.
   d. He walked in the meadow.

3. The white dome was actually

   a. a diamond.
   b. a roc.
   c. an egg.
   d. a salt mine.

4. Sinbad tied himself to the leg of the roc because he

   a. had always wanted to fly.
   b. wanted to eat the egg.
   c. was afraid of the roc.
   d. needed to escape.

5. How big was the roc?

   a. fifty paces around
   b. as big as a tree
   c. big enough to swallow an elephant
   d. bigger than all of the above

6. Why wasn't Sinbad interested in the diamonds?

   a. He had inherited a lot of money.
   b. He was too afraid of the serpents.
   c. He had decided to be poor.
   d. He did not know what diamonds were worth.

7. Why did Sinbad tie himself to a large piece of meat?

   a. He wanted to cook it.
   b. He wanted to eat it.
   c. He wanted diamonds to stick to it.
   d. He wanted to be lifted out of the valley.

8. Why did the merchants throw giant pieces of meat into the valley?

   a. They wanted to feed the serpents.
   b. They wanted diamonds to stick to them.
   c. They wanted to feed the eagles.
   d. They were afraid of the eagles.

9. Which of the following is the **best** adjective that could be used to describe Sinbad?

    a. clever
    b. clumsy
    c. panicked
    d. hot-tempered

10. Why was the merchant content with only one diamond?

from "TISH, THE CHRONICLES OF HER ESCAPADES AND EXCURSIONS"

by Mary Roberts Rinehart

That was how it happened that Bettina Bailey, sitting on Eliza Bailey's front piazza, decked out in chintz cushions,—the piazza, of course,—saw a dusty machine come up the drive and stop with a flourish at the steps. And from it alight, not one chaperon, but three.

After her first gasp Bettina was game. She was a pretty girl in a white dress and bore no traces in her face of any stern religious proclivities.

"I didn't know—" she said, staring from one to the other of us. "Mother said— that is—won't you go right upstairs and have some tea and lie down?" She had hardly taken her eyes from Tish, who had lifted the engine hood and was poking at the carburetor with a hairpin.

"No, thanks," said Tish briskly. "I'll just go around to the garage and oil up while I'm dirty. I've got a short circuit somewhere. Aggie, you and Lizzie get the trunk off."

Bettina stood by while we unbuckled and lifted down our traveling trunk. She did not speak a word, beyond asking if we wouldn't wait until the gardener came. On Tish's saying she had no time to wait, because she wanted to put kerosene in the cylinders before the engine cooled, Bettina lapsed into silence and stood by watching us.

Bettina took us upstairs. She had put Drummond's *Natural Law in the Spiritual World* on my table and a couch was ready with pillows and a knitted slumber robe. Very gently she helped us out of our veils and dusters and closed the windows for fear of drafts.

"Dear mother is so reckless of drafts," she remarked. "Are you sure you won't have tea?"

"We had some blackberry cordial with us," Aggie said, "and we all had a little on the way. We had to change a tire and it made us thirsty."

"Change a tire!"

Aggie had taken off her bonnet and was pinning on the small lace cap she wears, away from home, to hide where her hair is growing thin. In her cap

Aggie is a sweet-faced woman of almost fifty, rather ethereal. She pinned on her cap and pulled her crimps down over her forehead.

"Yes," she observed. "A bridge went down with us and one of the nails spoiled a new tire. I told Miss Carberry the bridge was unsafe, but she thought, by taking it very fast—"

Bettina went over to Aggie and clutched her arm. "Do you mean to say," she quavered, "that you three women went through a bridge—"

"It was a small bridge," I put in, to relieve her mind; "and only a foot or two of water below. If only the man had not been so disagreeable—"

"Oh," she said, relieved, "you had a man with you!"

"We never take a man with us," Aggie said with dignity. "This one was fishing under the bridge and he was most ungentlemanly. Quite refused to help, and tried to get the license number so he could sue us."

"Sue you!"

"He claimed his arm was broken, but I distinctly saw him move it." Aggie, having adjusted her cap, was looking at it in the mirror. "But dear Tish thinks of everything. She had taken off the license plates."

Bettina had gone really pale. She seemed at a loss, and impatient at herself for being so. "You—you won't have tea?" she asked.

"No, thank you."

"Would you—perhaps you would prefer whiskey and soda?"

Aggie turned on her a reproachful eye. "My dear girl," she said, "with the exception of a little home-made wine used medicinally, we drink nothing. I am the secretary of the Woman's Prohibition Party."

Bettina left us shortly after that to arrange for putting up Letitia and Aggie. She gave them her mother's room, and whatever impulse she may have had to put the *Presbyterian Psalter* by the bed, she restrained it. By midnight Drummond's *Natural Law* had disappeared from my table and a novel had taken its place. But Bettina had not lost her air of bewilderment.

That first evening was very quiet. A young man in white flannels called, and he and Letitia spent a delightful evening on the porch talking spark-plugs and carburetors. Bettina sat in a corner and looked at the moon. Spoken to, she replied in monosyllables in a carefully sweet tone. The young man's name was Jasper McCutcheon.

It developed that Jasper owned an old racing-car which he kept in the Bailey garage, and he and Tish went out to look it over. They very politely asked us all to go along, but Bettina refusing, Aggie and I sat with her and looked at the moon.

Aggie in her capacity as chaperon, or as one of an association of chaperons, used the opportunity to examine Bettina on the subject of Jasper.

"He seems a nice boy," she remarked. Aggie's idea of a nice boy is one who in summer wears fresh flannels outside, in winter less conspicuously. "Does he live near?"

"Next door," sweetly but coolly.

"He is very good-looking."

"Ears spoil him—too large."

"Does he come around—er—often?"

"Only two or three times a day. On Sunday, of course, we see more of him."

Aggie looked at me in the moonlight. Clearly the young man from the next door needed watching. It was well we had come.

"I suppose you like the same things?" she suggested. "Similar tastes and—er—all that?"

Bettina stretched her arms over her head and yawned.

"Not so you could notice it," she said coolly. "I can't think of anything we agree on. He is an Episcopalian; I'm a Presbyterian. He approves of suffrage for women; I do not. He is a Republican; I'm a Progressive. He disapproves of large families; I approve of them, if people can afford them."

Aggie sat straight up. "I hope you don't discuss that!" she exclaimed.

Bettina smiled. "How nice to find that you are really just nice elderly ladies after all!" she said. "Of course we discuss it. Is it anything to be ashamed of?"

"When I was a girl," I said tartly, "we married first and discussed those things afterward."

"Of course you did, Aunt Lizzie," she said, smiling alluringly. She was the prettiest girl I think I have ever seen, and that night she was beautiful. "And you raised enormous families who religiously walked to church in their bare feet to save their shoes!"

"I did nothing of the sort," I snapped.

"It seems to me," Aggie put in gently, "that you make very little of love." Aggie was once engaged to be married to a young man named Wiggins, a roofer by trade, who was killed in the act of inspecting a tin gutter, on a rainy day. He slipped and fell over, breaking his neck as a result.

Bettina smiled at Aggie. "Not at all," she said. "The day of blind love is gone, that's all—gone like the day of the chaperon."

Neither of us cared to pursue this, and Tish at that moment appearing with Jasper, Aggie and I made a move toward bed. But Jasper not going, and none of us caring to leave him alone with Bettina, we sat down again.

We sat until one o'clock.

At the end of that time Jasper rose, and saying something about it being almost bedtime strolled off next door. Aggie was sound asleep in her chair and Tish was dozing. As for Bettina, she had said hardly a word after eleven o'clock.

Aggie and Tish, as I have said, were occupying the same room. I went to sleep the moment I got into bed, and must have slept three or four hours when I was awakened by a shot. A moment later a dozen or more shots were fired in rapid succession and I sat bolt upright in bed. Across the street someone was raising a window, and a man called, "What's the matter?" twice.

There was no response and no further sound. Shaking in every limb, I found the light switch and looked at the time. It was four o'clock in the morning and quite dark.

Someone was moving in the hall outside and whimpering. I opened the door hurriedly and Aggie half fell into the room.

"Tish is murdered, Lizzie!" she said, and collapsed on the floor in a heap.

"Nonsense!"

"She's not in her room or in the house, and I heard shots!"

Well, Aggie was right. Tish was not in her room. There was a sort of horrible stillness everywhere as we stood there clutching at each other and listening.

"She's heard burglars downstairs and has gone down after them, and this is what has happened! Oh, Tish! Brave Tish!" Aggie cried hysterically.

And at that Bettina came in with her hair over her shoulders and asked us if we had heard anything. When we told her about Tish, she insisted on going downstairs, and with Aggie carrying her first-aid box and I carrying the blackberry cordial, we went down.

The lower floor was quiet and empty. The man across the street had put down his window and gone back to bed, and everything was still. Bettina in her dressing-gown went out on the porch and turned on the light. Tish was not there, nor was there a body lying on the lawn.

"It was back of the house by the garage," Bettina said. "If only Jasper—"

And at that moment Jasper came into the circle of light. He had a Norfolk coat on over his pajamas and a pair of slippers, and he was running, calling over his shoulder to someone behind as he ran.

"Watch the drive!" he yelled. "I saw him duck round the corner."

We could hear other footsteps now and somebody panting near us. Aggie was sitting huddled in a porch chair, crying, and Bettina, in the hall, was trying to get down from the wall a Moorish knife that Eliza Bailey had picked up somewhere.

"John!" we heard Jasper calling. "John! Quick! I've got him!"

He was just at the corner of the porch. My heart stopped and then rushed on a thousand a minute. Then:—

"Take your hands off me!" said Tish's voice.

16

The next moment Tish came majestically into the circle of light and mounted the steps. Jasper, with his mouth open, stood below looking up, and a hired man in what looked like a bed quilt was behind in the shadow.

Tish was completely dressed in her motoring clothes, even to her goggles. She looked neither to the right nor left, but stalked across the porch into the house and up the stairway. None of us moved until we heard the door of her room slam above.

"Poor old dear!" said Bettina. "She's been walking in her sleep!"

"But the shots!" gasped Aggie. "Someone was shooting at her!"

Conscious now of his costume, Jasper had edged close to the veranda and stood in its shadow.

"Walking in her sleep, of course!" he said heartily. "The trip today was too much for her. But think of her getting into that burglar-proof garage with her eyes shut—or do sleep-walkers have their eyes shut?—and actually cranking up my racer!"

Aggie looked at me and I looked at Aggie.

"Of course," Jasper went on, "there being no muffler on it, the racket wakened her as well as the neighborhood. And then the way we chased her!"

"Poor old dear!" said Bettina again. "I'm going in to make her some tea."

"I think," said Jasper, "that I need a bit of tea too. If you will put out the porch lights I'll come up and have some."

But Aggie and I said nothing. We knew Tish never walked in her sleep. She had meant to try out Jasper's racing-car at dawn, forgetting that racers have no mufflers, and she had been, as one may say, hoist with her own petard—although I do not know what a petard is and have never been able to find out.

We drank our tea, but Tish refused to have any or to reply to our knocks, preserving a sulky silence. Also she had locked Aggie out and I was compelled to let her sleep in my room.

I was almost asleep when Aggie spoke:—

"Did you think there was anything queer about the way that Jasper boy said good-night to Bettina?" she asked drowsily.

"I didn't hear him say good-night."

"That was it. He didn't. I think"—she yawned—"I think he kissed her."

1. It is likely that Bettina was expecting

    a. one chaperon.
    b. three chaperons.
    c. her mother.
    d. nobody.

2. Tish seems to be very

    a. delicate.
    b. talkative.
    c. mechanical.
    d. shy.

3. _____ thought she could get over the bridge safely by driving very fast.

    a. Bettina Bailey
    b. Eliza Bailey
    c. Letitia Carberry
    d. Aggie

4. With which of the following statements would Bettina and Aggie be **most** likely to disagree?

    a. It is important to visit friends and relatives often.
    b. When driving, women should always take a man with them.
    c. If a man is fishing under a bridge, someone will get a flat tire.
    d. Bridges can sometimes be unstable.

5. The narrator is

    a. Tish.
    b. Bettina.
    c. Aggie.
    d. Lizzie.

6. The man under the bridge was upset because

    a. he did not want to change a tire.
    b. he was hurt when the car crashed into him.
    c. the car had scared the fish away.
    d. he wanted to see the ladies.

7. What is the most likely reason why Jasper comes around as often as he does?

    a. He and Bettina talk about racing cars.
    b. He always comes around when Tish visits.
    c. He likes to argue with Lizzie.
    d. He is in love with Bettina.

8. Which of the following is **true** of Jasper?

    a. He wants to have a large family.
    b. He doesn't visit on Sundays.
    c. He believes women should have the right to vote.
    d. He has strong Presbyterian and Progressive views.

9. What led Bettina to claim that Aggie and Lizzie were "nice elderly ladies after all"?

    a. They did not approve of suffrage for women.
    b. They were very religious.
    c. They did not believe in discussing family size before marriage.
    d. Their children walked to church in their bare feet.

10. It is likely that John

    a. was a car thief.
    b. called, "What's the matter?"
    c. was a hired hand.
    d. fired the shots.

11. Tish sulked in silence because she was

    a. still sleepwalking.
    b. embarrassed about having been caught trying out Jasper's racecar.
    c. worried that someone was shooting at her.
    d. upset that someone had touched her.

12. Why do you think Tish removed the license plates? Do you think that it was a good idea?

_____

_____

_____

_____

_____

_____

_____

13. Do you think the women really don't drink alcohol? Why or why not?

_____

_____

_____

_____

_____

_____

_____

14. Why do you think Jasper stayed so late?

_____

_____

_____

_____

_____

_____

_____

15. Do you think Bettina is happy to have chaperons? Use evidence to support your opinion.

_____

_____

_____

_____

_____

_____

_____

_____

_____

_____

_____

21

16. Do you think Aggie was right at the end of the story? Why or why not?

_____

_____

_____

_____

_____

_____

_____

_____

_____

_____

_____

_____

_____

_____

_____

_____

_____

_____

THE BRAVE LITTLE TAILOR
by Wilhelm and Jacob Grimm

A tailor sat in his workroom one morning, stitching away busily at a coat for the Lord Mayor. He whistled and sang so gaily that all the little boys who passed the shop on their way to school thought what a fine thing it was to be a tailor, and told one another that when they grew to be men they'd be tailors, too.

"How hungry I feel, to be sure!" cried the little man, at last; "but I'm far too busy to trouble about eating. I must finish his lordship's coat before I touch a morsel of food," and he broke once more into a merry song.

"Fine new jam for sale," sang out an old woman, as she walked along the street.

"Jam! I can't resist such a treat," said the tailor; and, running to the door, he shouted, "This way for jam, dame; show me a pot of your very finest."

The woman handed him jar after jar, but he found fault with all. At last he hit upon some to his liking.

"And how many pounds will you take, sir?"

"I'll take four ounces," he replied, in a solemn tone, "and mind you give me good weight."

The old woman was very angry, for she had expected to sell several pounds, at least. She went off grumbling after she had weighed out the four ounces.

"Now for a feed!" cried the little man, taking a loaf from the cupboard as he spoke. He cut off a huge slice, and spread the jam on quite half an inch thick. Then he suddenly remembered his work.

"It will never do to get jam on the Lord Mayor's coat, so I'll finish it off before I take even one bite," said he. So he picked up his work once more, and his needle flew in and out like lightning.

I am afraid the Lord Mayor had some stitches in his garment that were quite a quarter of an inch long.

The tailor glanced longingly at his slice of bread and jam once or twice, but when he looked the third time it was quite covered with flies, and a fine feast they were having of it.

This was too much for the little fellow. Up he jumped, crying: "So you think I provide bread and jam for you, indeed! Well, we'll very soon see! Take that!" and he struck the flies such a heavy blow with a duster that no fewer than seven lay dead upon the table, while the others flew up to the ceiling in great haste.

"Seven at one blow!" said the little man with great pride. "Such a brave deed ought to be known all over the town, and it won't be my fault if folks fail to hear of it."

So he cut out a wide belt, and stitched on it in big golden letters the words "Seven at one blow." When this was done he fastened it round him, crying:

"I'm cut out for something better than a tailor, it's quite clear. I'm one of the world's great heroes, and I'll be off at once to seek my fortune."

He glanced round the cottage, but there was nothing of value to take with him. The only thing he possessed in the world was a small cheese.

"You may as well come, too," said he, stowing away the cheese in his pocket, "and now I'm off."

When he got into the street the neighbors all crowded round him to read the words on his belt.

"Seven at one blow!" said they to one another. "What a blessing he's going; for it wouldn't be safe to have a man about us could kill seven of us at one stroke."

You see, they didn't know that the tailor had only killed flies. They took it to mean men.

The little tailor jogged along for some miles until he came to a hedge, where a little bird was caught in the branches.

"Come along," said the tailor; "I'll have you keep my cheese company"; so he caught the bird and put it carefully into his pocket with the cheese.

Soon he reached a lofty mountain, and he made up his mind to climb it and see what was going on at the other side. When he reached the top, there stood a huge giant, gazing down into the valley below.

"Good day," said the tailor.

The giant turned round, and seeing nobody but the little tailor there, he cried with scorn:

"And what might you be doing here, might I ask? You'd best be off at once."

"Not so fast, my friend," said the little man: "read this."

"Seven at one blow," read the giant, and he began to wish he'd been more civil.

"Well, I'm sure nobody would think it to look at you," he replied; "but since you are so clever, do this," and he picked up a stone and squeezed it until water ran out.

"Do that! Why, it's mere child's play to me," and the man took out his cheese and squeezed it until the whey ran from it. "Now who is cleverer?" asked the tailor. "You see, I can squeeze milk out, while you only get water."

The giant was too surprised to utter a word for a few minutes; then, taking up another stone, he threw it so high into the air that for a moment they couldn't see where it went; then down it fell to the ground again.

"Good!" said the tailor; "but I'll throw a stone that won't come back again at all."

Taking the little bird from his pocket, he threw it into the air, and the bird, glad to get away, flew right off and never returned.

This sort of thing didn't suit the giant at all, for he wasn't used to being beaten by anyone.

"Here's something that you'll never manage," said he to the little man. "Just come and help me to carry this fallen oak-tree for a few miles."

"Delighted!" said the tailor, "and I'll take the end with the branches, for it's sure to be heavier."

"Agreed," replied the giant, and he lifted the heavy trunk on to his shoulder, while the tailor climbed up among the branches at the other end, and sang with all his might, as though carrying a tree was nothing to him.

The poor giant, who was holding the tree-trunk and the little tailor as well, soon grew tired.

"I'm going to let it fall" he shouted, and the tailor jumped down from the branches and pretended he had been helping all the time.

"The idea of a man your size finding a tree too heavy to carry!" laughed the little tailor.

"You are a clever little fellow, and no mistake," replied the giant, "and if you'll only come and spend the night in our cave, we shall be delighted to have you."

"I shall have great pleasure in coming, my friend," answered the little tailor, and together they set off for the giant's home.

There were seven more giants in the cave, and each one of them was eating a roasted pig for his supper. They gave the little man some food, and then showed him a bed in which he might pass the night. It was so big that, after tossing about for half an hour in it, the tailor thought he would be more comfortable if he slept in the corner, so he crept out without being noticed.

In the middle of the night the giant stole out of bed and went up to the one where he thought the little man was fast asleep. Taking a big bar of iron, he struck such a heavy blow at it that he woke up all the other giants.
"Keep quiet, friends," said he. "I've just killed the little scamp."

The tailor made his escape as soon as possible, and he journeyed on for many miles, until he began to feel very tired, so he lay down under a tree, and was soon fast asleep. When he awoke, he found a big crowd of people standing round him. Up walked one very wise-looking old man, who was really the King's prime minister.

"Is it true that you have killed seven with one blow?" he asked.

"It is a fact," answered the little tailor.

"Then come with me to the King, my friend, for he's been searching for a brave man like you for some time past. You are to be made captain of his army, and the King will give you a fine house to live in."

"That I will," replied the little man. "It is just the sort of thing that will suit me, and I'll come at once."

The little tailor had not been in the King's service long before everyone grew jealous of him. The soldiers were afraid that, if they offended him, he would make short work of them all, while the members of the King's household didn't fancy the idea of making such a fuss over a stranger.

So the soldiers went in a body to the King and asked that another captain should be put over them, for they were afraid of this one.

The King didn't like to refuse, for fear they should all desert, and yet he didn't dare get rid of the captain, in case such a strong and brave man should try to have his revenge.

At last the King hit upon a plan. In some woods close by there lived two giants, who were the terror of the countryside; they robbed all the travelers, and if any resistance was offered they killed the men on the spot.

Sending for the little tailor he said: "Knowing you to be the bravest man in my kingdom, I want to ask a favor of you. If you will kill these two giants, and bring me back proof that they are dead, you shall marry the Princess, my daughter, and have half my kingdom. You shall also take one hundred men to help you, and you are to set off at once."

"A hundred men, your Majesty! Pray, what do I want with a hundred men? If I can kill seven at one blow, I needn't be afraid of two. I'll kill them fast enough, never fear."

The tailor chose ten strong men, and told them to await him on the border of the wood, while he went on quite alone. He could hear the giants snoring for quite half an hour before he reached them, so he knew in which direction to go.

He found the pair fast asleep under a tree, so he filled his pockets with stones and climbed up into the branches over their heads. Then he began to pelt one of the giants with the missiles, until after a few minutes one of the men awoke. Giving the other a rough push he cried:

"If you strike me like that again, I'll know the reason why."

"I didn't touch you," said the other giant crossly, and they were soon fast asleep once more.

Then the tailor threw stones at the other man, and soon he awoke as the first had done.

"What did you throw that at me for?" said he.

"You are dreaming," answered the other, "I didn't throw anything."

No sooner were they fast asleep again, than the little man began to pelt them afresh.

Up they both sprang, and seizing each other, they began to fight in real earnest. Not content with using their fists, they tore up huge trees by the roots, and beat each other until very soon the pair lay dead on the ground.

Down climbed the little tailor, and taking his sword in his hand he plunged it into each giant, and then went back to the edge of the forest where the ten men were waiting for him.

"They are dead as two door nails," shouted the little man. "I don't say that I had an easy task, for they tore up trees by their roots to try to protect themselves with, but, of course, it was no good. What were two giants to a man who has slain seven at one blow?"

But the men wouldn't believe it until they went into the forest and saw the two dead bodies, laying each in a pool of blood, while the ground was covered with uprooted trees.

Back they went to the King, but instead of handing over half his kingdom, as he had promised, his Majesty told the little tailor that there was still another brave deed for him to do before he got the Princess for his bride.

"Just name it, then; I'm more than ready," was the man's reply.

"You are to kill the famous unicorn that is running wild in the forest and doing so much damage. When this is done you shall have your reward at once."

"No trouble, your Majesty. I'll get rid of him in a twinkling."

He made the ten men wait for him at the entrance to the wood as they had done the first time, and taking a stout rope and a saw he entered the forest alone.

Up came the unicorn, but just as it was about to rush at the man he darted behind a big tree.

The unicorn dashed with such force against the tree that its horn was caught quite fast and it was kept a prisoner.

28

Taking his rope, he tied it tightly round the animal and, after sawing off the horn, back he went to the palace, leading the unicorn by his side.

But even then the King was not satisfied, and he made the little tailor catch a wild boar that had been seen wandering in the woods.

He took a party of huntsmen with him, but again he made them wait on the outskirts of the forest while he went on by himself.

The wild boar made a dash at the little tailor; but the man was too quick for it. He slipped into a little building close by, with the animal at his heels. Then, catching sight of a small window, he forced his way out into the forest again, and while the boar, who was too big and clumsy to follow, stood gazing at the spot where he had disappeared, the tailor ran round and closed the door, keeping the animal quite secure inside. Then he called the hunters, who shot the boar and carried the body back to the palace.

This time the King was obliged to keep his promise; so the little tailor became a Prince, and a grand wedding they had, too.

When they had been married for about a couple of years, the Princess once overhead her husband talking in his sleep.

"Boy, if you have put a patch on that waistcoat, take the Lord Mayor's coat home at once, or I'll box your ears," he said.

"Oh, dear," cried the Princess, "to think that I've married a common tailor! Whatever can I do to get rid of him?"

So she told her father the story, and the King said she need not worry, for he would find a way out of the difficulty. She was to leave the door open that night, and while the tailor was sleeping, the King's servants should steal into the room, bind the tailor, and take him away to be killed.

The Princess promised to see that everything was in readiness, and she tripped about all day with a very light heart.

She little knew that one of the tailor's servants had overheard their cruel plot, and carried the news straight to his master.

That night, when the Princess thought her husband was sleeping fast, she crept to the door and opened it.

To her great terror the tailor began to speak.

"Boy, take the Lord Mayor's coat home, or I'll box your ears. Haven't I killed seven with one blow? Haven't I slain two giants, a unicorn, and a wild boar? What do I care for the men who are standing outside my door at this moment?"

At these words off flew the men as though they had been shot from a gun. No more attempts were ever made on his life. So the Princess had to make the best of a bad job.

He lived on and when the old King died he ascended the throne in his stead. So the brave little tailor became ruler over the whole kingdom; and his motto throughout his whole life was, "Seven at one blow."

1. The tailor was so _____ that he wasn't going to eat anything.
    a. happy
    b. hungry
    c. busy
    d. poor

2. Why was the woman with the jam angry?
    a. She did not like the tailor.
    b. She had expected a big sale.
    c. She did not like the tailor's choice.
    d. The tailor was rude.

3. The tailor decided to wait and eat until he had finished his work because
    a. the Lord Mayor was in a hurry.
    b. the Lord Mayor would pay for his meal.
    c. the Lord Mayor knew the old woman.
    d. he did not want to get jam on the Lord Mayor's coat.

4. Why were the stiches in the Lord Mayor's garment a quarter of an inch long?
    a. The tailor was hungry and in a hurry to finish.
    b. That was the style.
    c. The tailor wanted to do his best work.
    d. The Lord Mayor wanted them that way.

30

5. What was the tailor's mood when he had killed the flies on his jam and bread?

   a. He was proud.
   b. He was afraid.
   c. He was anxious.
   d. He was strong.

6. After killing the flies, the tailor

   a. went back to work on the Lord Mayor's coat.
   b. made a golden belt.
   c. made a belt with golden letters.
   d. decided to be a better tailor.

7. What did the neighbors think that the tailor had done?

   a. They thought he had killed seven men in one try.
   b. They thought he had killed seven flies with his jam and bread.
   c. They thought he had eaten seven pieces of bread.
   d. They thought he smelled like cheese.

8. The little tailor first outwitted the giant by

   a. squeezing water from cheese.
   b. throwing the cheese.
   c. squeezing the bird.
   d. squeezing milk from cheese.

9. How did the tailor surprise the giant?

   a. He squeezed water from cheese.
   b. He threw the cheese.
   c. He threw the bird.
   d. He squeezed a stone.

10. The tailor helped carry the oak tree

   a. by lifting the heavy end.
   b. by lifting the light end.
   c. by singing and walking alongside.
   d. not at all; instead he rode on it.

11. What is the **best** way to describe the tailor when he avoided being killed in bed by the giant?

    a. lucky
    b. tired
    c. smart
    d. quick

12. Why did the king's soldiers **not** want the tailor as their captain?

    a. They did not believe he was brave.
    b. They did not believe he had killed seven men at one blow.
    c. They were afraid he would kill them.
    d. They did not like such a fuss made over one stranger.

13. The king felt he

    a. could ignore what the soldiers wanted.
    b. could dismiss the tailor without fear.
    c. could not dismiss the tailor without fear of revenge.
    d. had no way to get rid of the tailor.

14. Why did the tailor go after the two giants alone?

    a. He did not want anyone to see his tactics.
    b. The king said he had to.
    c. The princess said he had to.
    d. He was afraid the men would attack him.

15. Which tactic did the tailor use to capture the unicorn and boar?

    a. He used himself as bait.
    b. He used a rope.
    c. He used a little building.
    d. He refused to do what the king asked.

16. The princess discovered she had married a tailor when he

    a. hired an assistant.
    b. began work again on the Lord Mayor's coat.
    c. talked in his sleep.
    d. told her so.

17. Why do you think the tailor decided he was a hero meant for better things?

_____

_____

_____

_____

_____

_____

_____

_____

18. Did the tailor lie when he answered the Prime Minister? Did he tell the truth? Why or why not?

_____

_____

_____

_____

_____

_____

_____

_____

_____

19. Do you think the tailor had planned his attack all along, or was he just lucky? What makes you say so?

_____

_____

_____

_____

_____

_____

_____

_____

20. Do you think the tailor and the princess lived happily ever after? Why or why not?

_____

_____

_____

_____

_____

_____

_____

_____

34

from "UNDERSTOOD BETSY"
by Dorothy Canfield

After the singing the teacher gave Elizabeth Ann a pile of schoolbooks, some paper, some pencils, and a pen, and told her to set her desk in order. There were more initials carved inside, another big H.P. with a little A.P. under it. What a lot of children must have sat there, thought the little girl as she arranged her books and papers. As she shut down the lid the teacher finished giving some instructions to three or four little ones and said, "Betsy and Ralph and Ellen, bring your reading books up here."

Betsy sighed, took out her third-grade reader, and went with the other two up to the battered old bench near the teacher's desk. She knew all about reading lessons and she hated them, although she loved to read. But reading lessons . . . ! You sat with your book open at some reading that you could do with your eyes shut, it was so easy, and you waited and waited and waited while your classmates slowly stumbled along, reading aloud a sentence or two apiece, until your turn came to stand up and read your sentence or two, which by that time sounded just like nonsense because you'd read it over and over so many times to yourself before your chance came. And often you didn't even have a chance to do that, because the teacher didn't have time to get around to you at all, and you closed your book and put it back in your desk without having opened your mouth. Reading was one thing Elizabeth Ann had learned to do very well indeed, but she had learned it all by herself at home from much reading to herself. Aunt Frances had kept her well supplied with children's books from the nearest public library. She often read three a week—very different, that, from a sentence or two once or twice a week.

When she sat down on the battered old bench she almost laughed aloud, it seemed so funny to be in a class of only three. There had been forty in her grade in the big brick building. She sat in the middle, the little girl whom the teacher had called Ellen on one side, and Ralph on the other. Ellen was very pretty, with fair hair smoothly braided in two little pig-tails, sweet, blue eyes, and a clean blue-and-white gingham dress. Ralph had very black eyes, dark hair, a big bruise on his forehead, a cut on his chin, and a tear in the knee of his short trousers. He was much bigger than Ellen, and Elizabeth Ann thought he looked rather fierce. She decided that she would be afraid of him, and would not like him at all.

"Page thirty-two," said the teacher. "Ralph first."

Ralph stood up and began to read. It sounded very familiar to Elizabeth Ann, for he did not read at all well. What was not familiar was that the teacher did not stop him after the first sentence. He read on and on till he had read a page, the teacher only helping him with the hardest words.

"Now Betsy," said the teacher.

Elizabeth Ann stood up, read the first sentence, and paused, like a caged lion pausing when he comes to the end of his cage.

"Go on," said the teacher.

Elizabeth Ann read the next sentence and stopped again, automatically.

"Go ON," said the teacher, looking at her sharply.

The next time the little girl paused the teacher laughed out good-naturedly. "What is the matter with you, Betsy?" she said. "Go on till I tell you to stop."

So Elizabeth Ann, very much surprised but very much interested, read on, sentence after sentence, till she forgot they were sentences and just thought of what they meant. She read a whole page and then another page, and that was the end of the selection. She had never read aloud so much in her life. She was aware that everybody in the room had stopped working to listen to her. She felt very proud and less afraid than she had ever thought she could be in a schoolroom. When she finished,

"You read very well!" said the teacher. "Is this very easy for you?"

"Oh, YES!" said Elizabeth Ann.

"I guess, then, that you'd better not stay in this class," said the teacher. She took a book out of her desk. "See if you can read that."

Elizabeth Ann began in her usual school-reading style, very slow and monotonous, but this didn't seem like a "reader" at all. It was poetry, full of hard words that were fun to try to pronounce, and it was all about an old woman who would hang out an American flag, even though the town was full of rebel soldiers. She read faster and faster, getting more and more excited, till she broke out with "Halt!" in such a loud, spirited voice that the sound of it startled her and made her stop, fearing that she would be laughed at. But nobody laughed. They were all listening, very eagerly, even the little ones, with their eyes turned toward her.

"You might as well go on and let us see how it came out," said the teacher, and Betsy finished triumphantly.

"WELL," said the teacher, "there's no sense in your reading along in the third reader. After this you'll recite out of the seventh reader with Frank and Harry and Stashie."

Elizabeth Ann could not believe her ears. To be "jumped" four grades in that casual way! It wasn't possible! She at once thought, however, of something that would prevent it entirely, and while Ellen was reading her page in a slow, careful little voice, Elizabeth Ann was feeling miserably that she must explain to the teacher why she couldn't read with the seventh-grade children. Oh, how she wished she could! When they stood up to go back to their seats she hesitated, hung her head, and looked very unhappy. "Did you want to say something to me?" asked the teacher, pausing with a bit of chalk in her hand.

The little girl went up to her desk and said what she knew it was her duty to confess: "I can't be allowed to read in the seventh reader. I don't write a bit well, and I never get the mental number-work right. I couldn't do anything with seventh-grade arithmetic!"

The teacher looked a little blank and said: "I didn't say anything about your number-work! I don't know anything about it! You haven't recited yet."

*   *   *

"Betsy, have you learned your spelling?"

"Yes, ma'am, I think so," said Elizabeth Ann, wondering very much why she was asked.

"That's fine," said the teacher. "I wish you'd take little Molly over in that corner and help her with her reading. She's getting on so much better than the rest of the class that I hate to have her lose her time. Just hear her read the rest of her little story, will you, and don't help her unless she's really stuck."

Elizabeth Ann was startled by this request, which was unheard of in her experience. She was very uncertain of herself as she sat down on a low chair in the corner of the schoolroom away from the desks, with the little child leaning on her knee. And yet she was not exactly afraid, either, because Molly was such a shy little roly-poly thing, with her crop of yellow curls, and her bright blue eyes very serious as she looked hard at the book and began: "Once there was a rat. It was a fat rat." No, it was impossible to be frightened of such a funny little girl, who peered so earnestly into the older child's face to make sure she was doing her lesson right.

Elizabeth Ann had never had anything to do with children younger than herself, and she felt very pleased and important to have anybody look up to HER! She put her arm around Molly's square, warm, fat little body and gave her a squeeze. Molly snuggled up closer; and the two children put their heads together over the printed page, Elizabeth Ann correcting Molly very gently indeed when she made a mistake, and waiting patiently when she hesitated. She had so fresh in her mind her own suffering from quick, nervous corrections that she took the greatest pleasure in speaking quietly and not interrupting the little girl more than was necessary. It was fun to teach, LOTS of fun! She was surprised when the teacher said, "Well, Betsy, how did Molly do?"

"Oh, is the time up?" said Elizabeth Ann. "Why, she does beautifully, I think, for such a little thing."

"Do you suppose," said the teacher thoughtfully, just as though Betsy were a grown-up person, "do you suppose she could go into the second reader, with Eliza? There's no use keeping her in the first if she's ready to go on."

Elizabeth Ann's head whirled with this second light-handed juggling with the sacred distinction between the grades. In the big brick schoolhouse nobody EVER went into another grade except at the beginning of a new year, after you'd passed a lot of examinations. She had not known that anybody could do anything else. The idea that everybody took a year to a grade, no MATTER what! was so fixed in her mind that she felt as though the teacher had said: "How would you like to stop being nine years old and be twelve instead! And don't you think Molly would better be eight instead of six?"

However, just then her class in arithmetic was called, so that she had no more time to be puzzled. She came forward with Ralph and Ellen again, very low in her mind. She hated arithmetic with all her might, and she really didn't understand a thing about it! By long experience she had learned to read her teachers' faces very accurately, and she guessed by their expression whether the answer she gave was the right one. And that was the only way she could tell. You never heard of any other child who did that, did you?

They had mental arithmetic, of course (Elizabeth Ann thought it just her luck!), and of course it was those hateful eights and sevens, and of course right away poor Betsy got the one she hated most, 7 x 8. She never knew that one! She said dispiritedly that it was 54, remembering vaguely that it was somewhere in the fifties. Ralph burst out scornfully, "56!" and the teacher, as if she wanted to take him down for showing off, pounced on him with 9 x 8. He answered, without drawing breath, "72." Elizabeth Ann shuddered at his

38

accuracy. Ellen, too, rose to the occasion when she got 6 x 7, which Elizabeth Ann could sometimes remember and sometimes not. And then, oh horrors! It was her turn again! Her turn had never before come more than twice during a mental arithmetic lesson. She was so startled by the swiftness with which the question went around that she balked on 6 x 6, which she knew perfectly. And before she could recover Ralph had answered and had rattled out a "108" in answer to 9 x 12; and then Ellen slapped down an "84" on top of 7 x 12. Good gracious! Who could have guessed, from the way they read, they could do their tables like this! She herself missed on 7 x 7 and was ready to cry. After this the teacher didn't call on her at all, but showered questions down on the other two, who sent the answers back with sickening speed. After the lesson the teacher said, smiling, "Well, Betsy, you were right about your arithmetic. I guess you'd better recite with Eliza for a while. She's doing second-grade work. I shouldn't be surprised if, after a good review with her, you'd be able to go on with the third-grade work."

Elizabeth Ann fell back on the bench with her mouth open. She felt really dizzy. What crazy things the teacher said! She felt as though she was being pulled limb from limb.

"What's the matter?" asked the teacher, seeing her bewildered face.

"Why—why," said Elizabeth Ann, "I don't know what I am at all. If I'm second-grade arithmetic and seventh-grade reading and third-grade spelling, what grade AM I?"

The teacher laughed at the turn of her phrase. "YOU aren't any grade at all, no matter where you are in school. You're just yourself, aren't you? What difference does it make what grade you're in! And what's the use of your reading little baby things too easy for you just because you don't know your multiplication table?"

1. Elizabeth Ann's desk was

    a. metal.
    b. new.
    c. a single board.
    d. old.

2. What is the **best** way to describe Betsy's thoughts after the teacher called her to the front of the classroom?

    a. She was making assumptions about what would happen.
    b. She was fearful of reading in front of the class.
    c. She thought that reading in front of the class was like reading the books her aunt had given her.
    d. She knew the other kids would taunt her because she didn't read well.

3. Betsy did **not** like reading lessons, although

    a. her classmates stumbled along.
    b. she was a very good reader.
    c. she only had to read a sentence or two.
    d. sometimes she did not get to read at all.

4. When Betsy's first reading group was called up, she thought it was funny because.

    a. the bench was old.
    b. the children were old.
    c. there were forty children.
    d. there were only three children.

5. What surprised Betsy about the reading lesson?

    a. Ralph had read well.
    b. Ellen did not read well.
    c. Everyone was allowed to read with few interruptions.
    d. The teacher did not let Betsy read a passage.

6. What made Betsy's class stop working?

    a. the teacher's sharp voice
    b. Betsy's reading
    c. a loud noise
    d. Betsy yelling, "Halt!"

7. The teacher asked Betsy to help _____ read.

    a. Eliza
    b. Molly
    c. Ralph
    d. Ellen

8. Elizabeth Ann was **not** frightened of helping the younger child because

    a. she had no experience with young children.
    b. no one had ever asked her to do such a thing.
    c. it was her first day at the new school.
    d. the little girl was so funny and eager.

9. Elizabeth Ann found that she enjoyed teaching, although she

    a. had to correct Molly frequently.
    b. had to correct Molly sharply.
    c. had never done it before.
    d. did not like having someone look up to her.

10. Betsy could **not** understand

    a. how the teacher could assign work without regard to grade.
    b. why the teacher did not ask her about Molly's reading.
    c. why the teacher did not treat her like an adult.
    d. why she was so bad at arithmetic.

11. Where had Betsy gone to school before she came to this one?

    a. She went to the big brick schoolhouse.
    b. Her aunt had taught her.
    c. She was self-taught.
    d. She learned from younger children.

12. How did Betsy's attitude change throughout this passage?

    a. At first, she was fearful of being at a new school, but then she made many new friends and was very happy.
    b. At first, she was arrogant about her skills, but then she grew hesitant and humiliated at her lack of them.
    c. At first, she was paranoid that the teacher would make fun of her, but then she remembered that it didn't matter what others thought of her.
    d. At first, she was sure she would fail out of her new school, but then she learned that most of the other students at the school weren't as smart as she was.

13. Why did Betsy think she could not read with seventh graders? Was she right to be worried? Why or why not?

_____

_____

_____

_____

_____

_____

_____

14. Why couldn't Elizabeth Ann figure out what grade she was in?

_____

_____

_____

_____

_____

_____

_____

15. Why do you think the author calls her Elizabeth Ann, but the teacher calls her Betsy?

_____

_____

_____

_____

_____

_____

_____

_____

16. Would you like to be in Elizabeth Ann's school? Why or why not?

_____

_____

_____

_____

_____

_____

_____

_____

from "UNDER THE ANDES"

by Rex Stout

At the entrance to the main room I met Bob Garforth, leaving. There was a scowl on his face and his hand trembled as he held it forth to take mine.

"Harry is inside. What a rotten hole," said he, and passed on. I smiled at his remark—it was being whispered about that Garforth had lost a quarter of a million at Mercer's within the month—and passed inside.

Gaudy, I have said it was, and it needs no other word. Not in its elements, but in their arrangement.

The rugs and pictures and hangings testified to the taste of the man who had selected them; but they were abominably disposed, and there were too many of them.

The room, which was unusually large, held two or three leather divans, an English buffet, and many easy chairs. A smoking-table, covered, stood in one corner.

Groups of men were gathered about each of the three roulette wheels arranged along the farther side. Through a door to the left could be seen the poker tables, surrounded by grave or jocular faces. Above the low buzz of conversation there sounded the continual droning voices of the croupiers as they called the winning numbers, and an occasional exclamation from a "customer."

I made my way to the center wheel and stood at the rear of the crowd surrounding it.

The ball rolled; there was a straining of necks amid an intense silence; then, as the little pellet wavered and finally came to a rest in the hole number twenty-four a fervent oath of disappointment came from someone in front of me.

The next moment, rising on tiptoe to look over the intervening shoulders, I found myself looking into the white face of my younger brother, Harry.

"Paul!" he exclaimed, turning quickly away.

I pushed my way through and stood at his side. There was no sound from the group of onlookers; it is not to be wondered at if they hesitated to offend Paul Lamar.

44

"My dear boy," said I, "I missed you at dinner. And though this may occupy your mind, it can scarcely fill your stomach. Haven't you had enough?"

Harry looked at me. His face was horribly pale and his eyes bloodshot; they could not meet mine.

"For Heaven's sake, Paul, let me alone," he said, hardly above a whisper. "I have lost ninety thousand."

In spite of myself I started. No wonder he was pale! And yet—

"That's nothing," I whispered back. "But you are making a show of yourself. Just now you were swearing like a sailor. See how your hand trembles! You were not made for this, Harry; it makes you forget that you're a gentleman. They are laughing at you. Come."

"But I say I have lost ninety thousand dollars," said the boy, and there was wildness in his eye. "Let me alone, Paul."

"I will repay you."

"No. Let me alone!"

"Harry!"

"I say no!"

His mouth was drawn tight and his eyes glared sullenly as those of a stubborn child. Clearly it was impossible to get him away without making a scene, which was unthinkable. For a moment I was at a complete loss; then the croupier's voice sounded suddenly in my ear:

"You are interrupting us, sir."

I silenced him with a glance and turned to my brother, having decided in an instant on the only possible course.

"Here, let me have your chair. I will get it back for you. Come!"

He looked at me for a moment in hesitation, then rose without a word and I took his place.

The thing was tiresome enough, but how could I have avoided it? The blood that rushes to the head of the gambler is certainly not food for the intellect;

and, besides, I was forced by circumstances into an heroic attitude—and nothing is more distasteful to a man of sense. But I had a task before me; if a man lays bricks he should lay them well; and I do not deny that there was a stirring of my pulse as I sat down.

Is it possible for a mind to directly influence the movements of a little ivory ball? I do not say yes, but will you say no? I watched the ball with the eye of an eagle, but without straining; I played with the precision of a man with an unerring system, though my selections were really made quite at random; and I handled my bets with the sureness and swift dexterity with which a chess-master places his pawn or piece in position to demoralize his opponent.

This told on the nerves of the croupier. Twice I corrected a miscalculation of his, and before I had played an hour his hand was trembling with agitation. And I won.

The details would be tiresome, but I won; and when, after six hours of play without an instant's rest, I rose exhausted from my chair and handed my brother the amount he had lost—I pocketed a few thousands for myself in addition. There were some who tried to detain me with congratulations and expressions of admiration, but I shook them off and led Harry outside to my car.

The chauffeur, poor devil, was completely stiff from the long wait, and I ordered him into the tonneau and took the wheel myself.

Partly was this due to pity for the driver, partly to a desire to leave Harry to his own thoughts, which I knew must be somewhat turbulent. He was silent during the drive, which was not long, and I smiled to myself in the darkness of the early morning as I heard, now and then, an uncontrollable sigh break through his dry lips. Of thankfulness, perhaps.

I preceded him up the stoop and into the hall of the old house on lower Fifth Avenue, near Tenth Street, that had been the home of our grandfather and our father before us. There, in the dim light, I halted and turned, while Evans approached from the inner rooms, rubbing eyes heavy with sleep. Good old Evans! Yet the faithfulness of such a servant has its disadvantages.

"Well?" said Harry in a thin, high voice.

The boy's nerves were stretched tightly; two words from me would have produced an explosion. So I clapped him on the shoulder and sent him off to bed. He went sulkily, without looking round, and his shoulders drooped like those of an old man; but I reflected that that would all be changed after a few hours of sleep.

"After all, he is a Lamar," I said to myself as I ordered Evans to bring wine and sandwiches to the library.

It was the middle of the following afternoon before Harry appeared downstairs. He had slept eleven hours. I was seated in the library when I heard his voice in the hall: "Breakfast! Breakfast for five at once!"

I smiled. That was Harry's style of wit.

After he had eaten his "breakfast for five" he came in to see me with the air of a man who was determined to have it out.

I myself was in no mood for talk; indeed, I scarcely ever am in such a mood, unless it be with a pretty woman or a great sinner. You may regard that sentence as tautological if you like; I shan't quarrel about it.

What I mean to say is that it was with a real effort I set myself to the distasteful task before me, rendered necessary by the responsibility of my position as elder brother and head of the family.

Harry began by observing with assumed indifference: "Well, and now there's the deuce to pay, I suppose."

"As his representative I am not a hard creditor," I smiled.

"I know, I know—" he began impetuously and stopped.

I continued:

"My boy, there is always the deuce to pay. If not for one thing, then for another. So your observation would serve for any other time as well as now. The point is this: you are ten years younger than I, and you are under my care; and much as I dislike to talk, we must reach an understanding."

"Well?" said Harry, lighting a cigarette and seating himself on the arm of a chair.

"You have often thought," I continued, "that I have been trying to interfere with your freedom. But you are mistaken; I have merely been trying to preserve it—and I have succeeded.

"When our father and mother died you were fifteen years of age. You are now twenty-two; and I take some credit for the fact that those seven years have left no stain, however slight, on the name of Lamar."

"Do I deserve that?" cried Harry. "What have I done?"

"Nothing irremediable, but you must admit that now and then I have been at no small pains to—er—assist you. But there, I don't intend to speak of the past; and to tell the truth, I suspect that we are of one mind. You regard me as more or less of an encumbrance; you think your movements are hampered; you consider yourself to be treated as a child unjustly.

"Well, for my part, I find my duty—for such I consider it—grows more irksome every day. If I am in your way, you are no less in mine. To make it short, you are now twenty-two years old, you chafe at restraint, you think yourself abundantly able to manage your own affairs. Well—I have no objection."

Harry stared at me.

"You mean—" he began.

"Exactly."

"But, Paul—"

"There is no need to discuss it. For me, it is mostly selfishness."

But he wanted to talk, and I humored him. For two hours we sat, running the scale from business to sentiment, and I must confess that I was more than once surprised by a flash from Harry. Clearly he was developing, and for the first time I indulged a Hope that he might prove himself fit for self-government.

At least I had given him the rope; it remained for time to discover whether or not he would avoid getting tangled up in it. When we had finished we understood each other better, I think, than we ever had before; and we parted with the best of feeling.

48

1. The narrator thought the room gaudy because

    a. the rugs, pictures, and hangings are in bad taste.
    b. the rugs, pictures, and hangings were displayed poorly.
    c. there were not enough rugs, pictures, and hangings.
    d. there was too much furniture.

2. Harry was playing

    a. poker.
    b. blackjack.
    c. craps.
    d. roulette.

3. How did Harry lose $90,000?

    a. He gambled it away.
    b. He donated it to a charity.
    c. He gave it to Paul.
    d. He was robbed.

4. Which of the following is the **best** way to describe Paul Lamar?

    a. poor
    b. not well known
    c. serious
    d. shy

5. How did Paul respond when he found out that Harry had lost so much money?

    a. He grew very angry and they left the establishment.
    b. He offered to win the money back so Harry wouldn't make a scene.
    c. He forced Harry to quit playing and then met with the owner to discuss payment.
    d. He allowed Harry to continue playing until he had won the money back.

6. Who was Evans?

    a. the chauffeur
    b. Paul and Harry's father
    c. Paul and Harry's grandfather
    d. a faithful servant

7. Harry ordered "breakfast for five" because

    a. he was very hungry.
    b. he wanted wine and sandwiches.
    c. he was feeding himself and four guests.
    d. it was the middle of the afternoon.

8. "There's the deuce to pay," probably refers to

    a. a pretty woman.
    b. a low card in the deck.
    c. the devil.
    d. a great sinner.

9. Does Paul Lamar remind you of any movie character? If so, who and why? Do you think this scene would make a good movie scene? Why or why not?

10. What has Paul decided to do about Harry and why?

_____

_____

_____

_____

_____

_____

_____

_____

_____

_____

_____

_____

_____

_____

_____

_____

_____

_____

51

WHAT THE OLD MAN DOES IS ALWAYS RIGHT

by Hans Christian Andersen

I will tell you a story which was told to me when I was a little boy. Every time I thought of the story, it seemed to me to become more and more charming, for it is with stories as it is with many people—they become better as they grow older.

I take it for granted that you have been in the country and seen a very old farmhouse with a thatched roof, with mosses and small plants growing wild upon the thatch. There is a stork's nest on the summit of the gable; for we can't do without the stork. The walls of the house are sloping and the windows are low, and only one of the latter is made so that it will open. The baking oven sticks out of the wall like a little fat body. The elder tree hangs over the paling, and beneath its branches, at the foot of the paling, is a pool of water in which a few ducks are disporting themselves. There is a yard dog too, who barks at all comers.

Just such a farmhouse stood out in the country, and in this house dwelt an old couple—a peasant and his wife. Small as was their property, there was one article among it that they could do without—a horse, which made a living out of the grass it found by the side of the highroad. The old peasant rode into the town on this horse, and often his neighbors borrowed it of him and rendered the old couple some service in return for the loan of it. But they thought it would be best if they sold the horse or exchanged it for something that might be more useful to them. But what might this something be?

"You'll know that best, old man," said the wife. "It is fair day today, so ride into town and get rid of the horse for money, or make a good exchange. Whichever you do will be right to me. Ride off to the fair."

And she fastened his neckerchief for him, for she could do that better than he could. And she tied it in a double bow, for she could do that very prettily. Then she brushed his hat round and round with the palm of her hand, and gave him a kiss. So he rode away upon the horse that was to be sold or to be bartered for something else. Yes, the old man knew what he was about.

The sun shone hotly down and not a cloud was to be seen in the sky. The road was very dusty, for many people, who were all bound for the fair, were driving or riding or walking upon it. There was no shelter anywhere.

Among the rest, a man was trudging along and driving a cow to the fair. The cow was as beautiful a creature as any cow can be.

52

"She gives good milk, I'm sure," said the peasant. "That would be a very good exchange—the cow for the horse."

"Hallow, you there with the cow!" he said. "I tell you what: I fancy a horse costs more than a cow, but I don't care for that. A cow would be more useful to me. If you like, we'll exchange."

"To be sure I will," said the man, and they exchanged accordingly.

So that was settled and the peasant might have turned back, for he had done the business he came to do. But as he had once made up his mind to go to the fair, he determined to go on, merely to have a look at it. And so he went on to the town with his cow.

Leading the animal, he strode sturdily on, and after a short time he overtook a man who was driving a sheep. It was a good fat sheep with a fine fleece on its back.

"I should like to have that fellow," said our peasant. "He would find plenty of grass by our palings, and in the winter we could keep him in the room with us. Perhaps it would be more practical to have a sheep instead of a cow. Shall we exchange?"

The man with the sheep was quite ready and the bargain was struck. So our peasant went on in the highroad with his sheep.

Soon he overtook another man, who came into the road from a field, carrying a great goose under his arm.

"That's a heavy thing you have there. It has plenty of feathers and plenty of fat, and would look well tied to a string and paddling in the water at our place. That would be something for my old woman. She could make all kinds of profit out of it. How often she has said, 'If we only had a goose!' Now perhaps she can have one, and if possible it shall be hers. Shall we exchange? I'll give you my sheep for your goose and thank you into the bargain."

The other man had not the least objection. And accordingly they exchanged, and our peasant became the proprietor of the goose.

By this time he was very near the town. The crowd on the highroad became greater and greater. There was quite a crush of men and cattle. They walked in the road, close by the palings, and at the barrier they even walked into the tollman's potato field, where his own fowl was strutting about with a string to its leg, lest it should take fright at the crowd and stray away, and so be lost. This fowl had short tail feathers, and winked with both its eyes, and looked very cunning, "Cluck, cluck!" said the fowl.

What it thought when it said this I cannot tell you, but directly when our good man saw it, he thought, "That's the finest fowl I've ever seen in my life! Why, it's finer than our parson's brood hen. On my word, I should like to have that fowl. A fowl can always find a grain or two, and can almost keep itself. I think it would be a good exchange if I could get that for my goose."

"Shall we exchange?" he asked the toll taker.

"Exchange?" repeated the man. "Well, that would not be a bad thing."

And so they exchanged. The toll taker at the barrier kept the goose and the peasant carried away the fowl.

Now he had done a good deal of business on his way to the fair, and he was hot and tired. He wanted something to eat and a glass of brandy to drink, and soon he was in front of the inn. He was just about to step in when the hostler came out, so they met at the door. The hostler was carrying a sack.

"What have you in that sack?" asked the peasant.

"Rotten apples," answered the hostler. "A whole sackful of them—enough to feed the pigs with."

"Why that's a terrible waste! I should like to take them to my old woman at home. Last year the old tree by the turf-hole bore only a single apple, and we kept it in the cupboard till it was quite rotten and spoiled. 'It was always property,' my old woman said. But here she can see a quantity of property—a whole sackful. Yes, I shall be glad to show them to her."

"What will you give me for the sackful?" asked the hostler.

"What will I give? I will give my fowl in exchange."

And he gave the fowl accordingly and received the apples, which he carried into the guest room. He leaned the sack carefully by the stove, and then went to the table. But the stove was hot: he had not thought of that. Many guests were present—horse dealers, oxherds, and two Englishmen. And the two Englishmen were so rich that their pockets bulged with gold coins and almost burst. And they could bet too, as you shall hear.

54

Hiss-s-s! hiss-s-s! What was that by the stove? The apples were beginning to roast!

"What is that?"

"Why, do you know—" said our peasant.

And he told the whole story of the horse he had changed for a cow, and all the rest of it, down to the apples.

"Well, your old woman will give it to you well when you get home!" said one of the two Englishmen. "There will be a disturbance."

"What? Give me what?" said the peasant. "She will kiss me and say, 'What the old man does is always right.'"

"Shall we wager?" said the Englishman. "We'll wager coined gold by the ton—a hundred pounds to the hundred-weight!"

"A bushel will be enough," replied the peasant. "I can only set the bushel of apples against it, and I'll throw myself and my old woman into the bargain. And I fancy that's piling up the measure."

"Done! Taken!"

And the bet was made. The host's carriage came up, and the Englishmen got in and the peasant got in. Away they went, and soon they stopped before the peasant's farm.

"Good evening, old woman."

"Good evening, old man."

"I've made the exchange."

"Yes, you understand what you're about," said the woman. And she embraced him, and paid no attention to the strange guests, nor did she notice the sack.

"I got a cow in exchange for the horse," said he.

"Heaven be thanked!" said she. "What glorious milk we shall now have, and butter and cheese on the table. That was a most capital exchange!"

"Yes, but I changed the cow for a sheep."

"Ah, that's better still!" cried the wife. "You always think of everything. We have just pasture enough for a sheep. Ewe's milk and cheese, and woolen jackets and stockings! The cow cannot give those, and her hairs will only come off. How you think of everything!"

"But I the changed away the sheep for a goose."

"Then this year we shall really have roast goose to eat, my dear old man. You are always thinking of something to give me pleasure. How charming that is! We can let the goose walk about with a string to her leg, and she'll grow fatter still before we roast her."

"But I gave away the goose for a fowl," said the man.

"A fowl? That was a good exchange!" replied the woman. "The fowl will lay eggs and hatch them, and we shall have chickens. We shall have a whole poultry yard! Oh, that's just what I was wishing for!"

"Yes, but I exchanged the fowl for a sack of shriveled apples."

"What! I must positively kiss you for that!" exclaimed the wife. "My dear good husband! Now I'll tell you something. Do you know, you had hardly left me this morning before I began thinking how I could give you something very nice this evening. I thought it should be pancakes with savory herbs. I had eggs, and bacon too. But I lacked herbs. So I went over to the schoolmaster's, as they have herbs there, I know. But the schoolmistress is a mean woman, though she looks so sweet. I begged her to lend me a handful of herbs. 'Lend!' she answered me, 'nothing at all grows in our garden, not even a shriveled apple. I could not even lend you a shriveled apple, my dear woman.' But now I can lend her ten, or a whole sackful. That I'm very glad of. That makes me laugh." And with that she gave him a resounding kiss.

"I like that!" exclaimed both the Englishmen together. "Always going downhill, and always merry! That's worth the money."

So they paid a hundredweight of gold to the peasant, who was not scolded, but kissed.

Yes, it always pays, when the wife sees and always asserts her husband knows best and that whatever he does is right.

You see, that is my story. I heard it when I was a child. And now you have heard it too, and know that "What the good man does is always right."

1. The farmhouse had plants growing on its

    a. summit.
    b. roof.
    c. walls.
    d. baking oven.

2. Which of the following animals did the farmer **not** have?

    a. cat
    d. dog
    c. stork
    d. duck

3. Which of the following did the farmer think they did **not** need?

    a. ducks
    b. dog
    c. stork
    d. horse

4. The farmer exchanged his sheep for a

    a. cow.
    b. horse.
    c. goose.
    d. chicken.

5. Why did the man want rotten apples?

    a. to feed the pigs
    b. He thought it was property.
    c. for its milk
    d. for its fleece

6. Who was **not** at the inn?

    a. horse dealers
    b. ox herds
    c. Englishmen
    d. the farmer's wife

7. What did the farmer **not** include in the bet?

    a. a bushel of apples
    b. himself
    c. his wife
    d. his home

8. The farmer's wife was happy with the apples because she

    a. needed bacon.
    b. needed eggs.
    c. needed herbs.
    d. could give them to the schoolmistress.

9. Why might someone think at first that the farmer is not smart? Give evidence for your answer.

_____

_____

_____

_____

_____

_____

_____

_____

_____

_____

_____

10. Did the farmer really win the bet? Why or why not?

_____

_____

_____

_____

_____

_____

_____

_____

_____

_____

_____

_____

_____

_____

_____

_____

_____

_____

11. What is the moral of this story? Do you agree with it? Why or why not?

_____

_____

_____

_____

_____

_____

_____

_____

_____

_____

_____

_____

_____

_____

_____

_____

_____

_____

from "WINESBURG, OHIO – 1919"

by Sherwood Anderson (1876–1941)

Joe Welling's love affair set the town of Winesburg on edge. When it began everyone whispered and shook his head. When people tried to laugh, the laughter was forced and unnatural. Joe fell in love with Sarah King, a lean, sad-looking woman who lived with her father and brother in a brick house that stood opposite the gate leading to the Winesburg Cemetery.

The two Kings, Edward the father, and Tom the son, were not popular in Winesburg. They were called proud and dangerous. They had come to Winesburg from some place in the South and ran a cider mill on the Trunion Pike. Tom King was reported to have killed a man before he came to Winesburg. He was twenty-seven years old and rode about town on a grey pony. Also he had a long yellow mustache that dropped down over his teeth, and always carried a heavy, wicked-looking walking stick in his hand. Once he killed a dog with the stick. The dog belonged to Win Pawsey, the shoe merchant, and stood on the sidewalk wagging its tail. Tom King killed it with one blow. He was arrested and paid a fine of ten dollars.

Old Edward King was small of stature and when he passed people in the street laughed a queer unmirthful laugh. When he laughed he scratched his left elbow with his right hand. The sleeve of his coat was almost worn through from the habit. As he walked along the street, looking nervously about and laughing, he seemed more dangerous than his silent, fierce-looking son.

When Sarah King began walking out in the evening with Joe Welling, people shook their heads in alarm. She was tall and pale and had dark rings under her eyes. The couple looked ridiculous together. Under the trees they walked and Joe talked. His passionate eager protestations of love, heard coming out of the darkness by the cemetery wall, or from the deep shadows of the trees on the hill that ran up to the Fair Grounds from Waterworks Pond, were repeated in the stores. Men stood by the bar in the New Willard House laughing and talking of Joe's courtship. After the laughter came the silence. The Winesburg baseball team, under his management, was winning game after game, and the town had begun to respect him. Sensing a tragedy, they waited, laughing nervously.

Late on a Saturday afternoon the meeting between Joe Welling and the two Kings, the anticipation of which had set the town on edge, took place in Joe Welling's room in the New Willard House. George Willard was a witness to the meeting. It came about in this way:

When the young reporter went to his room after the evening meal he saw Tom King and his father sitting in the half darkness in Joe's room. The son had the heavy walking stick in his hand and sat near the door. Old Edward King walked nervously about, scratching his left elbow with his right hand. The hallways were empty and silent.

George Willard went to his own room and sat down at his desk. He tried to write but his hand trembled so that he could not hold the pen. He also walked nervously up and down. Like the rest of the town of Winesburg he was perplexed and knew not what to do.

It was seven-thirty and fast growing dark when Joe Welling came along the station platform toward the New Willard House. In his arms he held a bundle of weeds and grasses. In spite of the terror that made his body shake, George Willard was amused at the sight of the small spry figure holding the grasses and half running along the platform.

Shaking with fright and anxiety, the young reporter lurked in the hallway outside the door of the room in which Joe Welling talked to the two Kings. There had been an oath, the nervous giggle of old Edward King, and then silence. Now the voice of Joe Welling, sharp and clear, broke forth. George Willard began to laugh. He understood. As he had swept all men before him, so now Joe Welling was carrying the two men in the room off their feet with a tidal wave of words. The listener in the hall walked up and down, lost in amazement.

Inside the room Joe Welling had paid no attention to the grumbled threat of Tom King. Absorbed in an idea he closed the door and, lighting a lamp, spread the handful of weeds and grasses upon the floor. "I've got something here," he announced solemnly. "I was going to tell George Willard about it, let him make a piece out of it for the paper. I'm glad you're here. I wish Sarah were here also. I've been going to come to your house and tell you of some of my ideas. They're interesting. Sarah wouldn't let me. She said we'd quarrel. That's foolish."

Running up and down before the two perplexed men, Joe Welling began to explain. "Don't you make a mistake now," he cried. "This is something big." His voice was shrill with excitement. "You just follow me, you'll be interested. I know you will. Suppose this—suppose all of the wheat, the corn, the oats, the peas, the potatoes, were all by some miracle swept away. Now here we are, you see, in this county. There is a high fence built all around us. We'll suppose that. No one can get over the fence and all the fruits of the earth are destroyed, nothing left but these wild things, these grasses. Would we be done

62

for? I ask you that. Would we be done for?" Again Tom King growled and for a moment there was silence in the room. Then again Joe plunged into the exposition of his idea. "Things would go hard for a time. I admit that. I've got to admit that. No getting around it. We'd be hard put to it. More than one fat stomach would cave in. But they couldn't down us. I should say not."

Tom King laughed good naturedly and the shivery, nervous laugh of Edward King rang through the house. Joe Welling hurried on. "We'd begin, you see, to breed up new vegetables and fruits. Soon we'd regain all we had lost. Mind, I don't say the new things would be the same as the old. They wouldn't. Maybe they'd be better, maybe not so good. That's interesting, eh? You can think about that. It starts your mind working, now don't it?"

In the room there was silence and then again old Edward King laughed nervously. "Say, I wish Sarah was here," cried Joe Welling. "Let's go up to your house. I want to tell her of this."

1. Sarah King lived near the

    a. cider mill.
    b. cemetery.
    c. shoe merchant.
    d. fairgrounds.

2. What did the people in town think Tom King may have done?

    a. killed a grey pony
    b. killed a dog
    c. killed a man
    d. carried a heavy, wicked-looking stick

3. How did the town residents feel about Joe Welling's feelings for Sarah?

    a. They had more respect for him because of it.
    b. They felt he would probably get hurt.
    c. They were worried for him.
    d. They thought it was natural.

4. Sarah King was probably _____ than her _____.

    a. heavier . . . brother
    b. darker . . . brother
    c. shorter . . . father
    d. taller . . . father

5. Who was the "young reporter"?

    a. George Willard
    b. Joe Welling
    c. Tom King
    d. Sarah King

6. Why was everyone so nervous about the meeting between Joe Welling and the two Kings?

    a. They were afraid Joe Welling would not like the Kings.
    b. They were afraid the Kings would not like Joe Welling.
    c. They were afraid the Kings would kill Joe Welling.
    d. They were afraid Sarah King would drop Joe Welling.

7. Which of the following is a **true** statement about Joe Welling?

    a. He had been frightened of the Kings from the start.
    b. He was not a very passionate man.
    c. He believed that George Willard could make him a famous man in town.
    d. He genuinely cared for Sarah King.

8. Do you think Joe Welling's ideas are interesting? Why or why not?

OWLS

Owls are incredible birds. They live all over the world. They live in tundra, forests, grasslands, and deserts. There are an estimated one hundred fifty species of owls in the world. There are nineteen in North America. Twelve of these have been seen in Big Bend National Park in Texas. Great horned owl, burrowing owl, elf owl, flammulated owl, and eastern and western screech owl nest in the park. The barn owl, northern pygmy owl, northern saw-whet owl, short-eared owl, and long-eared owl are rare or accidental visitors.

Owls are amazing creatures. They are well-adapted predators. Owls eat mice, voles, shrews, rats, squirrels, lemmings, grasshoppers, fish, snakes, birds, skunks, rabbits, insects, spiders, scorpions, reptiles, and even other owls. Some scientists estimate that one owl will eat two thousand rodents a year. That's five to six per night!

Each owl has a facial disk, which is an area of very short feathers arranged in a rounded pattern on the front of its head. The facial disk helps collect sounds. It funnels the sound to ears hidden beneath the feathers in the disk. Many owls have ear tufts. These are soft feathers that stick up and look like ears. However, in reality, you can't see the ears since the feathers hide them. Owls' ears are asymmetrical in shape, size, and placement. One ear is higher than the other so they can hear noises from above. One ear is lower to hear noises from below. This placement allows the owl to pinpoint the direction and location of sounds. Their hearing is so good that they can hear a mouse squeak up to a half-mile away! Owls can hunt by sound alone. Locating a mouse under leaf litter or snow is easy with their excellent hearing!

Owls have large, fixed eyes at the front of their heads. If our eyes were the same proportions as those of an owl, our eyes would be the size of grapefruits! Because their eyes are fixed and can't move, they must turn their heads to see an object to the side. Owls have very flexible necks with fourteen cervical vertebrae. They can turn their heads up to two hundred and seventy degrees in either direction. This allows them to see more than a full circle of vision. They can focus both eyes at once on an object for accurate depth perception. To adjust to bright daylight, owls can close their pupils to a pinhole and lower their top eyelid. Scientists believe owls are color-blind, seeing only shades of black, white, and gray. Their eyes have very few cones for color detection, but they have lots of rods for light reception. Their eyes are one hundred times more sensitive to light than human eyes.

The owls' excellent hearing and eyesight make them effective predators. They hunt at night when their prey is out. They fly silently through the sky when hunting. Their wings are very wide. They have soft, comb-like edges to their flight feathers. This decreases the amount of disturbance from the airflow around the wings. The velvety surfaces and fringes on the back edge of their flight feathers muffles more noise. The owl molts yearly. It only loses one feather at a time, so it can always fly silently. Owls use their beaks and claws to smooth and tidy their feathers. The feathers are waterproofed with oil from a special gland. Owls even have short, bristly feathers around their beaks that act like cat whiskers to help them sense objects around them.

Owls have sharp, curved, vice-like talons. They are made of keratin. The keratin surrounds a living core. As their talons wear down, they continue to grow and get sharper. They are designed for catching and killing their prey. The talons clamp tight around a perch so that the owl will not fall off a tree branch when sleeping. Owls have eight talons, one per toe, four per leg. Their hooked beaks are also made of keratin. They are used for tearing food when the owls catch larger prey.

Owls are best known for their hooting calls, but they also shriek, bark, hiss, whine, and whistle. Owls call to attract mates and defend their territories. Young owlets will call to beg for food from the adults. Owls will hiss or clack their beaks and tongues in self-defense and as a warning. Listening for owl calls is one way to locate them.

Owls are highly territorial. They often live in the same area for many years. Unfortunately, their populations are decreasing due to loss of habitat and nesting sites. Poisons in their food also affect them. Owls will eat rodents that have fed on poisons or plants that were sprayed with pesticides. These poisons then concentrate in the owl's body, causing illness or even death. Owls in Big Bend National Park are protected from habitat loss and contamination problems.

There are several ways to locate owls in the wild. Look for whitewash on trees and cliffs. Watch known holes in trees; they may be the home of an owl. If you see small birds chasing and dive-bombing a larger bird, check to see if the large bird is an owl. At night, shine a flashlight around the area where you are watching. It may pick up eye shine or reflected light from the eyes of owls.

Another way to look for owls is to locate their pellets. The pile of pellets under a tree indicates an owl roost site. Pellets are small, hard, rounded objects containing the fur, bones, and feathers that the owl can not digest. Eight to twelve hours after a meal, an owl will regurgitate or cough up the pellet and drop it to the ground below. Pellets are clean of all flesh and are virtually odorless. Scientists have used owl pellets to do small mammal studies. By breaking up the pellet and identifying the bones inside, they can determine which mammals live in an area. Not all the bones will be in the pellets. Many of the tiny bones are actually digested by the owl and provide a source of calcium.

1. Owls do **not** live

   a. in tundra.
   b. in forests.
   c. out at sea.
   d. in deserts.

2. How many species of North American owls have **not** been seen in Big Bend National Park?

   a. 7
   b. 12
   c. 19
   d. 150

3. How many species of owls nest in Big Bend National Park?

   a. 6
   b. 12
   c. 19
   d. 150

4. Which of these are rare or accidental visitors to Big Bend National Park?

   a. great horned owls
   b. eastern screech owls
   c. western screech owls
   d. barn owls

5. Which of these are rare or accidental visitors to Big Bend National Park?

   a. burrowing owls
   b. elf owls
   c. northern pygmy owls
   d. flammulated owls

6. Which of the following is **not** true about owls' ears?

    a. They are asymmetrical.
    b. They are in the ear tufts.
    c. One ear is higher than the other.
    d. One ear is lower than the other.

7. Which of the following is **not** true about owls' eyes?

    a. They are the size of grapefruits.
    b. They can't move.
    c. They can see at night.
    d. They are much more sensitive to light than human eyes.

8. What makes owls able to fly so quietly?

    a. small wings
    b. yearly molting
    c. soft edges and fringes on their feathers
    d. waterproofed feathers

9. Owls use their talons for all of the following **except**

    a. holding on tight to tree branches.
    b. catching prey.
    c. killing prey.
    d. tearing larger prey to pieces.

10. Owls are most famous for

    a. hissing.
    b. whining.
    c. whistling.
    d. hooting.

11. Owl populations have declined for all of the following reasons **except**

    a. living in Big Bend National Park.
    b. loss of habitat.
    c. poisoning due to eating poisoned rodents.
    d. poisoning due to eating plants sprayed with pesticide.

12. How would someone **best** characterize this passage?

    a. It tells stories about owls.
    b. It tries to get people to help save owls.
    c. It offers details about a certain kind of owl.
    d. It describes owls and their habitats.

13. Why and how are owl pellets made? Why are they useful?

_____

_____

_____

_____

_____

_____

_____

_____

_____

_____

_____

_____

_____

69

THE EARLY DAYS OF OKLAHOMA CITY

by Arthur W. Dunham

The early days of Oklahoma City were little different from those of other frontier towns, with respect to gambling and its attendant evils. The "sure thing" men and "Knights of the Green Cloth" were on the job. They were open for business early and late. Their field of operation was not restricted. They seemed to have preempted all that territory along the railroad from Main Street to Reno Avenue, with a few places on Grand and California.

The soap man, the "chuck-a-luck" game, fan-tan, faro, roulette, three card monte, stud-poker, and even keno were much in evidence.

Dance halls and "honky tonks" were well patronized. The bright lights were burning and joy was unconfined. Bootleggers were there; booze, White Mule and Choctaw beer with a kick could be had, although the troops were active and did suppress a great deal of this traffic.

I don't know how many people came to Oklahoma City. Many thousands came and moved away in every direction. I believe we had a town of ten thousand when the sun went down that day.

I witnessed several near riots over the city organization and election matters. I saw the infantry troops under Captain Stiles, charge the crowds. A few were clubbed with guns or jabbed with bayonets, but none seriously hurt.

The water supply was a problem. We furnished all the water we could *gratis* from the railroad tank, but had to place a guard over it to keep the water from being wasted, even then the supply was exhausted. We had to haul water in on cars for a while.

The excitement continued at fever heat. Gradually order was brought out of chaos. People had to have supplies; household goods, furniture, stoves, building material, vehicles, farm implements, live stock, groceries, clothing, etc. Everything had to be brought in by the railroad. There was an urgent demand for freight, as you might well know. While the railroad had fully anticipated this, and did all possible to expedite shipments, the facilities for the time being were inadequate. There was not enough track room to hold the cars. The volume of business was only limited by the number of cars we could release from their lading each day. By the time one lot of cars was unloaded another would take its place. This state of affairs continued quite a while.

One of the principle [*sic*] commodities handled was lumber. If my memory serves me right we released one hundred five cars in one day. The lumber was

70

disposed of as fast as it came from the cars. Dealers did a rushing business and could not supply the immediate demands. Many would buy it by the stick and by the arm full [*sic*]. They retailed lumber from cars.

The regular lumber dealers who early established themselves were fine fellows. We got along splendidly with them, but there were several "wild cat" outfits who were taking advantage of the peculiar conditions.

While we had watchmen patrolling our yards, some one got away with four cars of lumber. We did not discover it until checking up at night. I had to have the bills of lading and the freight money amounting to several hundred dollars. The case looked hopeless.

I remembered a certain party who had been at the office several days before making inquiry as to his shipments of lumber. Early next morning I got hold of a deputy United States marshal and we started a search of town. After spending several hours, we were about to give the matter up for the time, when in going into one of the tents we found our man. I immediately recognized him. He at first denied all knowledge of the matter. We told him the United States commissioner was a friend of ours and would he mind accompanying us before that official; that the commissioner took a great interest in strangers and would no doubt give him the opportunity to recite some of his life's history. Well, he produced the bills of lading and peeled from his roll enough bills to satisfy my demands, and the transaction ended. He had enough money to start a bank. I never saw him again.

There were many other trying incidents during this formative period, which if I attempted to describe would take up too much of your time.

The early business men were honest and capable. They wanted only what was right and were willing to co-operate for the best interests of the town. It was a pleasure to know and do business with them.

Pimm & Banks, I believe, had the first furniture store. They were also engaged in the undertaking business. One of them came to me and said he was preparing for shipment the body of a person who had been killed near Council Grove. He had no suitable place to keep it. He asked permission to let the casket rest in our freight house until train time the next day. I reluctantly assented. It was placed in one end of the building. It was quite impossible to find suitable lodging, so a few of our force slept on cots and improvised bunks in the freight room. I came along with a lantern just before daylight. To my surprise I found these fellows had put one end of the bed springs on the box containing the casket, the other end rested on some smaller boxes. Their astonishment and chagrin was complete, when it was found they had been peacefully slumbering with the dead.

The town site board and land office was kept busy. They furnished most of the excitement. After a while a reaction set in and Oklahoma City saw several dull years. Contests and litigation, I believe, was partly responsible for this. It was a big drain on the purse of the people. Large sums for permanent improvements were not available. Titles had to be perfected to get money for large enterprises.

Everyone took an interest in the several capital fights and there were indeed some hot times. I remember once when it was proposed to send a train load of our citizens to Guthrie to protect our legislators, but cooler heads prevailed. It would only have led to trouble and possible bloodshed.

It is surprising how people under adverse circumstances got together for the common good. Churches, schools, societies of all kinds, and organizations for public benefit, were functioning. They soon commenced to make preparations for the first Fourth of July celebration. It was advertised far and near, and the trains brought in good crowds. The citizens attended *en masse*. A large grand stand [*sic*] was erected on the military reservation, bordering on what was later Maywood. There were horse races, roping contests, Indian dances, and some athletic stunts. Public speakers were provided, in fact, the plans contemplated a first class celebration.

The grand stand was crowded to the limit. As the crowd had just gotten comfortably seated, the whole structure collapsed without warning. A good many were hurt. Dr. Ryan's child was killed. I was sitting near the top with two other companions. All three of us were covered with wreckage. I suffered no injury, but had my coat badly torn. The one next to me wearing a Derby hat, had the top cut off, causing his black bushy hair to show through the top of the hat. The other was one of the boys from my office. He was injured so badly that we carried him to a dray. I took him to my home where his injuries were examined by the doctor. Recovery, however was rapid, as no bones were broken. The next day several of the injured were taken out on the train. One poor fellow occupying a cot, was put in the baggage car. He had both legs broken.

The opening of Oklahoma came so late that the first year afforded little opportunity to prepare the ground and raise crops, and many had come from places where crops were poor. The second year saw a crop failure. This left some of the settlers in a deplorable condition; they had a hard time. They displayed a fortitude, courage and tenacity of purpose, worthy [of] the best traditions of our time.

72

Appeals were sent out for aid. The Santa Fe and the Rock Island furnished seed wheat to the farmers at actual cost on notes given, requiring payment the following year. I was custodian of these notes in the Oklahoma City district, and looked after their collection. Let it be said that most of the notes were paid. I feel sure the makers of the unpaid notes would have met their obligation had it been at all possible for them to have done so.

I lived in Oklahoma City for some years after this. I saw the city grow in size and importance. I saw peace, prosperity and happiness all around. Many of those who bore the hardships and weathered the storm were abundantly rewarded. All honor to the old settlers who blazed the way for the making of this great commonwealth. They had the same love of country, the same ideals, and are worthy descendants of those heroic souls who carried the banner of civilization across the continent to the golden West. In this day and age, when all of Europe and most of the world is in the throes of trouble, when discord and strife is the order of the day, where money is worthless, suffering and starvation on every hand, it is well for us to pause and reflect on our own state of affairs.

I thank God I live in a country like ours, where every man is as good as another, where rank or station is not the only attribute of manhood, where industry is justly rewarded, where every one can enjoy life, liberty and the pursuit of happiness. With such a people and such ideals, this Government will endure forever.

1. The "Knights of the Green Cloth" were

    a. dance hall men.
    b. warriors.
    c. gamblers.
    d. bootleggers.

2. White Mule was

    a. a cross between a white horse and a white donkey.
    b. a company that carried freight by mule train.
    c. a gambling game.
    d. liquor.

73

3. The railroad supplied _____ free of charge to people crowded into Oklahoma City.

   a. water
   b. food
   c. lumber
   d. freight

4. Who took four cars of lumber away?

   a. the watchmen, in between resting in the tents
   b. the deputy U.S. marshal
   c. a thief who managed to escape
   d. the owner, who did not want to pay the freight charges

5. A "capital fight," as mentioned in the sixteenth paragraph, means

   a. a fight over which place should be the state capital.
   b. a boxing match.
   c. a fight over money for a business.
   d. any really good fight.

6. The farmers who bought seed wheat "on notes given"

   a. paid with paper money.
   b. bought on credit with a promise to pay in the future.
   c. paid with a promise to replace the seed.
   d. agreed to pay with a portion of their crop.

7. Most of this story took place

   a. just after the Civil War, at the time of Reconstruction.
   b. around 1881, at the opening of the Indian Territory to settlers.
   c. at the turn of the century, during the years before and after 1900.
   d. around the time of World War I.

8. When was this speech delivered?

   a. just after the Civil War, at the time of Reconstruction
   b. around 1881, at the opening of the Indian Territory to settlers
   c. at the turn of the century, during the years before and after 1900
   d. around the time of World War I

9. What was the funniest part of this speech? What was the saddest? What was the most inspiring? What was the most interesting?

75

THE NIGHT BATTLE OF DECEMBER 23rd

Jackson's forces had advanced undetected. At 7:30 p.m., the *Carolina's* opening broadside hit the unsuspecting foe. Recovering from their consternation like the veterans they were, the British put their campfires out, and began to shoot at the schooner. Their muskets and rockets were of even less effect than their three-pounders—the biggest guns they had. The noise of the battle was heard by their troops on Lake Borgne, and by the people in New Orleans. The British troops under the schooner's fire could only lay close to the levee or hide behind buildings, while they listened to the moans and shrieks of the wounded. They were so impressed by the volume of cannon fire that their commander mistakenly reported "two Gun-vessels" besides the *Carolina*.

For ten minutes, "which seemed thirty," Jackson let the little ship carry on the fight alone. Then he ordered his division to advance. The accounts of what followed, on both sides, are confused and contradictory. In the darkness, troops in both armies became separated from each other. The battle broke up into many small fights. Men were captured because they did not know where they were. Troops fired into other units of their own forces. Such things happened to both armies as the battle swayed back and forth.

The infantry under Jackson got off to a bad start, some advancing in column and others in line. A company of the 7th Infantry was the first to clash with the enemy. The Americans drove the invaders back. Then the British were reinforced. The two forces continued to shoot at each other in the dark. This action was typical of the battle.

The main body of the 7th Infantry, coming on, engaged in a brisk fire, followed by the 44th Infantry, which also began to fire as the action became general. The artillery and marines advanced with the regulars. The two cannon were placed. They began to fire in the direction of the enemy. Flashes from the *Carolina*, and later from Coffee's men showed other actions of the battle. In Jackson's Division, the militia apparently lagged at first. They seem to have fired into the more advanced regulars. The British tried to turn the line by attacking the militia, but Plauche's and Daquin's battalions returned the fire and drove them back.

Then larger units of the British 85th and 95th regiments under Colonel William Thornton came into the fight. The Americans had to give ground. The two American fieldpieces were threatened. Jackson himself is said to have saved them. Reorganized somewhat, the Americans drove the enemy back again. The 93rd Highlanders arrived to reinforce the British. The *Carolina* ceased firing as a fog made all further action impossible.

In the meantime, Coffee and his men had moved to the left to attack the British flank. The Tennesseans dismounted and turned their horses loose. The cane fields where they fought were cut by ditches. The could not use horses there. Coffee's men were almost in position when the *Carolina* opened fire. Then they advanced, firing rifles and muskets into the British camp. Experienced in Indian warfare, and accustomed to night battles, the frontiersmen drove the British back. Fighting as individuals, they cut their way through the British camp. "In the whole course of my military career I remember no scene at all resembling this," a British officer wrote later. "An American officer, whose sword I demanded, instead of giving it up . . . made a cut at my head." Friend and foe were confused in the dark.

British reinforcements from Lake Borgne arrived. Their army found a position behind an old levee. Coffee's men could not dislodge them. The Tennesseans kept on shooting after Jackson's immediate command to stop doing so. Both wings of the American army withdrew to a place near the De La Ronde mansion. There they waited for daylight.

The Americans lost twenty-four killed. One hundred and fifteen were wounded and seventy-four missing. The British commander reported forty-six killed, one hundred and sixty-seven wounded, and sixty-four missing. Among the prisoners taken by the Americans was Major Samuel Mitchell. He was the person who was supposed to have set fire to the Capitol in Washington.

New Orleans was saved for the time being. Although Jackson had not driven the enemy from American soil, the results were important. The invader's surprise had been met by a defensive surprise. The British had been given a bad fright by the Americans. The invaders had been thrown off balance. They did not recover during the entire attack on New Orleans. The Night Battle of December 23rd went far toward making the British cautious, when they might still have captured their prize by moving fast.

It had been a close call. Jackson himself wrote that had the British arrived a few days sooner, or had the Americans failed to attack them in their first position, the invaders probably would have taken New Orleans.

1. How many ships did the British commander think were firing at him?

   a. 1
   b. 2
   c. 3
   d. 4

2. How many cannon did Jackson's forces have with them?

   a. 1
   b. 2
   c. 3
   d. 4

3. Which does **not** mean the same thing as "cannon"?

   a. fieldpieces
   b. artillery
   c. guns
   d. rockets

4. What eventually forced the Americans to retreat?

   a. the darkness and confusion of battle
   b. Some troops advanced in columns, some in lines.
   c. the British three-pounders
   d. British reinforcements

5. Who seems to have done the **best** in the battle?

   a. Coffee's Tennessee frontiersmen
   b. the 7th and 44th infantry regulars
   c. the militia
   d. Plauche's and Daquin's battalions

6. Why was this battle so important?

_____

_____

_____

_____

_____

_____

_____

_____

_____

_____

_____

_____

_____

_____

_____

_____

_____

_____

THE MUD RAMPART

Jackson's men were mostly militia and recruits. Jackson knew they could not stand up to a bayonet attack by the British veterans in daylight and in the open. Leaving cavalry to watch the enemy, the Americans withdrew soon after dawn on December 24, 1814, to the Rodriguez Canal. It was the best defensive position in the vicinity.

The Rodriguez Canal formed the boundary between the Chalmette and Macarty plantations. This shallow ditch was on the shortest line between river and swamp. Years before it had been used as a millrace. When the river was higher than the land, river water had operated a small mill. Then it had drained into the canal. It was directly astride the British route of advance across the Chalmette plantation. It was two miles from the scene of the night battle and six miles from the center of New Orleans.

Along the Rodriguez Canal, Jackson's men began to build the mud wall behind which a motley army would defend New Orleans. It would hold off three attacks. City and surrounding country were ransacked for tools and men. The ground was much too wet for trenches. Fence rails were driven into the soil along the canal. Dirt was piled against the rails. By nightfall, the mud wall had the semblance of a field fortification. The work went on. One shift relieved another. Jackson himself was seldom out of the saddle, day or night. (Nearly five thousand miles away, in Ghent, Belgium, the British and American envoys signed a treaty of peace on that Christmas Eve.)

On the morning of the 24th, the *Louisiana* came downstream. It anchored about a mile from the *Carolina*. Whenever redcoats showed that day, their appearance was followed by cannon fire from the ships. The British advance was effectively pinned down. During the day, troops from the British fleet landed at the Villeré plantation. The British advance forces withdrew after dark to join them out of range of the American ships' guns.

In the days following, Americans cut the levee below the Rodriguez Canal. This flooded the plain between their army and the British. The river soon subsided and left the plain dry. Work continued on the mud wall. A threat of attack on New Orleans from the northeast proved false, so General Carroll and his men moved to Jackson's line on the 26th. Pierre Lacoste's battalion also moved here.

Meanwhile, General Pakenham had arrived to take command of the British. His arrival on Christmas Day brought a momentary lift to the spirit of his depressed troops, but the situation of Pakenham and his second in command,

80

Sir Samuel Gibbs, was not good. The terrain made it hard to reinforce and supply their troops. This difficulty was increased by the shortage of pack animals. The Americans held a wall of mud, men, and artillery across the only dry ground on the way to the city which Pakenham had come to take. He must either break through that line or try another route. He decided to try for a break-through.

First, however, Pakenham felt he must rid himself of that intolerable nuisance, the *Carolina*, that kept shooting at the flanks of his army. So heavy guns and howitzers were brought from the fleet. A hot-shot furnace was built. Early on the morning of the 27th, British gunners began firing red-hot balls into the *Carolina*. It caught fire and blew up. Now Pakenham was ready.

That evening, the British drove in the U.S. outposts by a show of superior force. They then established artillery within range of the American lines. In withdrawing, the Americans blew up the buildings of Chalmette's plantation. They did so to give their own artillery a clearer field of fire.

The defenders had been strengthening their position in other ways. The crew of the *Louisiana* had towed that vessel out of range. This saved for a few days the only remaining armed ship on the river.

Some guns from the *Carolina* had been saved and mounted on Jackson's line. Expert gunners from Barataria manned a battery. Two regiments of Louisiana Militia had been added to the force behind the mud wall.

As soon as the mist cleared next morning, December 28th, Pakenham sent his troops forward in close-packed ranks across the cane stubble. The Britishers marched in two main columns. One advanced near the river. The other marched on the edge of the cypress swamp. Skirmishers were deployed between the two columns. A British subaltern later wrote of the approach:

> On we went for about three miles, without any let or hindrance from man or inanimate nature coming our way. But all at once a spectacle was presented to us, such indeed as we ought to have looked for, but such as manifestly took our leaders by surprise. The enemy's army became visible. It was posted in rear of a canal, and covered, though most imperfectly, by an unfinished breastwork.

The artillery of the British fired at the unfinished mud wall and at the *Louisiana*. The Americans returned the fire. In the artillery duel the British cannon were silenced. Then missiles from the ship and from American artillery on land broke up the attacking column along the river.

At the swamp end of the line, a detachment of Carroll's troops under Colonel Hutchinson was ordered to skirt the edge of the swamp and dislodge the invaders. The colonel was killed by the first British fire. The detachment withdraw in confusion.

The British column along the swamp advanced toward the left of the U.S. line. It was not as strong as the right side. On seeing his other column broken, however, Pakenham ordered all his forces back. His officers were bitter at the thought that they could have turned the American left if permitted to continue the attack. Said the subaltern quoted earlier: "There was not a man among us who failed to experience shame and indignation."

This second land battle for New Orleans, called by the British a "reconnaissance in force," did not last long. The Americans lost seven killed and ten wounded. British losses were nine killed and eight wounded.

1. What happened on December 24, 1814, that General Jackson did **not** know about?

    a. The Rodriguez Canal was six miles from the center of New Orleans.
    b. The Rodriguez Canal was no longer used to power a mill.
    c. A peace treaty had been signed in Ghent, Belgium.
    d. The river was higher than the land.

2. Which American tactic did **not** work?

    a. bringing the *Louisiana* downstream
    b. cutting the levee to flood the plain
    c. a false threat of an attack from the northeast
    d. moving Carroll and Lacoste's men to the front

3. What did the hot-shot furnace do?

    a. It helped Pakenham bring heavy guns from his fleet.
    b. It helped dry out the ground around it.
    c. It helped make up for the shortage of pack animals.
    d. It heated the cannonballs to be fired at the *Carolina*.

4. Why did the British attack the strong American position?

    a. It was across the only dry route to New Orleans.
    b. It was protecting the Carolina and the Louisiana.
    c. It was only a canal and a mud wall.
    d. They didn't know it was there.

5. Which of the following is **true**?

    a. The British soldiers on the left were not as strong as the British soldiers on the right.
    b. The British soldiers on the left thought they could defeat the U.S. soldiers on the right.
    c. The British soldiers on the left thought they could defeat the U.S. soldiers on the left.
    d. The British soldiers on the right thought they could defeat the U.S. soldiers on the left.

6. Why do you think the British retreated?

MARIE LAVEAU

Almost nothing written or recorded about Marie Laveau can be cited as fact. Everything that is known about her comes from local legend, hearsay and oral tradition. However, not a child grew up in New Orleans without knowing and fearing the great "Voodoo Queen," Marie Laveau.

It is accepted that she was born in 1794 in Vieux Carré. Her father, Charles Laveau, is said to have been a wealthy white planter. Her mother, Darcantel Marguerite, was a mulatto with a strain of Indian blood. Marie herself is described as being mulatto, quadroon (one-fourth black), and sometimes just as "yellow." She was a tall statuesque woman. She had "curling black hair, 'good' features, dark skin that had a distinct reddish cast, and fierce black eyes." She married Jacques Paris, a free man of color, on August 4, 1819. The ceremony was performed in St. Louis Cathedral. Her contract of marriage can still be found in the files there.

At the time of her marriage, there is no evidence that either she or Jacques were practicing voodoo. Marie and Jacques had both been raised Roman Catholic. She still practiced it devoutly. She attended daily worship at St. Louis Cathedral. Only a short while after the wedding, Jacques disappeared. Marie began calling herself the "Widow Paris." A record of his death did not appear until several years after he had been gone.

It was after the strange death of Jacques that Marie became a professional hairdresser. She began visiting the homes of wealthy white women. This is probably how Marie got her start in practicing voodoo. Women historically have confided things to their hairdressers that they normally would not tell a soul. "All the family skeletons must have come out to dance for Marie." Marie, being the shrewd businesswoman that she was, started cashing in on these secrets.

While she was working as a hairdresser, Marie became involved with Louis Christophe Duminy de Glapion. Just a few years after becoming a widow, Glapion moved into her home. He lived there until he died in 1835. All that is known of Glapion and his relationship with Marie is that he was a quadroon from Santo Domingo who had fought in the Battle of New Orleans. He and Marie had fifteen children.

One of the most famous Marie Laveau stories tells how she came into possession of her house on Rue St. Ann. There are various versions of the story, but this one is the most widely accepted. A man came to Marie early in her practice. He begged her to get his son declared innocent at his upcoming

84

trial. Some say the young man, the son of a wealthy white man, had murdered a young girl. Marie was promised a house as payment if the young man won. The night before the trial Marie put three guinea peppers in her mouth and prayed at St. Louis Cathedral. The next morning, she entered the courthouse. Somehow she put the peppers underneath the judge's chair. The young man was found innocent. He left the courtroom with his euphoric father. Marie was soon the proud owner of a pretty little house on Rue St. Ann.

Was this magic? Most doubt it. It was later discovered that Marie had approached a witness, who happened to be deathly afraid of voodoo. She had threatened him if he did not testify in favor of the young man. It seems that this was Marie's main style of magic: the manipulation of those she served.

When Marie was a hairdresser, she began what became her network of informers. She continued to build on it over the years. She later used her "spies" to find the best way to "cure" a cheating husband (which, incidentally, usually involved blackmailing the mistress), find true love for the lonely, and avenge the enemies of the angry.

However, there was another side to Marie that was more indicative of her Catholic upbringing. She helped nurse the wounded at the Battle of New Orleans. She nursed the sick during the yellow fever epidemic of the 1850s. She was a missionary to the convicts on death row in the New Orleans city prison. This was a side of Marie that a lot of her followers did not know about.

The are very few remaining facts known about Marie. One is that her longtime lover, Glapion, died in their home on June 27, 1835, at the age of sixty-six. Over the years to follow, there are several small articles that mention Marie appearing in the New Orleans newspapers. These mostly deal with small legal battles she had with various voodoo practitioners. Then, on June 16, 1881, the newspapers announced that Marie Laveau was dead. She would have been eighty-seven years old. The main mystery of Marie Laveau arises when people still claim to be seeing her long after her reported death. Who was it that died, and who did people continue to see? The widely accepted opinion is that it was the Widow Paris that died in 1881. Her daughter, Marie Glapion, a striking look-alike, then took over the role of Voodoo Queen. Marie II was about fifty years old when her mother died. This theory accounts for sightings all the way into the early twentieth century.

85

1. Of the following, which would the author of this passage believe to be **true**?

    a. Everything written about Marie Laveau should be taken as fact.
    b. Marie Laveau was born in 1794 in Vieux Carré.
    c. At the time of her marriage, Marie's husband was practicing voodoo.
    d. Jacques Paris was a mulatto with a strain of Native-American blood.

2. What solid piece of evidence exists to prove the marriage between Marie and Jacques Paris?

    a. a marriage contract
    b. an almanac from 1819
    c. records of their voodoo practices
    d. oral tradition

3. What does "All the family skeletons must have come out to dance for Marie" mean?

    a. Everyone must have loved her work as a hairdresser.
    b. People wanted her to meet their families.
    c. The women she worked for told her all their secrets.
    d. She must have dressed up in a skeleton costume.

4. Of the following, which is **not** true of Marie's relationship with Louis Christophe Duminy de Glapion?

    a. The couple had 15 children.
    b. Glapion died in 1835.
    c. The couple married just before Glapion moved into Marie's house.
    d. Marie was working as a hairdresser when she met Glapion.

5. How did Marie "cure" a cheating husband?

    a. by starting a network of informers
    b. by blackmailing his mistress
    c. by appealing to her Catholic roots
    d. by pretending to be dead

86

6. According to the author of this passage, what is most likely to be **true** about Marie Laveau's death?

    a. She died at the age of 50.
    b. The newspapers reported a lie about her death.
    c. Many people mistook Marie's daughter for Marie.
    d. She was playing a voodoo trick.

7. According to legend, how did Marie Laveau come to own her house on Rue St. Ann?

8. Make an argument claiming that Marie Laveau was not actually practicing voodoo throughout her life. Use details from the article to support your ideas.

_____

_____

_____

_____

_____

_____

_____

_____

_____

_____

_____

_____

_____

_____

_____

_____

_____

_____

BATTLE OF PILOT KNOB

Major General Sterling Price had led three divisions of Confederate troops into Missouri. With them he planned to attack St. Louis. The Union's General Rosecrans had sent St. Louis district commander General Thomas Ewing to cut them off at Pilot Knob. Pilot Knob was his only fortification in south central Missouri.

Price approached Pilot Knob. Two Confederate divisions, Fagan's and Marmaduke's, suffered more than two hundred casualties in the first evening and morning of fighting. Then, on September 27, 1864, they swarmed over the encircling hills. Ewing found himself completely bottled in the fort with no avenue of escape. Price determined that his big guns would be placed on top of nearby Shepherd Mountain. He then sent an emissary, Colonel Lauchlan Maclean, to the fort to ask for a Union surrender.

The Union general refused to surrender. Maclean returned to Price. He urged a frontal assault on the fort. Maclean argued that there was no time to bring up all of the Confederate artillery and place it on the mountain. Nevertheless, Price tried. The first attempt at placement saw a Confederate cannon disabled and its gunner killed by the first few volleys from the expert Federal artillerymen. Price soon became convinced that placing the big guns on the mountain would be no easy task.

Price was now determined to try a frontal assault. For nearly an hour, a hush fell over the peaceful valley. It was the silence before the storm. Among the heavy brush and timber on the mountains the Confederate commanders were forming their brigades for battle. In the fort, Ewing ordered his cannons run down from maximum elevation. They were to be trained across the flat. They could now shoot directly at an advancing army. Their load was to be canister rounds. Each would be filled with hundreds of half-inch lead balls. There was not enough room atop the walls of the fort for all the riflemen to fire. Details were assembled to tear cartridges, load rounds, and pass up the guns as they were needed. At the foot of the encircling mountains, nine thousand Confederates crouched down and waited.

The Storm

At two o'clock the silence was broken. Confederate cannons in the gap opened on the earthen fort. Soon waves of dismounted Southern cavalry poured into the open. The troops were formed in long columns three ranks deep. They slowly moved toward the fort. Inside the walled enclosure, the riflemen were ordered to hold their fire. The Union artillery was opened on the advancing Confederate lines. At short range across the flat, the big guns

89

could not miss. Dense clouds of smoke blanketed the fort and rose in columns hundreds of feet high.

The surrounding Confederate mass continued its ill-fated advance. The Confederate horde was only five hundred yards from the walls when Union riflemen were ordered to fire. Empty rifles were passed down. Loaded ones were handed up. The three hundred rifles along the top of the walls spewed forth lead as if from machine guns. Smoke from the heavy fire obliterated the Confederate lines.

At two hundred yards, the Southern brigades unleashed their first volley. They then broke into a crazed running charge. The Union gunners could see only the charging legs. The smoke blocked everything from view. The walls of Fort Davidson now blazed as fire leaped from the muzzles of the gun barrels. At thirty yards, Price's troops finally broke. Slowly they started to fall back.

Spurred on by their officers, the terrified southerners re-formed their lines and surged ahead. Again, they hesitated. Again their officers turned them about. This third charge saw some men actually charge into a dry moat which surrounded the fort. The Union gunners had artillery shells fused as grenades. They leaned over the walls and tossed them into the huddled Confederate soldiers.

The blood and confusion now was too much to bear. Just a few yards from the fort, Price's soldiers finally turned and ran. As the soldiers streamed away from the fort and the smoke had a chance to clear, the incredible carnage became apparent. For five hundred yards on the three sides of the fort that were attacked, the ground was covered with dead and wounded men. In the short few minutes that had just passed, one of the bloodiest clashes of the Civil War had taken place.

The Great Escape

The black rainy night which settled in the Arcadia Valley saw every shelter from Ironton filled with Confederate wounded. Price sent messages north toward the Union lines to beg for medical assistance. His entire command lay in a pitiful state of confusion. Most companies were scattered. Only a few posted sentries or maintained any semblance of military discipline.

Inside Fort Davidson, General Ewing was deciding on his next move. He correctly surmised that the new morning would dawn with Price's artillery perched on top of Shepherd Mountain. The fort could no longer be defended.

90

Near midnight, Ewing hit upon a daring plan. He would attempt to slip his troops out of the fort and through Confederate lines.

At midnight, Ewing muffled the wheels of the six field guns. With the 14th Iowa at the head the column marched silently out of the fort. The weary Union defenders moved north along the road to Potosi. Miraculously they marched unchallenged right through the loose Confederate lines. In a few hours, Ewing was miles away from the fort.

At two o'clock in the morning, a squad left behind in the fort blew up the powder magazine in the center of the earthen enclosure. Confederates roused by the blast thought the explosion was an accident. At dawn, Price's dwindling army awakened to find the fort empty. It had a giant smoking hole in the center. In a fit of rage, Price sent Marmaduke's division after the escaping Federals. Although Ewing ran headlong into Shelby, he was able to successfully fight his way to a strong Union fortification in Rolla. Marmaduke and Shelby wasted three days on futile pursuit.

With his best assault troops lost and two of his divisions in disarray, Price knew that an attack on the now reinforced city of St. Louis was out of the question. To salvage something from the ill-fated campaign, Price decided to turn northwest. He planned to capture Missouri's capital for the Confederacy. However, the week wasted at Pilot Knob and the crushing defeat there had cost him dearly. Price found that Jefferson City, too, had been reinforced. He fought only a brief, half-hearted skirmish.

Price had been forced to bypass St. Louis and Jefferson City because of overwhelming Federal strength there. Price's troops then struggled past Lexington and Independence. They finally lost a fight at Westport, near Kansas City. They retired, exhausted, into Arkansas. Westport was the last major Civil War battle west of the Mississippi River.

> General Price he made a raid, made a raid, made a raid
> General Price he made a raid
> An' lost many a soldier . . .
>
> —A game song

1. Who commanded the Union soldiers at Pilot Knob?

    a. Major General Sterling Price
    b. General Rosecrans
    c. General Thomas Ewing
    d. Fagan and Marmaduke

2. Who commanded the Confederate soldiers attacking Pilot Knob?

   a. Major General Sterling Price
   b. Colonel Lauchlan Maclean
   c. General Thomas Ewing
   d. Fagan and Marmaduke

3. Who commanded two of the three Confederate divisions?

   a. Major General Sterling Price
   b. Colonel Lauchlan Maclean
   c. General Thomas Ewing
   d. Fagan and Marmaduke

4. Why didn't the Confederate troops just go around Pilot Knob?

   a. Shepherd Mountain was in the way.
   b. Colonel Maclean argued for a frontal assault.
   c. The Union soldiers had ambushed them.
   d. If they had done so, Union soldiers could have attacked them from behind.

5. Why were the cannon in the fort pointed as high as possible before they were lowered?

   a. so they could shoot as far as possible
   b. to shoot Confederate soldiers as they approached across the plain
   c. because there was not enough room for every rifleman on top of the wall
   d. because they were loaded with canister rounds

6. How close to the Union walls did the Confederate troops get in the first charge before they started retreating?

   a. 30 yards
   b. 170 yards
   c. 200 yards
   d. 500 yards

7. How close did the Confederate troops get in the final charge?

   a. less than 10 yards
   b. 30 yards
   c. 200 yards
   d. 500 yards

8. What forced the first retreat?

   a. officers
   b. grenades
   c. intense rifle fire
   d. smoke

9. What forced the final retreat?

   a. officers
   b. grenades
   c. intense rifle fire
   d. smoke

10. Why did Ewing's forces retreat?

    a. They knew they could not withstand another charge.
    b. They knew the cannons on the mountain would be too much to fight.
    c. They knew the Confederates were getting reinforcements.
    d. They preferred to fight on open ground.

11. Price's last stand was at

    a. Rolla.
    b. St. Louis.
    c. Jefferson City.
    d. Westport.

12. Why didn't Ewing attack Price's troops after they gave up their attack?

_____

_____

_____

_____

_____

_____

_____

_____

_____

_____

_____

_____

_____

_____

_____

_____

JOHN DEERE

by Matthew K. Gumbel
Macomb Junior/Senior High School, Macomb
from Illinois History: A Magazine for Young People, 1992

John Deere was born February 7, 1804, in Rutland, Vermont. He was eight when he lost his father. His father had taught him to "let truth and honesty be your guide." The daily sight of his seamstress mother's shiny needles gliding easily in and out of fabrics also influenced his later work.

John attended school for a while. Being a practical boy, he apprenticed himself to Captain Benjamin Lawrence. He began learning the blacksmithing trade. The captain's insistence on superior workmanship instilled in his young apprentice an abiding concern for quality.

Blacksmithing soon earned John quite a reputation. Farmers bragged that "John Deere's shovels were like no others. . . . [They] scoured themself [sic] of the soil by reason of their smooth, satiny surface." His pitchforks "slipped in and out of the hay like needles."

Earning a living was difficult in Vermont. John decided to head west. He set up shop in Grand Detour, Illinois. He soon discovered that Illinois farmers faced a serious problem. The prairie soil was moist and sticky. Their heavy wood-and-cast-iron plows stuck in the gumbo. Farmers said it would be impossible to make a plow that would work in the sticky soil, but Deere had heard the word impossible before. When he was an apprentice, John could repair tools that farmers thought were unfixable.

One day in 1837, while repairing a broken shaft at the sawmill of fellow Vermont native, Leonard Andrus, John noticed a shiny broken sawblade in the corner. It gave him an idea. Why not use it to form a smooth, polished steel plow to slip through heavy Illinois soils? In the days that followed, no shoeing of horses or making of tools went on in Deere's shop. The only thing he was working on was his plow.

The "share," or sharp edge, he cut from the sawmill blade. The wrought-iron moldboard was first formed into a curve by bending it over a log. Then the blade was polished so that sticky earth would slide off. Deere took the finished plow to a neighboring field where he tested it in front of a crowd of doubtful spectators. The plow slipped easily through the gummy soil. By day's end Deere had orders for two more of what was called "the plow that broke the plains."

On March 20, 1843, Leonard Andrus and Deere became partners. They built a factory equipped with horse power and steam engines. They were soon selling $10 plows.

As business increased, the lack of transportation to remote Grand Detour either by rail or on the small Rock River grew to be a serious problem. Deere made the critical decision to leave. He dissolved his partnership with Andrus. He picked Moline, Illinois, as his new location. Moline was better suited for business. The Mississippi River was invaluable to ship raw materials and finished products.

There, in June 1848, he formed a partnership with Robert N. Tate. They constructed a factory. They were soon in business manufacturing plows. Although securing high-quality steel was difficult and expensive, Deere finally persuaded an American firm to produce the kind of steel he had been importing at high cost. The first slab of cast plow steel ever rolled in America was produced by Jones and Quigs of Pittsburgh for John Deere of Moline, Illinois.

In late 1848, Deere and Tate took on a new partner, John Gould. Deere concentrated on improvements. Production was left to Tate. Gould supervised finances. Deere developed new concepts of marketing. He set up a large sales operation. He advertised in papers and farm publications. He gave demonstrations on farms and at fairs. Business increased steadily. Soon farmers in surrounding states were buying Deere plows.

The company's continuing success grew from Deere's frequently expressed belief, "I will never put my name on a plow that does not have in it the best that is in me." Another philosophy that proved to be a sound business principle was, "If I don't improve my plow, somebody else will and I will lose my trade." Occasionally his eagerness to improve got him into legal trouble. Other manufacturers felt he borrowed ideas too freely.

In 1853, Deere decided to conduct business under his own name. He terminated the partnership with Tate and Gould. In the following years, Deere plow production soared. The late 1800s also brought many expansions in the company's line—planters, cultivators, harrows, and harvesters—to fill customers' needs. John Deere remained active as president of his company until his death in Moline on May 12, 1886, at the age of 82. After his death, family members continued to lead Deere and Company.

The success of John Deere's "self polisher" opened Illinois and the west to development and began a new era in agriculture. His genuine concern for the farmers and their problems, his commitment to quality, and his belief in continual improvement of products characterized his company. John Deere is still a household name on many farms. The invention of the steel plow was only the beginning. Today, Deere & Company products are sold around the world.

1. John Deere's mother was a

    a. teacher.
    b. seamstress.
    c. cook.
    d. blacksmith.

2. John Deere's father died in

    a. 1804.
    b. 1808.
    c. 1812.
    d. 1816.

3. John Deere learned the importance of quality workmanship from

    a. his father.
    b. his mother.
    c. Captain Benjamin Lawrence.
    d. Leonard Andrus.

4. Leonard Andrus was

    a. a blacksmith.
    b. a native of Illinois.
    c. a farmer.
    d. the owner of a sawmill.

5. John Deere noticed that sawblades were made from

    a. wood.
    b. cast-iron.
    c. roughened steel.
    d. smooth, polished steel.

6. John Deere knew that Illinois' soil was **not**

   a. moist.
   b. loose and dry.
   c. sticky.
   d. gummy.

7. John Deere decided to try to make the sharp edge of a plow from

   a. wood.
   b. cast-iron.
   c. roughened steel.
   d. smooth, polished steel.

8. John Deere's first partner was

   a. a blacksmith.
   b. a native of Illinois.
   c. a farmer.
   d. the owner of a sawmill.

9. John Deere decided to move to Moline because he wanted to

   a. get away from Leonard Andrus.
   b. be near the Rock River.
   c. be near the Mississippi River.
   d. be near a railroad.

10. At first, John Deere had to obtain high-quality steel from

    a. Europe.
    b. Pittsburgh.
    c. Robert N. Tate.
    d. Leonard Andrus.

11. For the company, Robert Tate was in charge of

    a. marketing.
    b. manufacturing.
    c. finances.
    d. improvements.

12. John Gould was in charge of

    a. marketing.
    b. manufacturing.
    c. finances.
    d. improvements.

13. Which do you think was more important to John Deere's success: his product improvements or his marketing innovations? Why?

14. Very few inventors make good businessmen. Why do you think this is? Was John Deere an exception? Why or why not?

_____

_____

_____

_____

_____

_____

_____

_____

_____

_____

_____

_____

_____

_____

_____

_____

FREDERICK DOUGLASS ESCAPES FROM MARYLAND

At the age of fifteen, Frederick Douglass was again put to work as a field hand. He was extremely unhappy about his situation. Thomas Auld starved his slaves. They had to steal food from neighboring farms to survive. Frederick received many beatings and saw even worse ones given to others. He then organized a Sunday religious service for the slaves. It met in nearby Saint Michaels. The services were soon stopped by a mob led by Thomas Auld. Thomas Auld had found Frederick especially difficult to control, so he decided to have someone tame his unruly slave.

In January 1834, Frederick was sent to work for Edward Covey, a poor farmer who had gained a reputation around Saint Michaels for being an expert "slave breaker." Frederick was not too displeased with this arrangement because Covey fed his slaves better than Auld did. The slaves on Covey's farm worked from dawn until after nightfall, plowing, hoeing, and picking corn. Although the men were given plenty of food, they had very little time allotted to eat before they were sent back to work. Covey hid in bushes and spied on the slaves as they worked. If he caught one of them resting, he would beat him with thick branches.

After being on the farm for one week, Frederick was given a serious beating for letting an oxen team run wild. During the months that followed, he was continually whipped until he began to feel that he was "broken." On one hot August afternoon, his strength failed him. He collapsed in the field. Covey kicked and beat Frederick to no avail. Finally, Covey walked away in disgust. Frederick mustered the strength to get up and walk to the Auld farm. He pleaded with his master to let him stay. Auld had little sympathy for him and sent him back to Covey.

Beaten down as Frederick was, he found the strength to rebel when Covey began tying him to a post in preparation for a whipping. "At that moment—from whence came the spirit I don't know—I resolved to fight," Frederick wrote. "I seized Covey hard by the throat, and as I did so, I rose." Covey and Frederick fought for almost two hours until Covey finally gave up, telling Frederick that his beating would have been less severe had he not resisted. "The truth was," said Frederick, "that he had not whipped me at all." Frederick had discovered an important truth: "Men are whipped oftenist who are whipped easiest." He was lucky. Legally, a slave could be killed for resisting his master. Covey had a reputation to protect; he did not want it known that he could not control a sixteen-year-old boy.

After working for Covey for a year, Frederick was sent to work for a farmer named William Freeland. Freeland was a relatively kind master but, by now, Frederick did not care about having a kind master. All Frederick wanted was his freedom. He started an illegal school for blacks in the area. It met secretly at night and on Sundays. He began to plan his escape to the North with five other slaves.

A year had passed since Frederick began working for William Freeland. His plan of escape had been completed. His group planned to steal a boat, row to the northern tip of Chesapeake Bay, and then flee on foot to the free state of Pennsylvania. The escape was supposed to take place just before the Easter holiday in 1836. Then one of Frederick's associates had exposed the plot. A group of armed white men captured the slaves and put them in jail.

Frederick was in jail for about a week. While imprisoned, he was inspected by slave traders. He fully expected that he would be sold to "a life of living death" in the Deep South. To his surprise, Thomas Auld came and released him. Then Frederick's master sent him back to Hugh Auld in Baltimore. The two brothers had finally settled their dispute. Frederick was now eighteen years old. He was six feet tall and very strong from his work in the fields.

Hugh Auld decided that Frederick should work as a caulker to earn his keep. A caulker was a man who forced sealing matter into the seams in a boat's hull to make it watertight. He was hired out to a local shipbuilder so that he could learn the trade. While apprenticing at the shipyard, Frederick was harassed by white workers who did not want blacks—slaves or free—competing with them for jobs. One afternoon, a group of white apprentices beat Frederick up and nearly took out one of his eyes. Hugh Auld was angry when he saw what had happened. He attempted to press charges against the assailants. However, none of the shipyard's white employees would step forward to testify about the beating. Free blacks had little hope of obtaining justice through the southern court system, which refused to accept a black person's testimony against that of a white person. Therefore, the case had to be dropped.

After Frederick recovered from his injuries, he began apprenticing at the shipyard where Hugh Auld worked. Within a year, he was an experienced caulker. He was being paid the highest wages possible for a tradesman at his level. He was allowed to seek his own employment and collect his own pay. At the end of each week he gave all his earnings to Hugh Auld. Sometimes he was allowed to keep a little money for himself but, as time passed, he became resentful of having to give up his hard-earned pay.

In Frederick's spare time, he met with a group of educated free blacks. He indulged in the luxury of being a student again. Some of the free blacks formed an educational association called the East Baltimore Mental Improvement Society, where Frederick had been admitted. This is where Frederick learned his debating skills. At one of the society's meetings, Frederick met a free black woman named Anna Murray. Anna was a few years older than Frederick. She was a servant for a wealthy Baltimore family. Although Anna was a plain, uneducated woman, Frederick admired her qualities of thriftiness, industriousness, and religiousness. Anna and Frederick were soon in love. In 1838, they were engaged.

Love and courtship increased Frederick's discontent with his status. After Frederick's escape attempt, Thomas Auld had promised him that if he worked hard, he would be freed when he turned twenty-five. Frederick did not trust his master and he resolved to escape. However, escaping would be very difficult due to professional slave catchers patrolling the borders between slave states and free states. Free blacks traveling by train or steamboat had to carry official papers listing their name, age, height, skin color, and other distinguishing features. In order to escape, Frederick needed money to pay for traveling expenses. Frederick arranged with Hugh Auld to hire out his time. That is, Frederick would take care of his own room and board and pay his master a set amount each week, keeping any extra money for himself. This also gave him the opportunity to see what it was like living on his own.

This arrangement worked out quite well until Frederick returned home late one night and failed to pay Hugh Auld on time. Auld was furious and revoked his hiring-out privilege. Frederick was so enraged over this that he refused to work for a week. He finally gave in to Auld's threats, but he also made a resolution that in three weeks, on September 3, 1838, he would be on a northbound train. Escaping was a difficult decision for Frederick. He would be leaving his friends and his fairly comfortable life in Baltimore forever. He did not know when and if he would see Anna Murray again. Furthermore, if he was caught during his escape, he was sure that he would be either killed or sold to slave traders. Taking all of this into consideration, Frederick resolved to escape to freedom.

With money that he borrowed from Anna, Frederick bought a ticket to Philadelphia, Pennsylvania. He also had a friend's "sailor's protection." That was a document that certified that the person named on it was a free seaman. Dressed in a sailor's red shirt and black cravat, Frederick boarded the train. Frederick reached northern Maryland before the conductor made it to the "Negro car" to collect tickets and examine papers. Frederick became very tense when the conductor approached him to look at his papers because he did not fit the description on them. However, with only a quick glance, the conductor walked on and the relieved Frederick sank back in his seat. On a couple of occasions, he thought that he had been recognized by other passengers from Baltimore but, if so, they did not turn him in to the authorities.

Upon arriving in Wilmington, Delaware, Frederick then boarded a steamboat to Philadelphia. Even after stepping on Pennsylvania's free soil, he knew he was not yet safe from slave catchers. He immediately asked directions to New York City. That night, he took another train north. On September 4, 1838, Frederick arrived in New York City. Frederick could not find the words to express his feelings of leaving behind his life in slavery. He later wrote, "A new world had opened upon me. . . . Anguish and grief, like darkness and rain, may be depicted, but gladness and joy, like the rainbow, defy the skill of pen or pencil."

In 1877, Douglass traveled to St. Michaels, Maryland, to visit old friends and to see the farms and plantations where he had worked as a slave. While there, he took the opportunity to visit his old master, Thomas Auld. Aged and feeble, Auld greeted his former slave as Marshal Douglass and the two men spoke for a long time. Auld both justified and apologized for his actions as a slaveholder. Overall, the former master and slave were able to part on good terms.

1. At first, Frederick Douglass was happy to be sent to the Covey farm because he

    a. could organize Sunday religious services there.
    b. knew he would not be beaten as often.
    c. liked to work in the field.
    d. could eat better there.

2. Frederick walked back to the Auld farm after

    a. being beaten for resting.
    b. being beaten for letting a team of oxen escape.
    c. being beaten after collapsing one afternoon.
    d. seizing Covey by the throat.

3. After Frederick fought with Covey, Covey pretended that

    a. he had given Frederick a beating.
    b. he and Frederick had not fought.
    c. he was going to have Frederick killed for resisting him.
    d. Frederick had received a less harsh beating.

4. _____ displayed some kindness in arranging to have Frederick released from jail after he had been caught planning to flee.

   a. Thomas Auld
   b. Hugh Auld
   c. Edward Covey
   d. William Freeland

5. Hugh Auld was Thomas Auld's

   a. father.
   b. son.
   c. brother.
   d. brother-in-law.

6. Hugh Auld angered Frederick by

   a. having Frederick learn a trade and working alongside him.
   b. trying to press charges when Frederick was attacked.
   c. allowing Frederick to hire out.
   d. withdrawing the hiring-out privilege.

7. Frederick was able to escape by borrowing money from

   a. Anna.
   b. Thomas.
   c. Hugh.
   d. a sailor.

8. Frederick was able to escape by using _____'s identification papers.

   a. Anna
   b. Thomas
   c. Hugh
   d. a sailor

9. From which kind of book did this passage likely come?

   a. a biography
   b. an autobiography
   c. a book of fables
   d. a collection of short stories

10. Which two parts of this story did you find the most surprising? Why?

_____

_____

_____

_____

_____

_____

_____

_____

_____

_____

_____

_____

_____

_____

_____

_____

_____

_____

106

LAND SHARKS

With the increase in the value of land came increased disputes over land ownership. Lawsuits brought disaster and ruin to many of the best people and best homes in Kentucky. With a class of men called "land sharks," it became a profitable business to hunt up problems with land ownership and to argue these in the courts. As a result, many titles of land ownership were found to be defective, and some had become worthless. For thousands of people, broken homes and broken hearts were the results. Many of Kentucky's worthiest people suffered.

By the ruinous land laws and litigation the veteran pioneer, Daniel Boone, lost all his fine lands in Kentucky. He came to such poverty as to lead him, in one of his petitions, to say, "I have not a spot of ground whereon to lay my bones." He left Kentucky, saying that he would never return to live in a country so ungrateful. About 1796 he moved to Missouri. He settled fifty miles west of St. Louis. Spain owned this territory then. The Spanish governor gave him a liberal grant of land, and appointed him to an office. Around him, his sons and daughters and their families settled.

The broad forests were full of game. Here Boone again indulged his passion for the hunter's life. The old hero neglected to complete his title to his new land and home in the foreign country. He lost this also. Congress afterward made him a smaller grant. He died in Missouri on the 26th of September, 1820, in the eighty-sixth year of his age. He was buried at the side of his wife. He lay in a coffin he had made for himself some years before. In 1845, the legislature of Kentucky had the remains of the pioneer and his wife removed and buried, with honor, in the cemetery at Frankfort. A suitable monument was erected on the spot.

There is a sadder story to tell than even that of Boone. George Rogers Clark was the greatest military genius in the early history of Kentucky. His greatest achievements had been accomplished before he was thirty years old. Settling about eight miles above Louisville, he fell into habits of intemperance, which unfitted him for public service. Virginia voted him large land bounties, as the only pay for the valuable services he had rendered. These were withheld for years. He was left, helpless and poor, upon the bounty of his kinsmen. At last when Virginia sent a messenger to present him with a jeweled sword, voted by her assembly, he responded, "Young man, go tell Virginia, when size needed a sword, I found one."

The young man brought back this message. Virginia, too late, made good her broken promises to Clark. The worn-out old man was buried at Locust Grove.

107

Now his remains rest beneath a plain headstone in Cave Hill Cemetery, at Louisville. It silently rebukes Kentucky and America for ingratitude to one of the greatest men of history.

The story is told that, after Yorktown, a French officer, who there met Clark, on his return to France, said to the king, "Sire, there are two Washingtons in America."

"What do you mean?" said the king.

"I mean," replied the officer, "that there is Washington, whom the world knows. And there is George Rogers Clark, the conqueror of the Northwest, as great a man as Washington in his field of action, for the opportunities given him."

Simon Kenton shared a like fate. Losing his lands, acre by acre, through the devices of the land sharks and the tortuous ways of the laws and the courts, this simplehearted old pioneer and hero found himself penniless in old age. As allowed by law then, to the shame of Kentucky and of civilization, his body was taken for debt. He was cast into prison by his creditors upon the very spot on which he built his first cabin, in 1775. In 1799, thus beggared, he shook the dust of Kentucky from his feet. He moved into Ohio, and settled near the site of Urbana. In 1813 he joined Governor Shelby's troops, and was with them in the battle of the Thames.

In 1820, Kenton moved from Urbana to the site upon the Scioto River, where the Native Americans, forty years before, had tied him to a stake to be burned. This was his last home. Here he died on the 29th of April, 1836, at the age of eighty-one. A few years before his death, he made a visit to Frankfort, Kentucky, in his pioneer garb. He was an unknown stranger for a time. He was finally recognized by an old comrade, General Thomas Fletcher, and treated with marked respect. The legislature promptly released him some mountain lands, which had been sold for taxes. Some friends soon after obtained a pension of two hundred and forty dollars a year, through an act of Congress.

1. Based on a reading of this passage, how do you think the author felt toward the people affected by the actions of the land sharks?

    a. sympathetic
    b. angry
    c. foolish
    d. disinterested

2. Why were land sharks unpopular?

   a. Land sharks would steal land from settlers.
   b. Land sharks would hunt down illegal land claims and cause settlers to lose their homes.
   c. Land sharks would raid the settlers' fields in the middle of the night, taking all the food they could.
   d. Land sharks would murder settlers who had staked illegal claims.

3. Why did Daniel Boone leave Kentucky, vowing never to return?

   a. He was upset when he was not elected governor.
   b. He fell in love with land in Missouri.
   c. He was paid good money by the Spanish to leave Kentucky.
   d. He felt that Kentucky did not give him the respect that he deserved.

4. The following sentence appears in this passage:

   Virginia, too late, made good her broken promises to Clark.

   Why was it too late?

   a. Clark no longer needed land.
   b. Clark no longer wanted anything from Virginia.
   c. Clark had died.
   d. Clark thought that the jeweled sword was enough of a gift for his years of service to the country.

5. Why was Simon Kenton imprisoned?

   a. He had become a thief and a murderer.
   b. He lost his land and went bankrupt.
   c. He became a spy for the British.
   d. He protested the election of Washington as president.

6. Which of the following most accurately depicts what became of Boone, Clark, and Kenton?

   a. They were treated like royalty by the United States government.
   b. They were awarded much land, money, and esteem for their valiant service in Kentucky.
   c. They struggled to maintain enough land and money to survive as they grew old.
   d. They were made honorary members of Congress.

7. Daniel Boone vowed never to return to Kentucky. However, after his death, his remains were returned to Frankfort with honors. How do you think he would have felt about this?

_____

_____

_____

_____

_____

_____

_____

_____

_____

_____

_____

_____

_____

_____

_____

_____

_____

8. Even today, some veterans of wars sometimes find themselves without enough food, money, medicine, or care, just like thousands of other citizens. What are your opinions about this? Do veterans of war deserve any extra assistance or special privileges as they age?

_____

_____

_____

_____

_____

_____

_____

_____

_____

_____

_____

_____

_____

_____

_____

_____

_____

_____

_____

_____

SHAWNEETOWN

by Julie Lea Wilson
Booth School, Carmi
from Illinois History: A Magazine for Young People, December 2000

Shawneetown is located on the Ohio River in southern Illinois. It is the oldest incorporated town in the state. It has been labeled by some as the "Gateway to Southern Illinois." Others have called it the "Gateway to the West." There is no doubt that it led the way to the early settlement and growth of southern Illinois.

Soldiers returning home with their families after the Revolutionary War were each given three hundred acres of land. Many settled near Shawneetown. These pioneers were from Ohio and Kentucky. Others left from Pittsburgh, Pennsylvania, and floated down the Ohio River. They loaded all their goods onto flatboats. The boats were large enough to hold a wagon, an ox, a horse, or a cow, and all the family with their belongings. Often these boats were built with log walls to protect them from Indians. A few settlers found their way across the Wabash from Indiana. Some came by roads or rivers in western Kentucky. They merely crossed the Ohio to reach the state.

Many settlers came looking for a place to live that did not allow slavery. Others wanted to practice their professions in a new territory. Some were looking to make money through land speculation.

One of these settlers was blacksmith Michael Sprinkle. He was the first white settler of Shawneetown in 1800. He built a log cabin and set up a forge. He could supply the needs of pioneers and Indians in hardware. Sprinkle was also a gunsmith. His business was the beginning of a growing town. It was a good place for people to settle. The river provided transportation. There was plenty of timber for building cabins. Game was plentiful. There were salt licks nearby.

In 1802 Alexander Wilson built a ferry. He began a business of ferrying settlers across the river. Wilson charged the following prices:

- Each wagon and team (4 horses or oxen)   **$1.50**
- Each wagon and team (not more than 2 horses)   **$1.00**
- 2 wheel carriages (not more than two horses)   **$.75**
- Mare and horse   **$.50**
- Each person (children under 7 excepted)   **$.25**
- Each horse, mare, or mule   **$.25**

- Each head of cattle   **$.125**
- Each head of sheep or hogs   **$.0625**

In 1804, John Marshall heard of the busy port of entry town in Illinois. He brought his stock of goods and opened one of the first stores in Shawneetown. He also owned a wagon train that hauled salt from the salt licks to the river. From there it was shipped away by boat.

Shawneetown grew rapidly. It was a town of many "firsts." Not only was it the first town settled by the English in Illinois, but it also had the first operating post office and the first bank. Some of the earliest churches were also founded in Shawneetown.

In 1810, eight years before Illinois became a state, a United States post office was established in Shawneetown. For a number of years Shawneetown served as a mail distribution center for a large area of Illinois, Indiana, Kentucky, Tennessee, and Mississippi. The first line of mail coaches had been established in the United States on September 7, 1785. As early as 1806 an overland mail route was established from Vincennes to Shawneetown. It was the oldest mail route in the Illinois Territory.

In the early days almost all goods were bartered for with animal hides, livestock, and eggs. There was very little money to be used for purchases. Later, as travelers began to come into the area with cash, a bank was needed. In 1816 John Marshall opened the Marshall Bank in his home. He lived there with his wife and seven children. The safe in the bank was a trap door that lifted over a wooden barrel in the cellar. At times the cashier slept nearby with a gun. The money issued by this bank was crude. A wave of counterfeiting swept the country. But banking in Shawneetown continued. The town was referred to as the financial capital of the state. A story is told by the residents of a time when several Chicago businessmen rode on horseback to Shawneetown to Marshall Bank asking for a loan of a few thousand dollars to help their struggling village of Chicago. The directors met and refused the loan saying, "Chicago is too far from Shawneetown to ever amount to anything."

Early Shawneetown had a reputation for lawlessness and not much concern for religion. However, there is documentary proof of Methodist circuit riders in the area as early as 1813. At first they met in homes but later bought a lot in town. Finally the First Methodist Church was built in 1842.

A missionary visiting in 1816 wrote that he had not found a single soul who made any pretense of religion. It was not until ten years later that the first Presbyterian Church was organized in Shawneetown.

Many famous people passed through the town in those early days. Some of those are Shawnee Chief Tecumseh, Marquis de Lafayette, Abraham Lincoln, General Grant, General Wilson, and many others.

The Ohio River played the most important role in the growth of Shawneetown, making it an important trading center in the west. Keelboats transported goods up and down the river. The river kept Shawneetown in touch with the world. As a result it advanced much faster than those villages that were landlocked. Shawneetown remained one of the most prosperous and important ports until the building of the railroad. With land travel so much faster and easier, the river ports became less important. The once-busy booming town that played such an important role in the settling and growth of the area eventually became just another small town in southern Illinois.

1. Shawneetown is **not**

    a. called the "Gateway to Southern Illinois."
    b. called the "Gateway to the West."
    c. on the Ohio River in southern Illinois.
    d. the oldest town west of the Mississippi.

2. Most of the pioneers from the east left from _____ and came down the Ohio River.

    a. Ohio
    b. Kentucky
    c. Pittsburgh
    d. Indiana

3. The settlers in southern Illinois who crossed the Wabash came from

    a. Ohio.
    b. Kentucky.
    c. Pittsburgh.
    d. Indiana.

4. The first settler in Shawneetown was

    a. Michael Sprinkle.
    b. Alexander Wilson.
    c. John Marshall.
    d. Michael Wilson.

5. _____ operated a ferry.

    a. Michael Sprinkle
    b. Alexander Wilson
    c. John Marshall
    d. Michael Wilson

6. _____ was a blacksmith.

    a. Michael Sprinkle
    b. Alexander Wilson
    c. John Marshall
    d. Michael Wilson

7. The author does **not** mention _____ as a reason to settle in Shawneetown.

    a. transportation
    b. lumber
    c. good land for farming
    d. game

8. One man leading three horses would have to pay _____ to use the ferry.

    a. 50¢
    b. 75¢
    c. $1.00
    d. $2.00

9. A family of four, with two children ages eight and four, would have paid _____ to use the ferry.

    a. 50¢
    b. 75¢
    c. $1.00
    d. $2.00

10. One of the first commodities shipped from Shawneetown was

    a. corn.
    b. soybeans.
    c. sheep.
    d. salt.

11. One piece of evidence of how important Shawneetown was early in its history is the

    a. mail.
    b. river.
    c. trains.
    d. ferry.

12. A bank was needed so that people could pay for goods with

    a. hides.
    b. livestock.
    c. eggs.
    d. money.

13. Do you think there were any farms around Shawneetown? Why or why not?

14. What was the most important factor in Shawneetown's growth? What was the most important factor in the town's decline?

_____

_____

_____

_____

_____

_____

_____

_____

_____

_____

_____

_____

_____

_____

_____

_____

_____

_____

117

THE WHEAT HARVEST
by Guadalupe Vallejo

A very important feature was the wheat harvest. Wheat was grown more or less at all the Missions. If those Americans who came to California in 1849 and said that wheat would not grow here had only visited the Missions they would have seen beautiful large wheat fields. Of course at first many mistakes were made by the fathers in their experiments, not only in wheat and corn, but also wine making, in crushing olives for oil, in grafting trees, and in creating fine flower and vegetable gardens. At most of the Missions it took them several years to find out how to grow good grain. At first they planted it on too wet land.

At the Mission San José a tract about a mile square came to be used for wheat. It was fenced in with a ditch. The ditch was dug by the Indians with sharp sticks and with their hands in the rainy season. It was so deep and wide that cattle and horses never crossed it. In other places stone or adobe walls, or hedges of the prickly pear cactus, were used about the wheat fields.

Timber was never considered available for fences. There were no sawmills. There were no roads to the forests. It was only at great expense and with extreme difficulty that we procured the logs that were necessary in building, and chopped them slowly, with poor tools, to the size we wanted. Sometimes low adobe walls were made high and safe by a row of the skulls of Spanish cattle, with the long curving horns attached. These came from the matanzas or slaughter corrals, where there were thousands of them lying in piles. They could be so used to make one of the strongest and most effective of barriers against man or beast. Set close and deep, at various angles, about the gateways and corral walls, these cattle horns helped to protect the enclosure from horse thieves.

When wheat was sown it was merely "scratched in" with a wooden plow, but the ground was so new and rich that the yield was great. The old Mission field is now occupied by some of the best farms of the valley, showing how excellent was the fathers' judgment of good land. The old ditches which fenced it have been plowed in for more than forty years by American farmers, but their course can still be distinctly traced.

A special ceremony was connected with the close of the wheat harvest. The last four sheaves taken from this large field were tied to poles in the form of a cross. They were then brought by the reapers in the "harvest procession" to the church. The bells were rung. The father, dressed in his robes, carrying the cross and accompanied by boys with tapers and censers, chanting the "Te

118

Deum" as they marched, went forth to meet the sheaves. This was a season of Indian festival also. One-fifth of the whole number of the Indians were sometimes allowed to leave the Mission for a certain number of days, to gather acorns, dig roots, hunt, fish, and enjoy a change of occupation. It was a privilege that they seldom, or never, abused by failing to return. That fact shows how well they were treated in the Missions.

As soon as the Missions had wheat fields they wanted flour, and mortars were made. Some of them were holes cut in the rock, with a heavy pestle, lifted by a long pole. When La Pérouse, the French navigator, visited Monterey in 1786, he gave the fathers in San Carlos an iron handmill, so that the neophyte women could more easily grind their wheat. He also gave the fathers seed potatoes from Chile. They were the first that were known in California. La Pérouse and his officers were received with much hospitality at San Carlos.

Early in the [nineteenth] century flour mills by water were built at Santa Cruz, San Luis Obispo, San José and San Gabriel. The ruins of some of these now remain. The one at Santa Cruz is very picturesque. Horse-power mills were in use at many places. At the time that the Americans began to arrive in numbers the Spanish people were just commencing to project larger mill enterprises and irrigation ditches for their own needs. The difficulties with land titles put an end to most of these plans. Some of them were afterward carried out by Americans when the ranches were broken up.

The principal sources of revenue which the Missions enjoyed were the sales of hides and tallow, fresh beef, fruits, wheat, and other things to ships, and in occasional sales of horses to trappers or traders. The Russians at Fort Ross, north of San Francisco, on Bodega Bay, bought a good deal from the Missions. Then too the Indians were sent out to trade with other Indians. So the Missions often secured many valuable furs, such as otter and beaver, together with skins of bears and deer killed by their own hunters.

The embarcadero, or "landing," for the Mission San José was at the mouth of a saltwater creek four or five miles away. When a ship sailed into San Francisco Bay the captain sent a large boat up this creek. There he arranged to buy hides. They were usually hauled there on an oxcart with solid wooden wheels, called a "carreta." But often in winter, there being no roads across the valley, each separate hide was doubled across the middle and placed on the head of an Indian. Long files of Indians, each carrying hide in this manner, could be seen over the unfenced level land through the wild mustard to the embarcadero. In a few weeks the whole cargo would thus be delivered. For such work the Indians always received additional gifts for themselves and families.

1. Why was the ditch at Mission San José dug in the rainy season?

    a. The missions did not yet know how to grow good grain.
    b. The land was too wet to grow good grain.
    c. The dirt was easiest to dig then.
    d. There were no sawmills.

2. Which of the following was never used to fence off and protect a wheat field?

    a. wood
    b. stone
    c. adobe
    d. hedges

3. What was used to make low adobe walls more effective?

    a. matanzas
    b. slaughter corrals
    c. logs
    d. cattle horns

4. The fact that only some of the Native Americans at the mission were allowed to leave for a certain number of days at the end of the wheat harvest indicates

    a. that they were well treated.
    b. that they were virtual prisoners.
    c. that they may have willingly given up their freedom in exchange for the material and spiritual support the missions offered.
    d. any or none of the above.

5. La Pérouse did **not**

    a. visit Monterey in 1786.
    b. give the fathers in San Carlos a mortar and pestle to grind wheat.
    c. give the fathers in San Carlos an iron hand mill to grind wheat.
    d. give the fathers in San Carlos seed potatoes from Chile.

6. _____ powered flour mills.

    a. Irrigation ditches
    b. Windmills
    c. Difficulties with land titles
    d. Water and horses

7. The missions obtained valuable fur from

    a. animals killed by their own hunters.
    b. trades made with other Indians.
    c. the Russians at Fort Ross.
    d. ships that landed in San Francisco Bay.

8. The "embarcadero" is

    a. an oxcart.
    b. a carreta.
    c. a waterfront or landing.
    d. wild mustard.

9. Do you think it took longer to fill a boat with fur and hides in the summer or in the winter? Why?

THE BATTLE RAGES ON

Mansfield Renews the Attack

The remnants of Hooker's command were under heavy attack by the Confederates. They sought shelter under the cover of powerful Federal batteries in front of East Woods. Now a new threat faced the Confederates at Antietam. Mansfield's XII Corps had encamped more than a mile to the rear of Hooker during the night. It had marched at the sound of Hooker's opening guns. On September 17, 1862, at 7:30 a.m., almost an hour and a half later, Mansfield's force was approaching from the north in heavy columns.

Seeing Hooker's plight, Mansfield now rushed to the forefront of his men. He urged them to the attack. However, his work was cut short by a Confederate ball. He was carried from the field mortally wounded.

Without pause, Brigadier General Alpheus Williams moved up to command. The attack swept on over ground just vacated by Hooker. On the right, Brigadier General Samuel Crawford's division bore down the Hagerstown Pike toward the Confederates in West Woods. Attacking in separate units, however, their lines were shattered by Brigadier General J.R. Jones's men. Jones's Confederates had the advantage of fighting from the cover of projecting rocks. J.E.B. Stuart's artillery, from the hill a half-mile to the west, rapidly dispersed the remnants.

On the left, the Federals fared better. They pounded Hood's men back across the fields toward the Dunkard Church. This opened a great gap in the Confederate line. Into the hole plunged Brigadier General George S. Greene's Union division. Only a desperate Confederate stand stopped Greene's men at the Dunkard Church. There they remained. They were an isolated salient beyond support. The Federal assault had shot its bolt.

Attacking separately, the two corps of Hooker and Mansfield had each come within a hair of breaking Jackson's line. What if they had attacked together? Again and again through this long day, the same question—changing only the names—would apply.

It may have been while observing this critical fight near the Dunkard Church that General Lee saw a straggler heading back toward camp lugging a pig that he had killed. With disaster so close and straggling one of its chief causes, Lee momentarily lost control and ordered Jackson to shoot the man as an example to the army. Instead, Jackson gave the culprit a musket and placed him where action was hottest for the rest of the day. He came through

122

unscathed. He was afterward known as the man who had lost his pig but saved his bacon.

Jackson Prepares an Ambush

By 9:00 a.m., three hours of killing had passed. The Miller cornfield had become a no-man's land. Its tall stalks had been trampled to the ground. It was strewn with blood-soaked corpses. Firing had been so intense, had so fouled the men's muskets, that some of them were using rocks to pound their ramrods home.

Jackson was in extreme danger. Greene's Federals still lurked near the Dunkard Church, waiting only for support to renew their attack on the frayed Confederate line. At this very moment, a mass of blue-clad infantry could be seen emerging from the East Woods half a mile away. It was part of Sumner's II Corps moving up for the morning's third major Federal attack.

Swiftly, Jackson gathered together reinforcements from other sectors of the battlefield. Some had just arrived from Harpers Ferry. These were McLaws's men. With hardly a pause, they moved north and disappeared into the West Woods. Lee ordered Walker's two brigades north from the Lower Bridge. They too disappeared into the West Woods.

For a moment, the fighting ceased. Then powerful reserves were rushed forward by commanders of both armies to renew the battle.

As soon as they came in, Jackson craftily placed these men behind the rocks and ridges at the western fringe of the woods. Soon they formed a great semicircle whose outer points perfectly encompassed the five thousand men in Sumner's approaching column. Ten thousand Confederates were there. Now they disappeared into the landscape and waited.

Sumner's II Corps had been under orders to support the attack on the Confederate left. It had prepared at dawn to cross Antietam Creek at Pry's Mill Ford. Impatiently, Sumner had awaited the signal to march while the battle raged with increasing violence on the ridge beyond the stream. Finally, at 7:30 a.m., he led Major General John Sedgwick's division across the ford. Brigadier General William French's division followed. However, it soon drifted to the south and lost contact with Sedgwick.

Believing that he still led two divisions, Sumner continued his march past the East Woods. By now he knew that the earlier Federal attackers could give him no support, but he believed that the Confederates who had repulsed them must be equally exhausted and disorganized. Striking now—immediately—he might turn the tide before the enemy had time to recover. In his hurry, Sumner neglected to make sure that French's division followed closely in his rear. Neither had he taken time to reconnoiter the Confederate front in the West Woods.

Soon after 9:00 a.m., Sedgwick's heavy column, with Sumner at the head, started toward the Hagerstown Pike. Battleflags waving, bayonets glistening, the division marched forward in brigade front—long swaying lines of two ranks each.

Unmolested, they crossed the pike and passed into the West Woods. Almost surrounding them were Jackson's quietly waiting ten thousand. Suddenly, the trap was sprung. Caught within a pocket of almost encircling fire, in such compact formation that return fire was impossible, Sedgwick's men were reduced to utter helplessness. Completely at the mercy of the Confederates on the front, flank, and rear, the Federal lines were shattered by converging volleys. So appalling was the slaughter, nearly half of Sedgwick's five thousand men were struck down in less than twenty minutes.

Nevertheless, the trap had not been completely closed. In the confusion of the surprise assault, many regiments on the Federal right found an opening. Hastily withdrawing to the northeast, they soon found cover under the protecting fire of Sedgwick's artillery in the cornfield. Other batteries in the East Woods and to the north joined in the cannonade.

Eagerly grasping the opportunity for a counterattack, Jackson's line now swept across the open fields and charged the Federal batteries in front of East Woods. The fire was more than sheer valor could overcome. Blasted with grape and canister from the crossfire of fifty guns, the Confederates staggered, then gave way and drew back to the cover of West Woods. There, protruding rock strata protected them. Meanwhile, from his menacing position near the Dunkard Church, Greene was driven back by Confederate reserves.

If McClellan now delivered simultaneous hammer blows from northeast, east, and southeast, he would surely destroy Lee's weak defensive setup. However, if he continued his piecemeal attacks, Lee could keep on shuttling his brigades back and forth to meet them. And this is what they both did.

124

1. Of the following, who was a Confederate general?

   a. Hooker
   b. Mansfield
   c. Williams
   d. Jones

2. Of the following, who was a Federal general?

   a. Crawford
   b. Hood
   c. Greene
   d. Jackson

3. "Saved his bacon," as used in the sixth paragraph, means

   a. brought home the ham.
   b. brought home the dough.
   c. saved his life.
   d. saved his pig.

4. Who saved the straggler's bacon?

   a. Lee
   b. Hooker
   c. Mansfield
   d. Jackson

5. Of the following, who was a Confederate general?

   a. Sumner
   b. McLaws
   c. Sedgwick
   d. French

6. How did French's division avoid the trap in the West Woods?

   a. They were warned in advance.
   b. They retreated as soon as the Confederates opened fire.
   c. They got lost.
   d. They attacked the East Woods instead.

7. Why do you think Jackson attacked the East Woods?

_____

_____

_____

_____

_____

_____

_____

_____

_____

_____

_____

_____

_____

_____

_____

_____

_____

THREE BOULDER COUNTY MINING COMMUNITIES

In the year 1859, gold was discovered near Denver. Thousands of pioneers flooded Colorado's Front Range. They panned every stream and blasted test pits all over the mountains. They dreamt of striking riches. Mining camps dotted the mountain landscape. Some of these became permanent towns and cities. Many disappeared almost without a trace. The "boom and bust" economy was the way of life in mining communities.

Fires posed a serious threat to any town's survival. The structures were often built of flimsy wood. The towns had no modern firefighting equipment, hoses, or hydrants. Fires easily spread from building to building and devastated towns.

Congress passed the Homestead Act in 1862. It attracted additional westward settlement. Homesteaders could claim one-hundred-and-sixty-acre tracts of unoccupied public land. Then they had to make improvements. They had to build a cabin and fences. They could till fields and raise livestock. After five years of residence and payment of a nominal fee, the land was theirs. Homesteads cropped up near mining camps to serve those communities.

Homesteading was not an easy way of life. To survive, families grew lettuce, turnips, potatoes and other root crops. They traded for what they could not grow. They slaughtered livestock and cut timber for sale in the mining communities. They worked the land all day to scrape out a living. These work-hardened pioneer miners and homesteaders were the foundation upon which modern-day Colorado was built.

Boulder

Boulder City, as it was first known, was established in 1859. It had building lots available for one thousand dollars each. Seventy cabins were built that first year. Boulder grew rapidly. It soon had a doctor and a minister. Goods were traded from wagons. There were no business buildings until 1860. Boulder built Colorado's first schoolhouse in 1860.

In 1861 Colorado became a territory. That year, the territorial legislature enacted a bill establishing a state university. It designated Boulder as the location. Construction of the university did not begin until 1875. The university opened in 1877.

Gold Hill

Boulder County's first gold claims were staked at Gold Run in 1859. That was near present-day Gold Hill. Gold Hill was the first mining town settled in Boulder County. Within a year there were over one thousand five hundred prospectors in the area. In fact, there were so many people working on the extensive placer (surface minerals) claims that the riches ran out in a few years. Many left Gold Hill. After tapping the resources of the placer claims, many mines around Gold Hill were deserted. Then, in 1869, new technologies became available. With these, lower-grade ores could now be profitably mined.

The best high-grade lode (vein of mineral ore) in the area was the Horsfal lode. It was discovered on June 13, 1859. It yielded one hundred thousand dollars in its first year. That is the equivalent of three million dollars today. As Gold Hill's mining activities waned through the 1860s and 1870s, Gold Hill's population dwindled. In 1887, the population there was only two hundred and thirty people. A bad fire in 1894 was followed by a flood that spring. It wiped the whole town out. Not much was rebuilt.

Today, Gold Hill is a small community of about two hundred people. The dirt road through town is lined with old buildings and houses. Some date to the town's beginnings. The Gold Hill Inn & Bluebird Lodge was built in 1872. It was originally called the Wentworth Hotel. It has been operating as a restaurant and lodge ever since. The Gold Hill General Store is in a false-front building. It is typical of the 1860s. It retains its historic character both inside and out.

Caribou

Sam Conger found silver on Caribou Mountain while hunting in 1860. It was not until he saw silver ore from Comstock, Nevada, that he realized what he had passed by in Boulder County. He hurried back to the mountain. He rediscovered what turned out to be "the greatest silver vein of the region" in 1869. Caribou City was established in 1870. It soon grew to be a thriving community of sixty businesses and four hundred people. They were supported by twenty producing mines. At its peak, Caribou was home to over three thousand people.

Caribou was noted for its weather. At ten thousand feet in elevation, the town was subject to thunderstorms, snow that buried buildings, and violent winds. Old-timers said that Caribou was "the town where the winds were born." When the wind blew in Nederland, four miles to the east, it was said that "someone in Caribou must have left the door open." Caribou was rebuilt after a devastating fire in 1879. The silver crash of 1893, along with epidemics of scarlet fever and diphtheria and a second fire in 1900, meant the end of Caribou.

128

Today, little remains of the historic town. Most of the town's streets and houses vanished without a trace. What is left is only the skeletons of two stone buildings. Crumbling mining structures are scattered throughout the area. One active mine remains in Caribou. The quest for the precious metals that put Caribou on the map is still very much alive there today.

1. The first influx of pioneers to Colorado were

    a. homesteaders.
    b. farmers.
    c. firefighters.
    d. miners.

2. How many years after the discovery of gold in Colorado could homesteaders claim ownership of land?

    a. 3
    b. 5
    c. 8
    d. 13

3. Why did Congress require improvements on a claim before homesteaders would be granted ownership?

    a. Improvement meant higher taxes.
    b. Improvement meant a commitment to the land.
    c. Improvement raised the value of the land.
    d. Homesteading was not an easy way of life.

4. How did homesteaders make a living?

    a. government assistance
    b. trading and farming
    c. selling real estate
    d. fighting fires

5. Which two events happened in Boulder (Boulder City) in the same year?

   a. Boulder City was established and business buildings were built.
   b. Seventy cabins were built and a bill was passed to establish a state university.
   c. Colorado's first schoolhouse and seventy cabins were built.
   d. A bill was passed to establish a state university and Colorado became a territory.

6. Which of the following was Boulder County's first mining town?

   a. Caribou
   b. Boulder
   c. Gold Hill
   d. Comstock

7. What caused Gold Hill's population to decline?

   a. diminished mining activities
   b. a flood
   c. a bad fire
   d. all of the above

8. What caused Sam Conger to return to Caribou Mountain?

   a. He realized that he had found valuable silver there.
   b. He crossed over the mountain to get to Nevada.
   c. He wanted to start a town.
   d. He liked the weather.

9. When would people say, "Someone in Caribou must have left the door open"?

   a. when it was destroyed by fire
   b. when scarlet fever and diphtheria ravaged the town
   c. when silver crashed in 1893
   d. when the wind blew in Nederland

130

10. Choose two towns described in this article. How are they similar? How are they different? Explain your answer using details from the passage.

_____

_____

_____

_____

_____

_____

_____

_____

_____

_____

_____

_____

_____

_____

_____

_____

_____

_____

_____

11. In which of these three towns would you have liked to live in the 1800s? Why? Which would you like to visit today? Why?

_____

_____

_____

_____

_____

_____

_____

_____

_____

_____

_____

_____

_____

_____

_____

_____

_____

_____

OKLAHOMA'S ONLY DAUGHTER
of the AMERICAN REVOLUTION
by Mrs. A.J. Arnote
September 1926

Mrs. Sarah Starns Ellis has the distinction of being Oklahoma's only real daughter of the Revolution. Her father served in Washington's army in the conflict for freedom.

In "The Kings Mountain Men" by Katherine Keogh White the following interesting sketch is given:

> Nicholas Starnes (Starns) enlisted under Arthur Campbell in 1775 for service against Tories and Indians on New River. After King's Mountain, where he was under William Campbell, the wounded were placed in his care. Later the same fall he served against the Cherokees, the expedition burning sixteen towns. He was born in Cecil County, Maryland, 1756. At the beginning of the Revolution the family were in Washington County, Virginia. He married Barbara Winters in 1816, in Rhea County, Tennessee. He died in 1836. Pension was allowed the widow.

At the national congress of the DAR held in April of this year, the organization voted to send each Real Daughter a hundred dollars as a Mothers' Day gift. Mrs. Ellis' check came in due time with a cordial letter from the treasurer: A pension of twenty-five dollars per month is also paid to Mrs. Ellis by this society. On her birthday she is never forgotten. Messages of good cheer come from members who live in various parts of the country. Thus does a patriotic society remember the daughter of the soldiers of the American Revolution.

Sarah Starns Ellis was born March 6th, 1833, in McNary County, Tennessee. Her father Nicholas Starns, as has already been stated, served in the war of the Revolution. Enlisted as a private, he was steadily advanced until, at the battle of King's Mountain, he was commissioned captain. He served also in the war of 1812.

Mrs. Ellis says she must have been very young when her father died, but that she remembers him quite well. After his death the family consisting of one brother, George Washington Starns, little Sarah, then five years old, and her mother emigrated to Arkansas. Many friends and neighbors went in the same wagon train to seek their fortunes in the new state. Two older daughters of Mrs. Starns had married and were already located in Arkansas. Mrs. Ellis says she remembers to this day the thrill of that journey.

The family located at Lewisburg, not far from Little Rock. Here Sarah spent her girlhood. She married young, and was soon left a widow with a baby daughter. Here too, she met and married the dashing young mechanic, Isaac Ellis. To them were born three children, William, John and Johanna. After living in various settlements in Arkansas, the Ellis family removed to the Indian Territory. They lived for a number of years at old Skullyville, in what is now Le Flore County. It was while living there that the Ellises built some of the substantial old homes that are over that part of the country. Mrs. Ellis says his biggest contract in this part of the state was the building of the Tuskahoma Female Academy.

In the war between the states, Isaac Ellis enlisted in the Confederate Army. Mrs. Ellis gave an interesting account of her husband's service in the war. "Once in an engagement near Helena, Arkansas, his horse was killed, and he was hit in the leg. After twenty-four hours, he was found by an old planter and his wife, pinned under his horse and nearly dead from loss of blood. They released him and took him to an old field and concealed him in a cotton pen, got a doctor and cared for him until he was well enough to be off again."

"Was he crippled?" Mrs. Ellis was asked.

"No," she replied, "his leg was scarred to the bone but he could dance with the best of em."

After Ellis was discharged from the army, he took his family to San Bois where he resumed his trade. Here on the famous trail to Fort Sill, their house was open to all travelers.

"Never a penny would we take for lodging and refreshment. Ike would not have it. He was too glad to see them," Mrs. Ellis said. "Three or four deer a week, seven or eight wild turkeys, fish in a great plenty, our own garden and fruit. It was possible to give them the best."

It was here that Ike Ellis's earthly career was closed. He sleeps in the peaceful valley of San Bois. That was forty-five years ago. White people could own no property in the Indian Territory, so the little family moved to a more thickly populated section of the country where the boys found work. Mrs. Ellis did fine sewing.

Granny, as Mrs. Ellis is called by all who knew her, has had a varied and interesting life. She has pioneered in two states, seen much hardship, experienced may sorrows, but she says "There was always pleasant things mixed with it."

Mrs. Ellis is keenly alert mentally. She has very decided opinions, though she doesn't give them unasked.

For many years Mrs. Ellis has made her home with her grandson, Clarence Ellis, at Antlers, Oklahoma. She is devoted to his three little children. She has a number of grandchildren and great grand-children. Her oldest daughter Mrs. Anna Townsend is still living. She makes her home in Tulsa.

1. Mrs. Ellis's father was a soldier in

   a. the Revolutionary War.
   b. the Civil War.
   c. the Spanish-American War.
   d. World War I.

2. Mrs. Ellis's father was originally from

   a. Oklahoma.
   b. Tennessee.
   c. Maryland.
   d. Virginia.

3. Nicholas Starns lived in _____ at the start of his military service.

   a. Oklahoma
   b. Tennessee
   c. Maryland
   d. Virginia

4. Nicholas Starns served in

   a. the Mexican War.
   b. the Civil War.
   c. the War of 1812.
   d. World War I.

5. Sarah Ellis's mother's name before she married was

   a. Sarah Starns.
   b. Barbara Starns.
   c. Barbara Winters.
   d. Sarah Ellis.

135

6. Sarah was born in the same state where her parents had been married,

    a. Oklahoma.
    b. Tennessee.
    c. Maryland.
    d. Virginia.

7. When Sarah was five years old, her family moved to

    a. Oklahoma.
    b. Tennessee.
    c. Maryland.
    d. Arkansas.

8. After getting married and having three children, Sarah and her family moved to what is now

    a. Oklahoma.
    b. Tennessee.
    c. Maryland.
    d. Arkansas.

9. Sarah's husband was a soldier in

    a. the Mexican War.
    b. the Civil War.
    c. the War of 1812.
    d. World War I.

10. Isaac Ellis's nickname was

    a. Willy.
    b. Bill.
    c. Johnny.
    d. Ike.

11. Isaac Ellis died in

    a. the Civil War.
    b. 1881.
    c. 1900.
    d. 1926.

12. Isaac Ellis made his living as a(n)

    a. teacher at Tuskahoma Female Academy.
    b. tailor.
    c. builder.
    d. innkeeper.

13. Anna Townsend's father was

    a. not named in this passage.
    b. Isaac Ellis.
    c. Clarence Ellis.
    d. Nicholas Starns.

14. Describe how Sarah Ellis's life reflected so much of American history. Use specific examples from the article to support your answer.

_____

_____

_____

_____

_____

_____

_____

_____

_____

_____

_____

_____

A PIONEER RAILROAD AGENT

by Arthur W. Dunham

I have lived and labored among you, I love this country and its people. I have shared your hardships and pleasures. They have left within me pleasant memories of the past. I am glad to be here.

If the pronoun "I" should appear quite often in the few remarks I am about to make, I want you to understand that it is not my desire to appear in the limelight, but the Oklahoma Historical Society has asked me to give some reminiscences. It necessarily follows that I must recite something within the scope of my activities.

My father was a soldier in the Civil War. After that memorable conflict was over, he came west from the State of Michigan to settle on one of Uncle Sam's 160-acre tracts in Kansas, so you see I was an original "boomer." At that time I was about eighteen months old. The Santa Fe had been completed as far West as Emporia. From there we continued overland sixty miles further.

Someone has suggested that I am a railroad man. My mother used to tell me the earliest evidence of that fact was shown on the way out to Kansas. I took great interest in transportation matters. Every time the engine would whistle I tried to imitate it. The friendly passengers observed that I was destined some day to engage in railroad service.

There were hard times in Kansas. We survived the grasshopper year. We finally located at Florence. At the age of five, I was placed in school. Later my spare time was spent as a boot-black, selling news papers [sic], herding cattle, working as a bell-boy and lunch counter attendant in Fred Harvey's hotel and eating house. I was also a news agent on a Santa Fe train.

I first gained prominence in local railway circles in this way. We boys had two good swimming holes, one at Doyle Creek, the other at a bend in the Cottonwood River; both close at hand. There was not enough novelty or adventure. As I had been around the railroad a good deal, I proposed that we climb up into the railroad tank for a swim, which was readily assented to. The tank was high and large. We stripped our clothes at the platform inside, near the top of the tank, and plunged into about fifteen feet of water. Somehow the railroad people got next to this. They raised quite a disturbance over it. The result was I was placed on my good behavior, but all the same I got acquainted with the minor officials of the road. I was given an opportunity to apply myself to some of the fundamentals of railroad operation. I acquired some knowledge of telegraphy, and clerical work around the station.

The first big money I ever earned was acting as a guide for the famous Doctor Pierce, of Buffalo, New York (Dr. Pierce's Favorite Prescriptions, you know). It was on a hunting trip around Florence. He was so well pleased that he gave me a twenty-dollar gold piece.

The next large sum of money I earned was for riding a fast horse to the county seat at Marion, ten miles away, to file some legal papers at the court house within a limited time. This netted me ten dollars.

Shortly after this I was made Santa Fe agent at Burns. I had then reached the age of fifteen. I was soon promoted to other Kansas stations. A little later I was asked to go to Oklahoma.

On one cold night, February 20th, 1888, to be exact, and at about 2:00 A.M., as near as I can remember, I got off the south-bound Santa Fe train at Oklahoma station, where this beautiful city now stands. I was accompanied by the traveling auditor of the railway, and the route agent for Wells Fargo & Company's Express. We made our way to a shack just across from the depot. This was then the pretentious abode of one George Gibson, where he fed and housed what we used to term "Mule skinners" and "Tender-feet" occasionally.

This building was made from rough lumber, a story and a half high, and had two or three sleeping rooms upstairs. The cracks were not closely battened, and the cold wind found its way through in unstinted measure. We knocked at the door, and soon made it understood who we were and what we wanted. George Gibson came down the steps holding a coal-oil lamp, to which was attached a tin reflector.

The light momentarily dazzled us, but we soon discerned a number of Indians on the floor, rolled up in their bright colored blankets. We had to step over one or two of them to get to the stairway, much to their disgust—and ours. They grunted and we passed on. Indians were no novelty to me at this early stage, as I had many times seen them in Kansas, and knew something of their habits. I was wondering whether there were still more Indians upstairs.

We were each given one blanket, and the bed had a thin cover. It was so cold I kept my clothes on, and used my overcoat as well. My other companions did the same.

When we came down to breakfast we were seated on benches at a long pine table. Our bill-of-fare consisted of the usual sow-belly, black coffee, soggy biscuits, and molasses.

I was finally checked in as railroad agent, express agent, manager of the Western Union Telegraph Company, and stage agent. My duties immediately commenced. My force consisted of one night operator. He was my only subordinate. I arranged my bunk in the depot, because I had to get up at 4:30 every morning to let the stage out and look after passengers, baggage and express. This took about one hour. I would then go back to bed and sleep a while longer.

There was considerable business transacted through this office, even before the country opened up, as Oklahoma was the only reporting or agency station between Arkansas City and Purcell, a distance of one hundred fifty-four miles. It is true there were some telegraph offices like Ponca City, Wharton (now Perry), Guthrie, Norman, but they were established primarily to take care of train service. Freight could be sent to these places if fully prepaid and put off at the risk of the owners, but there were no regularly authorized agents to handle it.

After I was there a short time I moved the family down to Oklahoma, which consisted of my mother, two sisters and a brother. We occupied the cottage built by the railway company to accommodate the agent. It had four rooms, and while not a thing of beauty, it was at least comfortable.

Business was increasing rapidly. I was permitted to employ my brother Van, as a helper. He was not an operator, and at that time had not been trained in railroad work, but we got along pretty well when we were not scrapping with each other. He was a year and a half younger than I.

The stage ran regularly between Oklahoma and Ft. Reno. The fare was $3.00 one way, or $5.00 for a round trip. Forty pounds of baggage were allowed free, anything over that took express rates. The old Concord style of stage was used. It had a boot in front and one behind. It was drawn by six horses.

Previous to my coming to the Indian Territory there had been an attempt made by the Government to suppress the cattle men, but there were still numerous herds left. During my first year we shipped out of Oklahoma station over a thousand cars of cattle. We also shipped a car or two of buffalo horns, and a number of cars of bones which had been gathered by enterprising nesters.

There were but few buildings in Oklahoma at this time. They were: the depot, the railway agent's cottage, section house, post office, with S.H. Radebaugh as postmaster, the Quartermasters agent's house, a boarding house run by George Gibson, and a stockade, belonging to C.B. Bickford, a contract Government freighter.

There was quite an abundance of game in the vicinity. We frequently had venison and quail. At times prairie chickens and wild turkey were brought in. I had little time for hunting but did kill wild turkey along the North Canadian river, and had sighted deer not far away.

Frequent bands of friendly blanket Indians passed through. Occasionally they camped several days. We could not converse with them freely but had a mutual understanding on some things. They gave us no trouble whatever, but we kept our eyes open to see that nothing of value was laying around loose to be carried off. We visited their camps to see them dance, a little of which was enjoyed for the novelty of the thing. I believe I can do some of their steps now.

1. How did the author and his family travel from Michigan to Emporia, Kansas?

   a. by train
   b. by covered wagon
   c. on horseback
   d. by boat

2. What is a news agent?

   a. a newspaper reporter
   b. a newspaper boy
   c. a representative of reporters
   d. a talent scout

3. "Somehow the railroad people got next to this," which appears in the sixth paragraph, means

   a. the train pulled up next to the water tank.
   b. some railroad employees arrived next to the water tank.
   c. the railroad employees almost found out about it.
   d. the railroad employees did find out about it.

4. Besides the author and some Native Americans, who spent the first night at George Gibson's?

   a. Dr. Pierce
   b. mule skinners
   c. a railroad conductor and a Wells Fargo agent
   d. tender-feet

142

5. "Sow-belly," as used in the fourteenth paragraph, was probably

   a. bread.
   b. cereal.
   c. eggs.
   d. bacon.

6. The author was trained as an operator in order to perform his duties as

   a. a railroad agent.
   b. an express agent.
   c. a manager of the Western Union Telegraph Company.
   d. a stage agent.

7. The author had to get up very early every morning to perform his duties as

   a. a railroad agent.
   b. an express agent.
   c. a manager of the Western Union Telegraph Company.
   d. a stage agent.

8. Business was brisk because it was the only place to _____ for a distance of 150 miles.

   a. catch a train
   b. send freight safely
   c. send a telegram
   d. catch the stage

9. What was the most popular shipment on the train?

   a. cattle
   b. buffalo horns
   c. bones
   d. game

10. What did you like most about this story? Why?

_____

_____

_____

_____

_____

_____

_____

_____

_____

_____

_____

_____

_____

_____

_____

_____

_____

144

JIMMIE DAVIS

Jimmie Davis was a country music superstar. He also served two separate terms as governor of the state of Louisiana. He was born on September 11, 1899, in Quitman (near Beech Springs). Quitman is a rural town located in the northeastern part of Louisiana. Jimmie was the oldest of eleven children. His parents were Sam Jones Davis and Sara Works. Sam only had a third-grade education. The family lived in a two-room shack. They worked as sharecroppers on a farm.

Jimmie graduated from high school in Beech Springs. He enrolled in Louisiana College, where he joined the glee club. He sang lead tenor for a quartet called the "Wildcat Four." He earned money by washing dishes. He also played music on street corners to make money. He received a master's degree from Louisiana State University. Later he was a professor of history at Dodd College, a Baptist school for women.

Country and gospel music was a part of everyday life. Jimmie learned to play guitar. He built a large repertoire of songs. He became interested in a musical career at the same time. In 1928, he went to work as a criminal court clerk in Shreveport. He was also singing in gospel concerts at church meetings. He performed on radio station KWKH. In 1929, a talent scout from RCA Records heard him sing and signed him to the label. For four years, he recorded songs. They imitated the style of the biggest star of the day, Jimmie Rodgers.

By 1934, Davis had developed his own vocal style. He relied less on the honky-tonk blues popularized by Rodgers. He became a softer crooner. In September 1934, he began recording for the new Decca label. It had been founded one month earlier. Jimmie also became a composer. He remained so throughout his life. In 1935, he earned enough money from his first big hit, "Nobody's Darling But Mine," to pay off old debts and purchase a farm. A year later, he had another major hit with a song that became a country standard, "It Makes No Difference Now." In 1938, *Collier's* magazine called Davis and Gene Autry the two biggest stars of country music. That same year, Davis first ran for office. He was elected commissioner of public safety for Shreveport.

By the end of the decade, Davis was a well-known recording artist. He was one of the biggest headliners in country music. As the new decade began, Davis recorded the song that would become his biggest hit all over the world. On February 4, 1940, Davis recorded his own composition "You Are My Sunshine." When it was released in March, it became a million-seller and an international hit. Gene Autry and Bing Crosby were among the first of over three hundred and fifty artists to record the song. Eventually it was translated into more than thirty languages.

In 1942, Davis made his film debut. He played himself in "Riding Through Nevada" and "Strictly in the Groove." That same year, he was named State Public Service Commissioner. Davis was a household name when he ran for governor of Louisiana on the Democratic ticket in 1944. He used "You Are My Sunshine" as his campaign song. He defeated the political machine of Huey Long and won the election on an anti-corruption slate. While governor, he had the biggest chart hit of his career. It was the song, "There's a New Moon Over My Shoulder." The single spent a week at No. 1 on Billboard's country chart in March 1945.

After completing his first term of office, Davis starred in "Louisiana." It was released in 1947. It was based on his own life. After making the movie he concentrated on his recording career again. This time his emphasis was on gospel music. In 1957, he was given the American Youth Singers Award for Best Male Sacred Singer.

Davis was elected to a second term as governor of Louisiana in 1960. While governor he returned to Billboard's country chart after an absence of almost fifteen years with a top 20 hit, "Where the Old Red River Flows."

Davis served as president of the Gospel Music Association in 1967. He was inducted into the Nashville Songwriters Hall of Fame in 1971. He was elected to the Country Music Hall of Fame and the Gospel Music Association's Hall of Fame in 1972. Davis appeared on a CBS special celebrating the Country Music Hall of Fame's 25th anniversary in the spring of 1992. He recorded a new version of "You Are My Sunshine" in 1998. Davis performed four songs at a one hundredth birthday party held in Baton Rouge in 1999. The affair was held as a benefit for the Jimmy Davis Tabernacle Fund.

Jimmie Davis passed away on November 5, 2000, in his sleep at his home in Baton Rouge. He was one hundred and one years old. Davis had lived in three different centuries.

1. Jimmie Davis signed to sing for RCA shortly after

   a. graduating from high school.
   b. joining the glee club at Louisiana College.
   c. composing "Nobody's Darling But Mine."
   d. taking a job in Shreveport.

146

2. From 1929 to 1933, Davis sang mostly

   a. the honky-tonk blues.
   b. as a crooner.
   c. country music.
   d. gospel music.

3. "You Are My Sunshine" was written by

   a. Jimmie Rodgers.
   b. Jimmie Davis.
   c. Gene Autry.
   d. Bing Crosby.

4. Jimmie Davis's first elected office was

   a. professor of history at Dodd College.
   b. criminal court clerk in Shreveport.
   c. commissioner of public safety in Shreveport.
   d. state public service commissioner.

5. Davis's only song to reach No. 1 on the hit parade was

   a. "Nobody's Darling But Mine."
   b. "It Makes No Difference Now."
   c. "You Are My Sunshine."
   d. "There's a New Moon over My Shoulder."

6. In 1944, Davis

   a. recorded "You Are My Sunshine."
   b. made his film debut.
   c. was elected governor of Louisiana.
   d. starred in the movie, "Louisiana."

7. After 1947, Davis focused on singing

   a. the honky-tonk blues.
   b. rhythm and blues.
   c. country music.
   d. gospel music.

8. While governor of Louisiana, in 1960, Davis recorded
   a. "Where the Red River Flows."
   b. "It Makes No Difference Now."
   c. "You Are My Sunshine."
   d. "There's a New Moon over My Shoulder."

9. What do you think Jimmie Davis should most be remembered for? Why?

_____

_____

_____

_____

_____

_____

_____

_____

_____

_____

_____

_____

_____

_____

LOGAN AND NATIVE AMERICAN ATTACKS, 1777

Harrodstown contained one hundred and ninety-eight people in 1777. Within the protecting walls of the fort, there was a school. There were no textbooks, and the methods were primitive. The children learned from letters and figures drawn on smooth bark or boards by teachers. They wrote from copies set in the same way, getting ink sometimes from oak balls and pokeberries. Bibles, hymn books, and other reading matter that came by chance, were used by the more advanced pupils. Progress was made by diligent study.

Among the pioneers, there was no truer, braver, nor better man than Colonel Benjamin Logan, who founded the station of St. Asaph, known as Logan's Fort, which is now Stanford, Kentucky. Colonel Logan had been born in Virginia, of Irish parentage. He was a large and commanding man, tall and dignified. His countenance was cast in a fine mold of intelligence, dark, grave, and thoughtful, showing firm and steady purpose, yet a kindly spirit. Logan had served as an officer in the Dunmore War, and before that, in the Native American wars. In 1775 he moved to Kentucky.

During the Revolutionary War, England had made allies of the Native Americans. Now, she was supplying them with arms. The Shawnee and other tribes were tempted by such rewards to violate their peace agreements with Virginia. They decided to wage a war against the frontier settlements. On May 20, 1777, one hundred Native Americans laid siege on Logan's Fort.

In the morning, while the women were milking, and some men on guard, the Native Americans fired on them. One man was killed and two wounded. One of the wounded lay helpless between the fort and the Native Americans. The heroic Logan boldly rushed forward from the opened gate into what seemed the jaws of death. He lifted the wounded man in his powerful arms. Amid a shower of bullets from the foe he bore him safely back inside.

During this attack, the ammunition of the fort began to run low. It desperately needed to be replenished. The closest settlement was Holston, one hundred and fifty miles away. Logan, with two picked men, snuck through the Native American lines and set out, over mountains and through forests, to secure the needed relief.

On July 4, 1777, two hundred warriors, painted and armed, next attacked Boonesborough. Smaller groups were also sent against Harrodstown and again, to Logan's Fort. For two days the Native Americans attacked. They were defeated and baffled at every point. In despair, they withdrew.

1. Which of the following **best** describes the conditions of the Harrodstown school in 1777?

   a. disgraceful
   b. primitive
   c. protected
   d. unsafe

2. With whom did the British form an alliance?

   a. Colonel Benjamin Logan
   b. Daniel Boone
   c. Mrs. William Coomes
   d. Native Americans

3. Colonel Logan was of _____ descent.

   a. Irish
   b. English
   c. French
   d. Virginian

4. Give at three examples from the text that help readers to understand just how noble and brave Colonel Logan was.

   _____

   _____

   _____

   _____

   _____

   _____

   _____

   _____

5. How do you think stories such as this one about the heroic Colonel Benjamin Logan make their way into history books?

CALIFORNIA CUSTOMS AND TRANSPORTATION

by Guadalupe Vallejo

Harvesting, with the rude implements, was a scene. Imagine three or four hundred wild Indians in a grain field. Some were armed with sickles. Some had butcher knives. Some had pieces of hoop iron roughly fashioned into shapes like sickles. Many had only their hands with which to gather by small handfuls the dry and brittle grain. As their hands would soon become sore they resorted to dry willow sticks. These were split to afford a sharper edge with which to sever the straw.

The wildest part was the threshing. The harvest of weeks, sometimes of a month, was piled up in the straw in the form of a huge mound in the middle of a high, strong, round, corral. Then three or four hundred wild horses were turned in to thresh it. The Indians whooped to make them run faster. Suddenly the Indians would dash in before the band of horses at full speed. Their motion became reversed, with the effect of plowing up the trampled straw to the very bottom. In an hour the grain would be thoroughly threshed. The dry straw became broken almost into chaff. In this manner I have seen two thousand bushels of wheat threshed in a single hour.

Next came the winnowing. It would often take another month. It could only be done when the wind was blowing. It was done by throwing high into the air shovelfuls of grain, straw and chaff. The lighter materials were wafted to one side. The grain, comparatively clean, would descend and form a heap by itself. In this manner all the grain in California was cleaned. At that day no such thing as a fanning mill hand ever been brought to this coast.

The kindness and hospitality of the native Californians have not been overstated. Up to the time the Mexican regime ceased in California they had a custom of never charging for anything; that is to say, for entertainment— food, use of horses, etc. You were supposed, even if invited to visit a friend, to bring your blankets with you. It would be thoughtless if he traveled and did not take a knife with him to cut his meat. When you had eaten, the invariable custom was to rise, deliver to the woman or hostess the plate on which you had eaten the meat and beans—for that was about all they had—and say, "Muchas gracias, Senora" ("Many thanks, madame"). The hostess invariably replied, "Buen provecho" ("May it do you much good"). The missions in California invariably had gardens with grapes, olives, figs, pomegranates, pears, and apples, but the ranches scarcely ever had any fruit. When you wanted a horse to ride, you would take it to the next ranch—it might be twenty, thirty, or fifty miles—and turn it out there. Sometime or other the

152

owner would get it back. In this way you might travel from one end of California to the other.

The ranch life was not confined to the country, it prevailed in the towns too. There was not a hotel in San Francisco, or Monterey, or anywhere in California, till 1846, when the Americans took the country. The priests at the missions were glad to entertain strangers without charge. They would give you a room in which to sleep, and perhaps a bedstead with a hide stretched across it, and over that you would spread your blankets.

At this time there was not in California any vehicle except a rude California cart. The wheels were without tires. They were made by felling an oak tree and hewing it down. It made a solid wheel nearly a foot thick on the rim and a little larger where the axle went through. The hole for the axle would be eight or nine inches in diameter. After a few years use it would increase it to a foot. To make the hole, an auger, gouge, or chisel was sometimes used, but the principal tool was an ax. A small tree required but little hewing and shaping to answer for an axle. These carts were always drawn by oxen, the yoke being lashed with rawhide to the horns.

To lubricate the axles they used soap (that is one thing the Mexicans could make), carrying along for the purpose a big pail of thick soapsuds which was constantly put in the box or hole. But you could generally tell when a California cart was coming half a mile away by the squeaking. I have seen the families of the wealthiest people go long distances at the rate of thirty miles or more a day, visiting in one of these clumsy two-wheeled vehicles. They had a little framework around it made of round sticks, and a bullock hide was put in for a floor or bottom. Sometimes the better class would have a little calico for curtains and cover. There was no such thing as a spoked wheel in use then.

Somebody sent from Boston a wagon as a present to the priest in charge of the mission of San José, but as soon as summer came the woodwork shrunk, the tires came off, and it all fell to pieces. There was no one in California to set tires. When Governor Micheltorena was sent from Mexico to California he brought with him an ambulance. It was not much better than a common spring wagon, such as a marketman would now use with one horse. It had shafts, but in California at that time there was no horse broken to work in them, nor was there such a thing known as a harness. The governor had two mounted vaqueros to pull it, their reatas being fastened to the shafts and to the pommels of their saddles.

The first wagons brought into California came across the plains in 1844 with the Townsend or Stevens party. They were left in the mountains. They lay buried under the snow till the following spring. Moses Schallenberger, Elisha Stevens (who was the captain of the party), and others went up and brought some of the wagons down into the Sacramento Valley

Elisha Stevens was from Georgia. He had there worked in the gold mines. He started across the plains with the express purpose of finding gold. When he got into the Rocky Mountains, Stevens said, "We are in a gold country." One evening (when they camped for the night) he went into a gulch. He took some gravel and washed it. He got the color of gold, thus unmistakably showing, as he afterwards did in Lower California, that he had considerable knowledge of gold mining. But the strange thing is, that afterwards, when he passed up and down several times over the country between Bear and Yuba rivers, as he did with the party in the spring of 1845 to bring down their wagons, he should have seen no signs of gold where subsequently the whole country was found to contain it.

1. Wild horses were used in _____ the grain.

   a. planting
   b. harvesting
   c. threshing
   d. winnowing

2. The Native Americans who used dry willow sticks to harvest began with

   a. sickles.
   b. butcher knives.
   c. iron hoops.
   d. their bare hands.

3. In harvesting grain, _____ were used.

   a. about the same number of wild horses and Native Americans
   b. more wild horses than Native Americans
   c. more Native Americans than wild horses
   d. there is no way to tell how many Native Americans and wild horses

4. What does the author mean when she says, "The kindness and hospitality of the native Californians have not been overstated," in the fourth paragraph?

    a. She needs to say much more about how kind and hospitable the native Californians were.

    b. It is not an exaggeration to say that the native Californians were kind and hospitable.

    c. Too many people have already said how kind and hospitable the native Californians were.

    d. Native Californians want others to say over and over again how kind and hospitable they are.

5. Which of the following was a traveler **not** expected to bring with him?

    a. knife
    b. blanket
    c. plate
    d. horse

6. Which of the following could be found at most ranches?

    a. grapes
    b. beans
    c. olives
    d. figs

7. Where did people who were traveling stay in California towns before 1846?

    a. ranches
    b. farms
    c. hotels
    d. missions

8. The oak wheel was

    a. the same dimension throughout.
    b. thicker in the middle.
    c. thicker on the outer edge.
    d. thicker on top than on the bottom.

9. Which of the following is the most likely reason why the author wrote this passage?

    a. to inform others of her culture
    b. to teach someone how to be Native American
    c. to keep people interested in working in the fields
    d. to teach children the importance of being a hard worker

10. The axle was made from

    a. a piece of metal.
    b. rawhide.
    c. a tree.
    d. an ax.

11. Despite being lubricated with soapsuds, what could be heard squeaking from a far distance?

    a. wheels
    b. yoke
    c. rawhide
    d. axles

12. Which of the following is **not** a reason why carriages were useful in California?

    a. The roads were not good enough.
    b. No one could repair tires.
    c. No horses had been broken to pull carriages.
    d. There were no harnesses available.

13. _____ could **not** find gold in California even though he knew how and where to look for it.

    a. Governor Micheltorena
    b. Elisha Stevens
    c. Moses Schallenberger
    d. Dr. Townsend

14. Compare some harvesting or visiting practices in California today with those of 200 years ago. How are things the same, if at all? How are they different?

15. Do you think that gold would have been discovered earlier in California if they had had better transportation? Why or why not?

MARYLAND IN THE AMERICAN REVOLUTION

Maryland's reaction to the increasingly strict British policies of the 1760s and early 1770s was not as strong as that of its neighboring colonies. This was due largely to the fact that Marylanders were fighting among themselves. Some were trying to gain more rights from the proprietor. Others were resisting that effort. Absorbed in that struggle, they were not too concerned about what the British were doing in America.

Nevertheless, in 1774, Maryland reacted strongly to the Tea Act Crisis and the resulting Boston Port Bill. Anthony Stewart was a ship owner. He brought the ship *Peggy Stewart* into Annapolis harbor. He planned to pay the tax and sell his cargo of tea. He had two thousand three hundred pounds of tea on board. The more independent-minded members of the colony opposed his plan. Stewart chose principle over profit. He sailed the ship into full view of the city, then set it on fire. None of the of tea reached shore.

Maryland was not the scene of significant military action during the War for Independence. She made contributions by supplying men, arms, and ships. In November 1776, the British threatened Philadelphia. The Continental Congress moved to Annapolis where it remained until the following spring.

George Washington is reported to have spoken admiringly of Maryland's soldiers as the "Old Line." From that Maryland got its nickname, "Old Line State." Annapolis was a focal point for Maryland's war effort. It was a center for collecting supplies and troops. The new state of Maryland leased many homes in town as housing for soldiers waiting to be sent out to battle. At times, there were more soldiers in the city than residents. The soldiers had to endure some hardships, even when barracked in a thriving town such as Annapolis. There was very little extra food available for them. The homes were meagerly furnished. Their supplies did not include fuel for warmth and cooking. What furniture there was in the houses was probably burned in an effort to keep warm during the winter months.

There is a building in Annapolis known as the Barracks. The Barracks is located on land that was leased for use by the troops. Although constructed after the war, this house is typical of the homes used as barracks. Buildings like this one would have been occupied by successful craftsmen or artisans living and working in the waterfront area of Annapolis. There are two main rooms on the first floor. There are two rooms on the second. There is an interior kitchen in the basement, which includes the remains of the original bake oven in the back wall.

The Barracks is owned by the state of Maryland and managed by the Historic Annapolis Foundation. It has been restored as part of a bicentennial project grant. The first floor is furnished as a home for soldiers quartered in town during the Revolutionary War.

During the American Revolution, some Marylanders remained loyal to England. Most of them lived on the Eastern Shore of Maryland. They were shunned by former friends and neighbors. They were forced from their homes. They fled to British-occupied Philadelphia. Some just wanted to escape the Rebels. Some wanted to fight them. Those who took up arms ravaged parts of Maryland before being sent to fight in Florida.

The loyal Marylanders were a varied lot. Reverend Jonathan Boucher preached loyalty from his pulpit in Annapolis. He did so with two loaded pistols in easy reach. Maryland's last British governor, Robert Eden, was well-liked in the Maryland colony. Even those who favored separation from England had little to say against him. Robert Alexander lived in Cecil County. He had been a member of the Continental Congress. Philip Barton Key later became a U.S. congressman despite his misplaced loyalty during the Revolution. He was Francis Scott Key's uncle.

A regiment of Maryland Loyalists was organized in 1777. Kent County planter James Chalmers was its lieutenant colonel. It was officially commissioned as the First Battalion of Maryland Loyalists. The name was somewhat misleading. Less than half the unit was actually from Maryland. The rest of the unit were poor and homeless Tories who had made their way into British-occupied Philadelphia. They had been persuaded to join up over a glass of rum and bold promises from a recruiting officer.

William Augustus Bowles was one of the very few loyalists west of the Chesapeake Bay to join the British cause. He had been born in Frederick, Maryland, in 1763. In the spring of 1778, while still a young teenager, he was commissioned with the rank of ensign in the First Battalion of Maryland Loyalists.

The British army evacuated the city of Philadelphia in June 1778. They headed toward New York City and Long Island. The British rear guard clashed with Washington's army in the Battle of Monmouth a short time later. The Marylanders had been among the first to leave Philadelphia. They were already a day's march to the north. No military glory awaited them in this endeavor. As part of the advance guard, they had little to do except stand around and wait for the rear guard to finish battling the Rebels and catch up. Upon reaching Long Island, many Loyalists deserted.

160

After spending the summer of 1778 on Long Island, the Marylanders were shipped off to Pensacola, Florida, to fight the Spanish (and smallpox). The commander of the post did not welcome them. He dismissed them as "Irish vagabonds." While stationed at Pensacola, a number of loyal Marylanders were sent aboard the H.M.S. *Mentor* to serve as marines. Ironically, the H.M.S. *Mentor* had been built in Maryland in 1778. It had started life as a rebel privateer named *Who's Afraid*. It was later captured by the British.

William Bowles followed the regiment to Pensacola. He quickly resigned, but returned more than a year later. In the spring of 1781, Spanish forces besieged the British stronghold in Florida: Fort George. After a five-week siege, the British and provincial regiments at Fort George were forced to surrender. Despite being hopelessly outnumbered, the fort had held out much longer than was expected. That was due partly to the heroic defiance of the untested Maryland and Pennsylvania Loyalist units. The Marylanders had even executed a successful bayonet charge on one of the Spanish redoubts. This brief encounter would be their only real taste of battle.

Shipped back to New York, the troops uneventfully sat out the rest of the war. Bowles became an actor and performed in several theater productions with British officers. The United States offered no place for Loyalists when the war ended. Most of them were forced to pack up and leave for Nova Scotia. Their transport ship, *Martha*, shipped out for Saint John in September 1783. Less than one hundred of the original three hundred members of the regiment were aboard. Half the unit had deserted over time; the rest had died of smallpox.

Bad luck struck on the way. The transport ship struck a ledge of rocks near the shore of Nova Scotia. Half the Maryland Loyalists and their families drowned. The survivors were brought to Saint John. They had no clothing, blankets, or weapons. Winter was approaching. The fifty surviving Marylanders made their way to the northern shore of the St. John River at Fredericton. They had received land grants there, in the newly-created province of New Brunswick.

William Augustus Bowles did not join his fellow Tories in their trip to Canada. After the war, he returned to Florida to live with his friends, the Creek Native Americans. He became their leader of sorts. He kept Spain and the United States terrified of Indian uprisings in the Florida territory. Bowles married a Creek woman. He adopted the Creek ways. He often visited London in his native Creek garb. He attracted considerable attention. Eventually, however, his old Spanish enemies caught up with him. He was imprisoned in Cuba and died there in 1805.

1. Before 1774, the citizens who in other states were protecting British behavior were, in Maryland, probably

   a. defending the proprietor.
   b. attacking the proprietor.
   c. even more strongly opposed to the British.
   d. uninterested in politics.

2. Anthony Stewart showed himself to be a patriot

   a. during the Tea Act Crisis.
   b. during the War of Independence.
   c. when the British threatened Philadelphia.
   d. when the Continental Congress moved to Annapolis.

3. Maryland did **not** see any major battles during the Revolutionary War because the

   a. British were too strongly entrenched to be attacked.
   b. British fleet could not get near Maryland.
   c. British focused on New York and Philadelphia.
   d. Americans focused on New York and Philadelphia.

4. The soldiers who gathered in Annapolis were apparently most in need of

   a. ammunition.
   b. clothing.
   c. food.
   d. firewood.

5. Who had been a member of the Continental Congress, but sided with England during the War of Independence?

   a. Robert Alexander
   b. Jonathan Boucher
   c. Philip Barton Key
   d. Robert Eden

6. Maryland Loyalists fought

   a. Washington's army at the Battle of Monmouth.
   b. the Rebel privateer *Who's Afraid* on board the H.M.S. *Mentor*.
   c. the Spanish at Fort George, Florida.
   d. the British at Fort George, Florida.

7. How many soldiers from the First Battalion of Maryland Loyalists deserted?

   a. 56
   b. 75
   c. 100
   d. 150

8. About how many soldiers from the First Battalion of Maryland Loyalists died of smallpox?

   a. 56
   b. 75
   c. 100
   d. 150

9. Why do you suppose most Loyalists came from Maryland's Eastern Shore?

_____

_____

_____

_____

_____

_____

_____

_____

_____

_____

_____

10. Write a story about a Loyalist family who made it to New Brunswick, or about William Bowles and his family in Florida.

SARAH LINCOLN GRIGSBY

(February 10, 1807–January 20, 1828)

Sarah Lincoln Grigsby, sister of Abraham Lincoln, would never know her younger brother's success and fame, nor how he would be remembered. As a result of her brother's fame, however, her own life has become part of our national heritage.

She was born in Elizabethtown, Kentucky, on February 10, 1807. With her younger brother, she attended a basic ABC school taught by Zachariah Riney and later by Caleb Hazel. From her mother she learned the arts of spinning, soap making, and cooking over an open fire. Most significant of all, she and her brother listened to stories told by travelers on the Louisville-Nashville Road. It ran directly in front of the Lincoln cabin. Sarah had the benefit at least of some schooling when many pioneer children learned only the tasks for farming or housekeeping.

When Thomas Lincoln moved his family to Indiana in 1816, Sarah's responsibilities increased. She worked hard to help her mother establish a home on this new frontier. However, the autumn frosts of 1818 had already colored the foliage of the huge trees of oak, hickory, maple and walnut when her mother Nancy became desperately ill. Her mother was stricken with milk sickness; a poisoning caused by the plant, white snakeroot. Cows ate this abundant weed and passed the poison on in their milk. On October 5, 1818, Nancy died. Death in a one-room cabin in the wilderness was a grim experience for the survivors. Sarah helped the neighbor women prepare, dress, and place her mother's body into the casket. Her mother was then taken to her final resting-place overlooking the Indiana farm she so dearly loved.

Her mother had been kind to Sarah. She had raised her in an environment of love, trust, and understanding. As Sarah matured, she built her life upon this solid foundation.

It was a difficult time for Sarah. She had to take over all the household chores. Her mother's death left Sarah with the formidable task of caring for the house, her father, her brother, and an orphaned eighteen-year-old cousin, Dennis Hanks, whose guardians had also died from the milk sickness. The absence of a mother was very painful for the whole family.

Thomas remarried to Sarah Bush Johnston. She was a widow with three children of her own. Sarah had to adjust to having a stepmother and a stepbrother and stepsisters. Her new mother did relieve Sarah of much of the

166

domestic labor in the Lincoln household. Her new stepsisters and stepbrother became playmates.

During her thirteenth year, Sarah attended Andrew Crawford's subscription school. Two years later she attended, infrequently, a school taught by James Swaney. Then, in her 17th year, she attended Azel Dorsey's school. The Lincoln children probably received their best education from him.

Sarah joined the Little Pigeon Baptist Church on April 8, 1826. On August 2, 1826, she married Aaron Grigsby. The new couple moved into a cabin two miles south of the Lincolns. Nine months after their marriage, Sarah announced to her family that she was pregnant. However, unknown complications during the delivery claimed both her life and that of her infant child. A neighbor is recorded as saying; "I remember the night she died. My mother was there at the time. She had a strong voice, and I heard her calling her father. He went after a doctor, but it was too late. They let her lay too long." Sarah died January 20, 1828 at the age of twenty-one.

A description of Sarah comes to us from her stepmother who said she was "short of stature and somewhat plump in build. Her hair was dark brown and her eyes were gray." John Hanks, a cousin, said, "She was kind, tender, and good natured and is said to have been a smart woman." Her brother-in-law, Nathaniel Grigsby, said that Sarah "was a woman of extraordinary mine [sic]. Her good-humored laugh I can hear now, is as fresh in my mind as if it were yesterday. She could, like her brother, meet and greet a person with the kindest greeting in the world, make you easy at the touch of a word, an intellectual and intelligent woman."

Sarah Lincoln was an important person in Abraham Lincoln's life. When she had started to school, while the family was living in Kentucky, she had taken Abraham with her. She had probably helped him learn his letters and numbers. When their mother died, they helped each other through the grief. Their relationship was characterized by a deep affection. As a neighbor said, "They were close companions and were a great deal alike in temperament." Sarah's kind and loving care of him may have had much to do with Abraham's development of these same traits.

Sarah Lincoln Grigsby, sister of the sixteenth president, was buried with her infant in her arms in the Little Pigeon Baptist Church Cemetery, which is located today in Lincoln State Park. Her husband, Aaron, is buried beside her.

1. How did Sarah Lincoln learn her ABCs?

   a. She went to school in Kentucky.
   b. She went to school in Indiana.
   c. from her mother
   d. from travelers

2. The Louisville-Nashville Road went right in front of the Lincoln cabin in

   a. Indiana.
   b. Kentucky.
   c. Illinois.
   d. Tennessee.

3. Sarah Lincoln's mother died when Sarah was _____ years old.

   a. 9
   b. 11
   c. 13
   d. 17

4. Based on a reading of the passage, what characteristic is most likely to be attributed to Sarah Lincoln?

   a. generous
   b. selfish
   c. wealthy
   d. artificial

5. What event lightened Sarah's responsibilities in the cabin?

   a. joining Little Pigeon Baptist Church
   b. attending a subscription school
   c. marrying Aaron Grigsby
   d. her father's remarriage

6. What was Nathaniel Grigsby's impression of Sarah Lincoln?

   a. He thought her to be good-natured and kind.
   b. He found her to be boorish and brainless.
   c. He believed that she was intelligent and approachable.
   d. He considered her to be the smartest person in town.

168

7. How do you think Abraham Lincoln's life might have been different if his sister had not died so young?

_____

_____

_____

_____

_____

_____

_____

_____

_____

_____

_____

_____

_____

_____

_____

_____

_____

_____

LIFE ON KEYS RANCH

Bill Keys thrived in the desert because of his resourcefulness and the diversity of his tasks. He built a wooden ranch house, work sheds, and guest cabins. He quarried rocks to build walls. He raised goats, chickens, and cattle for food. He grew fruits and vegetables. He owned at least thirty mining claims. He mined for gold and gypsum. "Gypsum" is a soft mineral used for ornamental objects. To make money, he operated a stamp mill. A "stamp mill" is a machine that crushes rock in order to remove gold or other minerals. Area miners brought their ore to Keys, who crushed it for a fee. None of these activities alone could have supported his family. Combined, they provided for their needs.

Lack of water was the first and most constant obstacle Keys faced. He dug deep wells by hand. He constructed windmills to draw water up from deep underground. He dammed up the rocky canyons surrounding the ranch to create a lake. The lake irrigated the orchard and vegetable garden through a sophisticated system of piping. It served as an emergency supply of drinking water if the wells dried up. It also provided recreation in the form of fishing, swimming, and ice skating.

Keys's ability to repair machines and household items often came in handy. Since the ranch site was far from town, the family rarely threw anything away that they might use to fix a broken item. Keys scavenged abandoned ranches and mines for rails, wire, pipes, household items, old cars, and tires left behind by less successful people. He even purchased an entire junkyard. He organized it into neat piles on the ranch to use as a supply yard.

The Keys family knew the importance of working as a team. With the nearest doctor more than fifty miles away, the family depended on each other for treatment of minor afflictions. They traded or bartered with local homesteaders and business owners in Twentynine Palms for items they could not produce on the ranch. These included salt, coffee, flour, and sugar.

Most of the surrounding homesteaders and miners viewed Keys's ranch as the center of their desert network. They regarded its owner as a helpful friend. Miners appreciated his knowledge of mines in the area and his milling capabilities. Keys built a one-room schoolhouse for his children and others in the area. He did so to ensure they received a proper education despite their isolation. He provided the teacher with a cabin on the ranch.

Like the typical self-reliant 19th-century homesteader, Keys adamantly protected the needs and interests of his family. This attitude sometimes caused him to be at odds with people around him. Disagreements over water

170

rights led cowboys working for a nearby cattle company to label Keys as a troublemaker. Keys acquired large sections of land surrounding public water sources. Access to the water was cut off once Keys fenced the land. The cattle company still ran three hundred to four hundred head of cattle there. They caused damage to Keys's fences. They also put a heavy strain on the water supply. The cowboys further retaliated by cutting his fences, shooting his cattle, or driving them to market with the company's herd.

Another problem arose in 1936 when a citizen-led campaign to preserve the unique desert environment of the region resulted in the creation of Joshua Tree National Monument. This new unit of the National Park Service (which became Joshua Tree National Park in 1994) completely surrounded Keys's ranch. Keys had a volatile relationship with park service personnel. New regulations limited his cattle grazing, opened his water holes to the public, and restricted his homesteading and mining activities. Keys, who had lived in the area for twenty-five years, resented the government regulations.

Keys had more serious problems with another neighbor, Worth Bagley. He had built a road leading to one of his mining claims on land Bagley later purchased. Despite repeated warnings by Bagley, Keys believed the road belonged to him and continued to use it. To retaliate, Bagley set up an ambush for Keys one day in 1943. Keys proved to be a better shot, however. The confrontation ended in Bagley's death. Believing he had acted in self-defense, Keys turned himself in to the authorities. He was convicted of manslaughter. He was sentenced to five years in San Quentin prison. After his release from jail in 1948, Keys worked to earn a pardon. It finally came eight years later.

Bill Keys returned to the ranch at the age of sixty-nine to resume the active life he had left behind. In his seventies, he built two more dams behind the house. He enlarged the orchard and garden areas. He assessed his mining properties. He temporarily reopened his mill. He even played the role of a prospector in the Disney Company's film *The Wild Burro of the West*.

When his wife died in 1963, Keys sold the ranch to Henry Tubman. Tubman traded the property with the government for federal land elsewhere. Thus, the ranch became the property of the National Park Service. Keys lived on the ranch until his death on June 28, 1969.

While the world outside the ranch had changed dramatically, Keys's way of life had remained remarkably constant. In 1994, the town of Twentynine Palms commissioned a mural to commemorate Bill Keys and to illustrate the impact he had on the area.

1. Bill Keys did **not** raise

   a. goats.
   b. sheep.
   c. chickens.
   d. cattle.

2. A "stamp mill"

   a. turns grains to flour.
   b. stamps designs into metal.
   c. creates ornamental objects from gypsum.
   d. crushes rock.

3. The most useful improvement Keys made was

   a. building guest cabins out of wood.
   b. building walls out of rock.
   c. mining for gold.
   d. damming a lake.

4. The Keys family obtained salt, flour, and sugar by

   a. repairing machines.
   b. trade or barter.
   c. scavenging.
   d. buying a junkyard.

5. What is a synonym for "volatile," as used in the seventh paragraph?

   a. unpredictable
   b. good-natured
   c. calm or soothing
   d. long

6. Keys got in trouble with the local cattle company by

   a. using lots of water.
   b. cutting their fences.
   c. shooting or stealing their cattle.
   d. fencing off public water sources.

7. Which of the following National Park Service regulations did Keys object to?

   a. limiting his cattle grazing
   b. opening his water holes to the public
   c. restricting his mining activities
   d. all of the above

8. Why was the Keys family successful in the desert? Give some examples.

9. How did Keys modify his environment? How did he adapt to it?

_____

_____

_____

_____

_____

_____

_____

_____

_____

10. How did the creation of Joshua Tree National Monument affect Keys's life?

_____

_____

_____

_____

_____

_____

_____

_____

_____

11. Why did Keys spend five years in prison? How else might Keys and
    Bagley have resolved their problem?

LOUISIANA BECOMES SPANISH

The long colonial rivalry of France and England was again coming to a head. In 1754, the French and Indian War burst out. It was the American segment of the great Seven Years' War. In America this bitter struggle reached its climax in September 1759. On a dark night a thirty-two year old British general, Major-General James Wolfe, led his troops up a narrow ravine and formed them at daybreak on the Plains of Abraham before the citadel of Quebec. Wolfe formed his men only two deep. He led them against the battalions of the French, massed six deep before the city. Quebec fell, along with both Wolfe and Montcalm, the young French commander. The next year Montreal surrendered. Canada was in English hands. Such colonial victories made England willing to listen to peace proposals.

Our scene now shifts to Europe and from battlefields to conference tables. In 1761, although the war was still in progress, France and England began negotiating for peace. The fate of Louisiana was one of the things that hung in the balance. The great continental empires of Canada and Louisiana were rather less interesting to the great powers than the little fever-ridden sugar islands of the West Indies. At first, it seemed that England would give both Canada and Louisiana back to France in return for Caribbean islands. When it became evident that the British would demand Canada, France still hoped to retain Louisiana. Finally, in order to keep the little island of St. Lucia, near Guadeloupe and Martinique, France offered England all of Louisiana east of the Mississippi—all, that is, except the Isle of Orleans.

The Isle of Orleans is an area of about two thousand eight hundred square miles. It lies between the Mississippi and Lakes Maurepas and Pontchartrain. On that so-called island stands the city of New Orleans. France kept that small segment east of the river by some close bargaining. One might say they stretched the truth a little. The English demanded free navigation of the Mississippi. The French assured them that the lakes bordering the Isle of Orleans constituted a navigable mouth of the Mississippi. To be sure they are connected with the Mississippi by bayous, but the route was hardly navigable.

The peace negotiations were in progress during 1761 and 1762, before the war was over. While France was dealing with England on the one hand, she was dickering with Spain in a very different light on the other. In 1761, the two Bourbon cousins, Louis XV of France and Charles III of Spain, secretly renewed the family compact of mutual assistance. They agreed that if England did not accede to reasonable terms, Spain would join the war. They hoped that by a combined sudden onslaught they could turn the tables. The

176

day after New Year's, 1762, Spain declared war on England. It turned out to be an unhappy solution. A few months later Havana—key to Spain's New World empire—fell to the British. Havana had to be bought back at any price. The price was Florida. Spain ceded it to England.

This unexpected outcome placed France in a rather delicate position. Spain, her friend, had come to her rescue and lost a valuable possession in consequence. There were three things to be done. Spain should be compensated for the loss of Florida. She should be kept in line for the next war with England. She should be induced to make peace at once before any more was lost.

To accomplish all three objectives, France gave Spain all that was left of Louisiana, that is, the Isle of Orleans and all the territory west of the Mississippi. At first Spain was inclined to look a gift horse in the mouth. Probably France didn't think much of this territory she was giving away. On second thought, however, the Spanish could see the advantages and accepted. That was in 1762. The following year the treaty of peace with England was signed. France gave up the eastern half of La Salle's Louisiana.

For nearly forty years what was left of Louisiana remained a Spanish possession. The business of taking over the administration from France was a long process. Inquiries, studies and plans all had to be made. The official notice to the French governor at New Orleans that Louisiana had been given to Spain was not sent from Paris until the spring of 1764. At that time the first buildings of St. Louis were being constructed on what the workers believed was French soil. The news was not published in New Orleans until October 1764.

A Spanish governor finally arrived at New Orleans in 1766, but the French garrison that was supposed to carry out his orders refused to serve under him. In 1768, he proclaimed major commercial restrictions. The inhabitants of the city revolted. They threw him out. The next year a new Spanish governor arrived. He was backed by troops. His name was Alexander O'Reilly. With Irish vigor he established the Spanish administration of the colony. He executed the ringleaders of the revolt. The same year a lieutenant governor was sent up to St. Louis to look after the upper part of the territory.

Under Spain, Louisiana had a fairly prosperous existence. New Orleans, in particular, grew in importance, for it was discovered that sugar cane could be grown in the vicinity with profit. Trade and population increased. The city's promise as a great world port came to be realized. During this period, 1788 to 1794, two great fires swept the city. The rebuilding reflected some Spanish influence. Few Spanish came to live in Louisiana, however. The French cultural presence remained strong.

1. Canada fell to the British during

   a. King Willliam's War.
   b. the War of Spanish Succession.
   c. the Seven Years' War.
   d. the War of 1812.

2. Canada fell to the British in

   a. 1754.
   b. 1759.
   c. 1760.
   d. 1761.

3. The crucial battle of the French and Indian War occurred on the Plains of Abraham in front of the city of

   a. Quebec.
   b. Montreal.
   c. New Orleans.
   d. St. Lucia.

4. France was willing to give up all of Louisiana east of the Mississippi except the Isle of Orleans in order to keep

   a. Quebec.
   b. Guadeloupe.
   c. Martinique.
   d. St. Lucia.

5. The Spanish entered the war against England only to have their prize possession, _____, fall to the British.

   a. Florida
   b. Havana
   c. Martinique
   d. St. Lucia

6. France gave what was left of Louisiana to Spain to compensate for the loss of

   a. Florida.
   b. Havana.
   c. Martinique.
   d. St. Lucia.

178

7. In what type of book would this passage most likely be found?

    a. a comic book
    b. a history book
    c. a geography book
    d. a journal

8. Why do you think Louisiana prospered under the Spanish to a far greater degree than it had under the French?

_____

_____

_____

_____

_____

_____

_____

_____

_____

_____

_____

_____

_____

_____

_____

THE WESTERN GRAY SQUIRREL

This is a guide to distinguish the state-threatened western gray squirrel from other native squirrels (Douglas', red, and flying) and from three introduced species (Eastern gray, fox, and California ground squirrel). Western gray squirrels can be readily confused with these other species. The Washington Department of Fish and Wildlife (WDFW) maintains records on the distribution of western gray squirrels in Washington. Your assistance is appreciated. Western gray, Douglas', red, and flying squirrels are all protected species in Washington.

The Decline of the Western Gray Squirrel

The western gray squirrel was added to Washington's list of state-threatened species in 1993. At that time surveys indicated a decline in its geographical distribution. The species was once common from low to mid-elevations in dry forests where oak, pine, and Douglas fir mix. It is now limited to three areas in Washington. One is the southern Puget Trough. Here they can be found primarily on Fort Lewis Military Reservation. A second area is the Methow Valley in Okanogan County and the north shore of Lake Chelan in Chelan County. The third area is in the river valleys of Klickitat and southern Yakima Counties. Threats to the species include habitat loss and degradation, fluctuating food supplies, disease, and deaths resulting from road-kill and illegal hunting. State law protects the nest trees used by western gray squirrels. WDFW biologists will consult with landowners to protect and enhance oak/conifer habitat.

Distribution

Several species of squirrel occur in the three areas occupied by western gray squirrels in Washington. Eastern gray, Douglas', and flying squirrels are present in the southern Puget Trough. All species except California ground squirrels are found in Chelan and Okanogan Counties. Klickitat and southern Yakima Counties are home to all but fox and red squirrels.

Western Gray Squirrel (*Sciurus griseus*)

BODY: 12 INCHES   TAIL: 12 INCHES

Western gray squirrels are the largest native tree squirrels in Washington. They are salt-and-pepper to steel gray on the back with contrasting white underparts. They are distinguished by their very long and bushy white-edged tails, large feet and prominent ears, which are reddish-brown at the back in winter. Western gray squirrels forage in trees for acorns and conifer seeds. They also search the ground for mushrooms and bury acorns. They travel

180

from tree to tree or on the ground in graceful, wave-like leaps. They may vocalize in the fall with a hoarse bark: "chuff–chuffchuff."

Douglas' Squirrel (*Tamiasciurus douglasii*)

BODY: 7 INCHES   **TAIL: 5 INCHES**

Douglas' squirrels are small native tree squirrels. They are dark chestnut on the back fading to a reddish- or brownish-gray on the sides. Their underparts are orange to gray and are offset by short black stripes. The eye ring is pale orange. Their tails are somewhat bushy, slightly flattened and have a black tip. Douglas' squirrels vocalize often and have a range of calls from a low "chirr" to a sharp staccato "cough."

Red Squirrel (*Tamiasciurus hudsonicus*)

BODY: 8 INCHES   **TAIL: 6.5 INCHES**

Red squirrels are native and closely resemble their cousin the Douglas' squirrel. Their coat is typically reddish-brown on the back, fading to brown on the sides. A black line contrasts with the white belly in summer, but fades as the whole coat brightens in winter. The eye has a prominent white ring. The ranges of red and Douglas' squirrels overlap in the North Cascades Mountains.

Northern Flying Squirrel (*Glaucomys sabrinus*)

BODY: 5 INCHES   **TAIL: 7 INCHES**

Northern flying squirrels are native and are found throughout forested parts of the state. They have dense, silky cinnamon to gray-brown fur above cream-colored bellies. They have wide, flat tails, large dark eyes and relatively long ears. A fur-covered fold of skin stretches from the wrist to the ankle and is extended outward when they glide. They are rarely seen because they are nocturnal and sleep in tree cavities or stick nests during the day.

Eastern Gray Squirrel (*Sciurus carolinensis*)

BODY: 10.5 INCHES   **TAIL: 8 INCHES**

Eastern gray squirrels are mid-sized, with relatively narrow tails and short ears compared to western gray squirrels. They have a pale gray coat with a reddish-brown wash on the face, back and tail. Their underparts are creamy white. Eastern gray squirrels were first introduced into Washington in 1925. They are now common in many cities, and thrive in developed areas. Live-trapped squirrels should not be released outside their known Washington range.

Fox Squirrel (*Sciurus niger*)

BODY: 13 INCHES   TAIL: 11 INCHES

Fox squirrels are large with variable reddish-brown to pale gray backs and red to yellow-orange underparts. They have broad tails, coarse, grizzled fur and short ears. Fox squirrels can be found in habitats with fewer trees than most other tree squirrels. They were introduced into Washington from the southeastern United States. They occur in urban and rural environments in several parts of the state.

California Ground Squirrel (*Spermophilus beecheyi*)

BODY: 11 INCHES   TAIL: 7 INCHES

California ground squirrels have large heads and stout bodies. Their upperparts are gray-brown with light flecks and their bellies are off-white. A triangle of dark fur on the back contrasts with white-tinged shoulders. Their tails are gray above and off-white below, and can be narrow or bushy.

They may be seen in trees, but spend most of their time on the ground, where they run belly to the ground. This species entered Washington in 1912 when bridges were built across the Columbia River. California ground squirrels are also called "gray diggers." They are hunted in Washington. Special care should be taken to distinguish between these and western gray squirrels.

Signs of Squirrels

All tree squirrels may build or use stick and leaf nests and some use tree cavities for denning. Western gray squirrel nests are large. They are often clustered in dry oak/conifer forests, not far from water. Occupied nests may have fresh leaves, conifer boughs, or lichen on top. California ground squirrels nest in underground burrows. Chewed cones and needle clusters on the ground may be a sign of western gray squirrel feeding activity. Large piles of cone scales generally indicate Douglas' or red squirrels.

1. Which of the following is a species of squirrel native to Washington?

    a. eastern gray squirrel
    b. red squirrel
    c. fox squirrel
    d. California ground squirrel

2. Why does the article say your assistance is appreciated?

   a. The article is addressed to people who have helped to count squirrels.
   b. The Department of Fish and Wildlife would like readers to inform them whenever they see western gray squirrels in Washington.
   c. The Department of Fish and Wildlife would like readers to inform them whenever they see introduced species of squirrels in Washington.
   d. The Department of Fish and Wildlife would like readers to inform them whenever they see other native species of squirrels in Washington.

3. Why was the western gray squirrel added to Washington's list of threatened species?

   a. The federal government told the state of Washington to do it.
   b. The federal government had already done it.
   c. There were fewer squirrels in three areas of Washington, including the Fort Lewis Military Reservation.
   d. There were few or no squirrels outside of three areas in Washington.

4. Which threat to western gray squirrels is a direct result of people violating the law?

   a. habitat loss
   b. loss of food supply
   c. road-kill
   d. hunting

5. Fox squirrels can be found in

   a. the southern Puget Trough.
   b. Chelan County.
   c. Klickitat County.
   d. southern Yakima County.

6. What is the **best** way to distinguish between a western gray squirrel and a California ground squirrel?

   a. A western gray squirrel is much bigger.
   b. A western gray squirrel does not forage on the ground.
   c. A western gray squirrel has a triangle of dark fur on its back.
   d. A California ground squirrel has a triangle of dark fur on its back.

7. Which kind of squirrel are you **least likely** to see in Washington?

   a. red squirrel
   b. fox squirrel
   c. northern flying squirrel
   d. Douglas' squirrel

8. What could the state of Washington do to better protect western gray squirrels?

WALNUT CANYON

Take a trip into the pine forests near Flagstaff, Arizona. There you will find a steep canyon. It sits in the midst of a rolling plateau. It is twenty miles long. It is four hundred feet deep and a quarter-mile wide. It was carved by Walnut Creek over a period of sixty million years. Within its winding walls are natural riches. There is a large mix of plants and animals. They have been drawn there by water and the rich earth. It seems a timeless place.

Walls of buff sandstone form the canyon's inner gorge. The rocks reveal their origins. You can still see the dunes of an ancient desert. The limestone ledges of the upper canyon contain delicate marine fossils. They are remnants of a sea that later covered that ancient desert. Then, much later, the people of this canyon built their sturdy homes in shallow hollows along these ledges.

For a brief time, from about 1100 to 1250 C.E., the canyon echoed with the rhythmic beat of a stone ax. The voice of an aged storyteller could be heard. Children laughed on the rocky slopes. The walls they built can still be seen in places. They hint of this past. It was a time when one hundred or more people made their homes here. These people well understood the gifts of the natural world. Deer, bighorn sheep, other wild game, and wild plants added to the corn, beans, and squash grown in fields on the canyon rim. Water sometimes flowed on the canyon floor. It provided the lifeblood of the community. Shaded pools in the bottom held precious water between rains. In the spring, melted snow roared through the narrow passage. It carried rich silt with it.

Today the canyon resonates with birdsong. Jays yammer, solitaires peep, and canyon wrens whistle their musical songs. There have been changes, but the canyon remains, as does the diversity of plants and animals that sustained a human community.

Walnut Canyon is now a national monument. It serves as sanctuary for a larger community. Six miles of the canyon's length are protected within the monument's three thousand six hundred acres. Walnut Canyon offers the perfect opportunity to admire nature and to learn from the past. Thousands of people visit every year. With continued protection and cooperation from visitors, this intimate canyon will educate and inspire for years to come.

Animals

For a small area, Walnut Canyon National Monument has a lot of wildlife. This is due in part to its rugged canyon terrain, vegetation cover, minimal human disturbance, and the presence of water. Also, several different ecological communities overlap here. This creates a variety of microhabitats. It creates a mix of species that are usually found in different places and at different elevations. Scientists have identified at least sixty-nine species of mammals in the monument. There are twenty-eight species of reptiles and amphibians. They have found one hundred and twenty-one species of birds.

Wildlife commonly seen includes coyotes, mule deer, cottontail and jack rabbits, rock squirrels, golden-mantled ground squirrels, cliff chipmunks, pinyon jays, white-throated swifts, and turkey vultures. There are lots and lots of lizards. Large mammals—including elk, mountain lions, black bear, and pronghorn antelope—are also in the area. The south side of the canyon provides habitat for wild turkey. The steep terrain and secluded side canyons provide habitat for birds of prey like the Cooper's hawk, sharp-shinned hawk, red-tailed hawk, golden eagle, prairie falcon, flammulated owl, and great grey owl. In addition, the Mexican spotted owl, peregrine falcon, and northern goshawk, among the rarest raptors in the southwestern United States, are residents of Walnut Canyon.

Animal populations at Walnut Canyon vary with the seasons and from one year to the next. How many there are of each kind depends on temperature, rainfall, snowpack, and other environmental conditions, both locally and throughout the region. Larger animals can move easily about the landscape in search of the best food and water sources. In some seasons, Walnut Canyon suits these needs. At other times, it provides a protected natural corridor for wildlife on the move. In all seasons, it is a natural sanctuary and scenic resource located near an expanding area of human development.

Ancient People

The forests surrounding Walnut Canyon National Monument contain hundreds of archaeological sites and artifacts. A few are Archaic sites; they show that people were here between 2500 B.C.E. and 1 C.E. Most are from a prehistoric farming culture that flourished around Flagstaff from about 600 C.E. until 1400. According to archaeologists, this was part of the Sinagua culture. The name comes from the Spanish *sin agua*, meaning "without water." Sinagua refers to various archaeological sites and objects found in this part of Arizona that share similar characteristics. It is not the name of a tribe or clan of people. In fact, it is unknown how these people thought of themselves and their neighbors, or what they called themselves.

At first, scattered families grew corn, squash, and beans above the canyon rim. In the late 1000s, following the eruption of nearby Sunset Crater Volcano, the population began to grow. In about 1150 C.E., many people started moving down into Walnut Canyon. There they built the cliff dwellings that line the canyon walls today. There was water at times in Walnut Creek. The canyon held a rich assortment of plants and animals that could be harvested.

The Walnut Canyon community thrived here for about one hundred and fifty years. They grew crops in small plots above the rim. Here they raised their children. They made stone tools and implements. They followed the ancient ceremonial cycles that had been passed down for generations. Then they moved on. By the early 1300s, the canyon ledges were quiet.

The Walnut Canyon cliff dwellings are unique. They are the only known such remains of the northern Sinagua culture. They are constructed in rock alcoves within the canyon. They protected their occupants from the elements. Almost seven hundred years later, their walls and the artifacts within are still remarkably well preserved. We can learn much from these dwellings and from the many masonry pueblos, rock shelters, campsites, agricultural fields, and objects still in place at Walnut Canyon National Monument.

1. How long was the period of time that people lived in Walnut Canyon?

    a. 60 million years
    b. 1,250 years
    c. 1,100 years
    d. 150 years

2. How did deer, sheep, and wild plants add to the corn, beans, and squash grown in the fields?

    a. They supplied fertilizer.
    b. They were additional sources of food.
    c. They helped turn up the dirt.
    d. They helped weed.

3. How long is Walnut Canyon?

    a. 1/4 mile
    b. six miles
    c. 12 miles
    d. 3,600 acres

4. How much of the canyon is within the Walnut Canyon National Monument?

   a. 1/4 mile
   b. six miles
   c. 12 miles
   d. 3,600 acres

5. Which has the most varied number of species present in the monument?

   a. mammals
   b. reptiles
   c. birds
   d. amphibians

6. Which of the following is the most common in the Southwest?

   a. Mexican spotted owl
   b. peregrine falcon
   c. northern goshawk
   d. red-tailed hawk

7. In Spanish, *sin agua* means

   a. without water.
   b. archaelogical site.
   c. prehistoric farming culture.
   d. a tribe or clan of people.

8. Archaic sites were inhabited by people who lived

   a. 2,000 to 4,500 years ago.
   b. 1,400 to 600 years ago.
   c. in the 1300s.
   d. 150 years ago.

9. Why would people decide to live on the side of a canyon?

_____

_____

_____

_____

_____

_____

_____

_____

_____

_____

_____

_____

_____

_____

_____

_____

_____

_____

189

SETTLERS SAIL TO MARYLAND

Armed with a charter, young Lord Baltimore set about the business of colonizing his domain. On November 22, 1633, Leonard Calvert and his brother, Cecilius, "with very near twenty other gentlemen of very good fashion, and three hundred laboring men," sailed from Cowes in the Isle of Wight. They sailed in two ships, the *Ark* and the *Dove*. The Calverts and the other gentlemen were Roman Catholics. While some of the laborers were also Roman Catholic, an even greater proportion were Protestant. The emigrants were accompanied by two Jesuit priests, Fathers Andrew White and John Altham. They performed religious ceremonies at the site where they were planning to depart from, while a gentle east wind blew, "committing the principal parts of the ship to the protection of God especially, and of His most Holy Mother, and St. Ignatius, and all the guardian angels of Maryland."

The colonists took the tedious southern route by way of the Canaries and the West Indies. They had just escaped the perils of The Needles on the coast of the Isle of Wight when the fear of the Turkish cruisers—then the terror of all Christian seamen—possessed them. This fear was soon relieved by the appearance of a large English merchantman called *The Dragon*. It was well armed and bound for Angola. It would convoy them beyond the line of danger.

When only two days' journey away, the group was overtaken by a furious gale. *The Dragon* turned back. The emigrant vessels went forward. The tempest increased when night fell. The people of the *Dove*, the smaller vessel, notified the officers of the staunch *Ark* that they would hang out a lighted lantern at the masthead in case of danger. That signal of distress appeared at midnight for a few minutes, then suddenly vanished. "All are lost!" thought the tenants of the *Ark*, and they grieved sorely. They had no doubt that the *Dove*, with her precious freight, had gone to the bottom of the sea.

For three days, the storm swept the ocean. Suddenly, the clouds gathered and rain fell in torrents. For a few minutes, a dreadful hurricane threatened instant destruction to all in its path. It seemed as if "all the malicious spirits of the storm, and all the evil genii of Maryland had come forth to battle" against the *Ark*. Her mainsail was split from top to bottom. Her rudder was torn away. She was left at the mercy of the winds and waves. In mortal terror, the emigrants fell on their knees and prayed. The Roman Catholics uttered vows in honor of "the Blessed Virgin Mary and her Immaculate Conception; of St. Ignatius, the patron saint of Maryland; St. Michael, and all the guardian angels of the same country."

"I had betaken myself to prayer," said Father White, "when the sea was raging its worst, and (may this be to the glory of God) I had scarcely finished, when they observed that the storm was abating." After that, the voyagers had delightful weather for three months both on sea and on land.

The *Ark* finally entered a harbor of the island of Barbados, on the eastern edge of the Antilles islands. The emigrants, all regarded as Roman Catholics, were coldly received. They were charged extravagant prices for provisions that they had to purchase. The voyagers learned that they had escaped a Spanish fleet lying at Bonavista, as well as another peril in the port at which they had arrived. The slaves on the island had conspired to murder their masters, seize the first ship that should appear, and put to sea. The conspiracy had just been discovered. The men were further thrilled by the arrival of the pinnace *Dove* after a separation of six weeks. In the terrible gale, the ship had taken refuge in the Scilly Isles, before sailing with a fair wind in search of the *Ark*. After perilous wanderings over the waters, the *Dove* had returned.

The emigrants left Barbados after a short stay. They passed several islands of the Antilles, near one where they encountered canoes full of naked and painted cannibals. Late in February 1634, they sailed in between the Capes of Virginia. They touched at Point Comfort before traveling up to Jamestown. They landed in Virginia full of doubt lest the inhabitants, who were very angry at their coming, should be plotting something against them. However, royal letters borne by Calvert secured a friendly reception from Governor Harvey. They rested pleasantly for nine days there.

They then sailed for the Chesapeake and entered the broad mouth of the Potomac River. They were delighted with the great stream and the scenery on its banks. They gave it the name of St. Gregory, in honor of the canonized pope of that name. Father White wrote the following:

> Never have I beheld a larger or more beautiful river. The Thames seems a mere rivulet in comparison with it; it is not disfigured by any swamps, but has firm land on each side. Fine groves of trees appear, not choked with briers or bushes or undergrowth, but growing at intervals as if planted by the hand of man, so that you can drive a four-horse carriage, wherever you choose, through the midst of the trees. Just at the mouth of the river we saw the natives in arms. That night fires blazed throughout the whole country, and since they had never seen so large a ship, messengers were sent in all directions, who reported that a canoe, like an island, had come with as many men as there were trees in the woods.

The colonists sailed up the Potomac to the Heron Islands. They landed on Black-stone, which they named St. Clements, a little past the middle of

March. The air was balmy and sweet with opening spring flowers. Birds were filling the groves with rich melody. The shy natives came to them one after another and were disarmed of all hostility by the kindness of the new arrivals.

As Calvert stepped ashore, a salute was fired from the boats. Then, reverently kneeling, the colonists listened while Mass was said for the first time in English America. Mass being over, they formed a procession. At its head a rough wooden cross was carried. Then, when they reached a spot chosen beforehand, they planted the cross. Kneeling around it, they chanted the Litany of the Sacred Cross with great fervor.

And thus a new colony was begun.

1. Most of the _____ on the *Ark* and *Dove* were Protestants.

   a. priests
   b. leaders
   c. gentlemen
   d. laborers

2. Who did the priest pray to for probably the very first time?

   a. "His most Holy Father"
   b. St. Ignatius
   c. all the guardian angels of Maryland
   d. the gentle east wind

3. The first danger the ships avoided was

   a. The Needles.
   b. *The Dragon.*
   c. Turkish cruisers.
   d. a furious gale.

4. In the gale, _____ turned back and _____ was thought lost.

   a. the *Dove* . . . *The Dragon*
   b. *The Dragon* . . . the *Dove*
   c. *The Dragon* . . . the *Ark*
   d. the *Ark* . . . the *Dove*

5. Once the storm abated, the *Ark*'s crew must have

    a. left the ship at the mercy of the wind and the waves.
    b. headed for Angola.
    c. headed back to England.
    d. repaired the mainsail and rudder.

6. The **worst** part of being in Barbados was

    a. the slave revolt.
    b. the Spanish fleet at Bonavista.
    c. religious hostility and overpriced goods.
    d. the reappearance of the *Dove*.

7. The **best** part of being in Barbados was

    a. the end of the slave revolt.
    b. avoiding the Spanish fleet.
    c. refuge in the Scilly Isles.
    d. the reappearance of the *Dove*.

8. Where did the emigrants expect the most hostility?

    a. Angola
    b. Barbados
    c. Virginia
    d. Black-stone

9. Where did the emigrants find the most hostility?

    a. Angola
    b. Barbados
    c. Virginia
    d. Black-stone

10. Do you think the colonists' first impressions of Maryland were on the whole accurate or misleading? Why?

_____

_____

_____

_____

_____

_____

_____

_____

_____

_____

_____

_____

_____

_____

_____

_____

_____

_____

194

SCIENTISTS TRACK ELUSIVE SEADUCKS
by Karl Blankenship

Last summer (2003), a group of ducks led some Chesapeake Bay scientists on a wild goose chase. Tipped off that a group of surf scoters were nesting on a lake in Labrador, Canada, a research team headed north.

They searched the area with a helicopter. They hired a guide with trained dogs. They even got help from people at a nearby NATO base.

They crawled through forest underbrush in densely vegetated roadless areas, swatting mosquitoes every foot of the way. But in the end, the team of scientists from the U.S. Geological Survey's Patuxent Wildlife Research Center in Maryland never found a nest.

"It's very much like trying to find a needle in a haystack," said Alicia Wells. She was one of the scientists involved. "I had tons of people out there with me. We found five females on five different ponds, but they never even once acted like they were nesting."

Such frustrations are one of the reasons why seaducks, such as the surf scoter, are the most poorly studied waterfowl of North America. One thing is known: "The long-term trend is the species are declining," said Matt Perry. He is a research biologist who is leading the center's seaduck effort.

That's true for the Chesapeake Bay, one of the most important wintering areas for the birds, as well as for many other populations. The reason, like the answer to many questions about seaducks, comes in three words: No one knows.

The decline could be due to degraded water quality in the Bay and other wintering areas. It could be caused by disturbances in their summer nesting grounds. It might be increased hunting pressure. Or it could be all of the above.

But no one knows. The 15 species of seaducks—that's 42 percent of all duck species—are so poorly studied that much about them remains a mystery even as other waterfowl have been studied for a century.

When the authoritative book, *Ducks, Geese and Swans of North America*, was published in 1980, everything known about surf scoter nesting was based on a single study of one nest. "You come across those kinds of things and it's just hard to believe," Perry said.

Part of the lack of interest stems from the fact that seaducks historically were not a main target of hunters. "They don't taste good," Perry noted. Most attention went to waterfowl that had more recreational value.

Further, seaducks are particularly hard to study. They get their name because they stay a mile or more out in the water, where they are hard to find. And because they are darker than many other birds, they are hard to see during aerial surveys compared to other, lighter duck species. "When you fly over them, and they are relatively scattered over a large area of water, they just disappear," Perry said.

Compounding those problems is that the birds nest over huge areas of Canada and Alaska. Nests are widely scattered in roadless areas. Researchers have to fly into areas and literally crawl through brush so dense they could easily overlook a nest only a few feet away.

"A whole team will spend weeks searching for nests and maybe find one," Perry said. Black scoters have been particularly difficult. None of the scientists has even seen one of their nests yet.

Things are beginning to change, in part as a result of the 1989 Exxon Valdez disaster in Alaska. It left a huge number of seaducks soaked in oil. Because no one knew much about the birds, scientists had trouble quantifying how important the disaster was to the overall population. "If a judge asks you what a duck is worth," Perry noted, "you need to know how to answer."

Research has been stepped up since then. The Patuxent scientists, whose work is being funded by the U.S. Fish and Wildlife Service, U.S. Geological Survey, and the Sea Duck Joint Venture, are one of the key research teams in the effort. They are focusing on birds using the hugely important Chesapeake Bay.

Although seaducks spend their winters anywhere along a 2,000-mile range from Labrador to Florida, it's estimated that between a quarter and a third of the entire Atlantic Flyway population is concentrated in the Bay.

The Chesapeake has eight seaduck species. The researchers are focusing on the four which are least studied. They are the black scoter, surf scoter, white-winged scoter and the long-tailed duck (formerly known as the oldsquaw).

Although those birds winter in the Bay, no one actually knew where the birds were spending their summer breeding seasons. To find out, the scientists in recent years have tried various techniques to capture live ducks on the Bay so they could be implanted with transmitters and tracked.

Catching the birds is no easy task. The scientists tried various techniques. One was chasing seaducks in speeding boats while firing a net from a specially designed gun. What they learned, Perry said, is that the ducks are difficult to catch. Perry's team has managed to capture 23 surf scoters. No black scoter has ever been successfully caught in the Chesapeake, despite weeks of effort, because of their low numbers.

To tag that species, the scientists finally had to go to the Restigouche River in New Brunswick, Canada. The birds congregate there during migration. Their flocks add up to nearly 100,000 ducks. There, teams of Canadian and American scientists used nightlighting techniques to daze the ducks and capture them.

Radio transmitters were implanted. A short antenna sticks out the back of the ducks. That allows the birds to be tracked by satellite. It's expensive. The transmitter, and the cost of the satellite data, adds up to about $5,000 a bird.

But it is revealing new information about the birds' migration routes, important staging areas for migration and—most importantly—where they are nesting.

The transmitters also give the scientists an important edge in finding nests in the wilderness. "These birds nest in dense, woody vegetation," Perry said. "To get through, you have to get down on your hands and knees and crawl." Using hand-held tracking devices, they can find the nests and determine what types of habitat the birds are using.

In some cases, they are also swiping some eggs. The eggs, usually from abandoned nests, are put in incubators and brought back to the Patuxent Center. There scientists are rearing a colony to study in captivity so they can better understand their diet in the Bay.

One thing that tracking has shown, Perry said, is that the birds return to the same location each winter. "They come back because they know where the groceries are."

It's possible, though, that the groceries in the Bay have changed because of poor water quality. Because they live far from shore, seaducks find their food by diving 20–40 feet to the bottom. They root around for clams, mussels and other bottom-dwelling creatures in deep habitats. Those habitats have been affected by low-oxygen conditions in recent decades.

1. Of the following, which is **not** true of the surf scoter?

    a. It is a seaduck.
    b. Its habits are well known.
    c. It is declining in number.
    d. It spends time in Labrador, Canada.

2. Where do some surf scoters spend winter?

    a. ponds in Labrador, Canada
    b. the Chesapeake Bay
    c. Restigouche River, New Brunswick, Canada
    d. No one knows.

3. How many species of seaducks are there?

    a. 15
    b. 25
    c. 35
    d. 45

4. About how many species of ducks are there?

    a. 15
    b. 25
    c. 35
    d. 45

5. In 1980, how many surf scoter nests had been studied?

    a. 15
    b. 5
    c. 1
    d. 0

6. Seaducks are studied now more than they were 20 years ago because

    a. the Exxon Valdez disaster left many coated with oil.
    b. they don't taste good.
    c. hunters aren't interested in them.
    d. they are hard to see.

7. Studying seaducks is

    a. easy because they stay a mile out in the water.
    b. easy because they nest over huge areas.
    c. easy because they nest in heavy underbrush.
    d. funded by government agencies.

8. The hardest seabird to study has been the

    a. black scoter.
    b. surf scoter.
    c. white-winged scoter.
    d. long-tailed duck.

9. The seaduck that was given a nicer name is the

    a. black scoter.
    b. surf scoter.
    c. white-winged scoter.
    d. long-tailed duck.

10. Do you think it is right for scientists to steal eggs and raise birds in captivity? Why or why not?

199

11. Write a story about trying to catch seaducks in Chesapeake Bay.

_____

_____

_____

_____

_____

_____

_____

_____

_____

_____

_____

_____

_____

_____

_____

_____

_____

200

201

ENDURANCE AND OPPORTUNITY
by Rolf Peterson

The Middle Pack was intent on expanding its territory. After spending five weeks at the west end of the island, the Pack moved twenty miles east. Two days later, tracks showed that the Middle Pack had encountered a wolf pair and had given chase. By aircraft we followed these tracks for six miles. We caught up to the eleven-member pack at water's edge just before noon. They were vigorously shaking themselves dry. Twenty feet out in Lake Superior, standing on a submerged rock in ten inches of water, stood a bedraggled wolf, cowering, its hindquarters almost underwater.

During the next hour we circled overhead. After several minutes of rolling in the snow to dry off, Middle Pack wolves either lay in the snow, watching the victim in the lake, or strutted stiffly back and forth along the shore in front of the hapless wolf. Suddenly, in quick succession, three wolves jumped into shallow water and leaped for the rock where their quarry stood quivering. Confronted by this snarling trio, it fought for its life, snapping furiously toward the lunging pack members. The lone wolf was forced backward into neck-deep water, but it retained its footing and held the attackers at bay. They retreated to shore to shake and roll again in the snow.

While we watched the pack led a series of attacks on the wolf on the rock. There were a dozen attacks in all. The desperate defense of the lone wolf was effective, but the ordeal, including standing neck-deep in ice-water, took its toll. During the last few encounters the loner adopted a new strategy. When attacked on its rock it retreated into the lake and swam along the shore about thirty feet to another submerged rock, buying a few moments before the pack members jumped back to shore and ran down to the new location where they renewed their attack.

We became aware of a new element when the breeding male of the Middle Pack jumped to the rock to confront the lone wolf. Instead of pressing the attack, however, he slowly wagged his raised tail. Then he circled around to the wolf's side and regarded its hindquarters. The male was interested in courting the stranger, a newly arrived female in heat. His arousal prompted the alpha female to jump to the rock, along with a helper. A severe attack then followed. Middle Pack wolves firmly grabbed the female and threw her on her back in the water. Soon all eleven wolves of the Middle Pack were involved in the melee. In less than a minute, however, the pack retreated and the lone female rose to her feet.

After forty-five minutes the lone female, once again facing a violent attack, swam out into Lake Superior, heading for a rocky point about fifty yards down

202

the shore. Her "dog-paddle" strokes seemed vigorous. I thought she might be able to hit shore and get away with an all-out run. But she could only crawl out of the water and stiffly walk a few steps before starting to shake her drenched fur.

Within seconds the Middle Pack arrived and knocked her over. The whole pack crowded around and bit her, shaking their heads as they held on. When the pack pulled back briefly, the female snapped at the wolves that surrounded her. The last wolf pressing the attack held the female's throat for several seconds, then left her lying motionless on the shoreline rocks. The Middle Pack retreated toward the forest edge, huddled excitedly, and then lay down in the bright afternoon sun, keeping an occasional eye on their victim. We thought the female was dead, but she raised her head briefly, which brought the pack running. They crowded around, vigorously biting her legs and throat.

Five minutes later, at 1:00 p.m., the female appeared to be dead at last. We flew to a nearby frozen lake and landed, to conserve our fuel supply. A half-hour later we checked the scene and found no change. The pack was sleeping and the carcass of the lone female had not been moved. We headed back to our base camp to refuel.

At 3:30 p.m. we found the pack heading into the island's interior. We planned to land to collect the carcass, but as we circled we saw a wolf approaching the attack scene in the tracks of the Middle Pack. This was the trailing member of the Middle Pack. As it drew near the attack scene, this new wolf became very uneasy. He looked all around with tail tucked between its legs. Eventually it followed tracks to the water's edge and saw the dead wolf. Without hesitation the newcomer approached and, when only two feet away, the lone female raised her head! The oncoming wolf kept its distance but moved near the female's hindquarters, revealing himself to be a potential suitor. Perhaps the female mustered a low growl from her torn throat. For some reason the male retreated a few feet, climbed up on a nearby rock, and lay down to watch. The female laid her head back on the bedrock shore.

Periodically the male approached the female. His attention seemed to breathe life into her. Almost an hour after his arrival, she managed to hold her head up. We left the pair alone for two hours, returning for our final check of the day at 6:00 p.m. The male and female were both gone, and we marveled at her resilience.

The next day the Middle Pack was miles away, busy with other matters. From the aircraft we could find no sign of the wounded female and her new friend.

We then landed on a nearby lake. We snowshoed to the attack scene. Not surprisingly, about fifty yards into the woods we found a succession of three bloody beds of the female. The snowy imprints of her throat and hindquarters were saturated with blood. We followed parallel tracks of both wolves, with occasional drops of blood marking the female's path, as far as we could.

Five days later we were rewarded with a clear view of the wounded female and her suitor standing on a rocky knoll, about a half-mile from the site of the attack. The female was standing while the male faced her and attentively licked her wounded neck for several minutes. The pair had occupied the site for a day or two, judging from the number of icy beds nearby, and there were just a few drops of blood in the area. Obviously the female was getting better. Her companion provided much-needed attention to her neck wound and may have saved her life, but now he became quite a pest, displaying an array of courtship behavior. The female had no evident interest, and she had to expend valuable energy to whirl and snap at his unwelcome advances. She tried to curl up and lie down but was forced to stay on her feet to fend him off. Standing tall and wagging his tail nearly vertically in the air, the male moved constantly round and round the female, and she reluctantly moved in circles. For almost an hour we circled overhead. We watched the female ward off all physical contact with the male except his attention to her wounded neck. Twice she grabbed a mouthful of snow. It seemed she had not been able to get to the lake for water, about a hundred yards distant. Prevented from displaying common courtship behavior, such as pawing the female's back, inspecting or mounting her rear, and playfully chasing in mutual excitement, the male tried a new approach. It was something I'd never seen before in wolf courtship. He stood in front of the female and quickly dug a deep hole in the snow, as though caching food. This was similar to some of the hunting-related courtship behavior of red foxes.

Two hours later, when we checked the pair for the last time, the male was still making a nuisance of himself. The female continued to snap at him. They were two individuals, one focused on mere survival and the other on reproductive imperatives. Neither had much chance of success outside the existing pack hierarchy. We felt fortunate to observe the pair again, but this was our last flight of the winter season. In this case, a final outcome would be known only to the wolves.

1. After the Middle Pack moved east, they chased a pack of wolves. What happened to the male of the pair?

    a. He was killed by the pack.
    b. He drowned.
    c. He was stuck on a rock in the middle of Lake Superior.
    d. The author doesn't know.

2. Why did the alpha female lead the attack of all eleven wolves on the lone wolf in the lake?

    a. She was jealous of the breeding male's interest in the newcomer.
    b. Her helper led the attack.
    c. The breeding male led the attack.
    d. The alpha female was in heat.

3. When the lone wolf reached shore, why did the pack initially retreat after knocking her over and biting her?

    a. The lone wolf fought back viciously.
    b. The author thought the lone wolf was dead.
    c. The pack thought the lone wolf was dead.
    d. The last pack wolf held the lone wolf's throat for several seconds.

4. The plane landed on a frozen lake to

    a. collect the carcass.
    b. conserve fuel.
    c. refuel.
    d. snowshoe to the attack scene.

5. The male's unique courtship behavior was

    a. pawing the female's back.
    b. inspecting her rear.
    c. playfully chasing.
    d. digging a deep hole in the snow.

6. What do you think happened to the wolf pair? Why?

_____

_____

_____

_____

_____

_____

_____

_____

_____

_____

_____

_____

_____

_____

_____

_____

_____

DANIEL BOONE AND THE LONG HUNTERS VISIT KENTUCKY

In 1767, John Finley, then residing in the Yadkin River valley in North Carolina, led a party into the wilderness. His object was to hunt and to trade with the Native Americans. His route was along the "Warrior's Path." This road had been laid out on an early map of Kentucky. Finley and his party roamed and hunted through the broad forests. They gazed with wonder and delight at the richness of the soil, the fine growth of vegetation, and the boundless supply of game. Late in the year they returned to their homes laden with the trophies of their hunt. They spread abroad among the people stories of the wonderland they had seen. Enough was now known about the Kentucky wilderness to inspire others to venture into it.

The spirit of adventure soon inspired men accustomed to Native American warfare, to hunting, and to all the perils of frontier life. In 1769, a group, with John Finley to guide them, and Boone as their leader, banded together for an excursion into the depths of the great wilderness.

They reached the foothills of the mountains in June, thirty-eight days after their departure. They built their camp cabin not far from Finley's old site. Besides Boone and Finley there were John Stewart, Joseph Holden, James Mooney, and William Cool.

The typical camp cabin was the structure of just a few hours' work. The hunters would fell a large tree, to lie nearly north and south, to protect from the westerly winds and gales. Two forks were set in the ground on the east side. They were ten or twelve feet apart, and the same distance from the body of the tree. Poles were placed, one end in the forks and the other on the body of the tree. Other poles were laid across these. They were about two feet apart. The bark was stripped from the fallen tree. It was laid board-shape upon the cross poles to keep off the sun and rain. The two sides were also covered with bark, and sometimes protected with logs. The front end was left open.

Just outside of the camp cabin, the fire was built for cooking and for warmth when needed. If the embers died out, the fire was rekindled by sparks that fell from the flint and steel struck together into some dry leaves or tinder placed underneath. Then the twigs and wood were added. Over these fires the kettle boiled. In the embers, delicious venison or bear, on the end of a pointed stick, roasted to a turn.

From June until December, the huntsmen ventured forth from their retreat. They roamed through river valleys and pastures. They were happy and content in the shadows of the wilderness. Nothing as yet had occurred to mar the pleasures of their adventure. At the base of the great forests and rich herbage they found that the soil was rich and fertile. It contrasted greatly with the sterile land in the east.

Amid these scenes of forest beauty roamed the timid deer, the stately elk, the surly bear, the cunning wolf, the crafty panther, the majestic buffalo, the shy turkey, and many, many more. From flowing springs, cool and refreshing waters sprang out of the ground, and coursed their way amid banks of bordering grass and flowers, or under hanging vines, to the creeks and rivers. No wonder that Daniel Boone said that he had found a paradise in the great wilds beyond the mountains. However, a shadow at last fell upon the paths of their good fortune. Hostile Native Americans had discovered their forest retreat and were on their trail.

While hunting one day, Boone and John Stewart were captured. Boone says:

> In the decline of the day, near Kentucky river, a number of Native Americans rushed out of a canebrake upon us and made us prisoners. The time of our sorrow was now arrived. They plundered us of what we had and kept us in confinement seven days, treating us with common savage usage. During this time we showed no uneasiness or desire to escape. This made them less suspicious of us. But in the dead of night, as we lay in a thick canebrake, by a large fire, when sleep had locked up their senses, I touched my companion and gently awoke him. We took the opportunity and departed, Leaving [*sic*] them to take their rest. We speedily directed our course toward our old camp; but found it plundered and the company dispersed and gone home.

The two companions lived on for a time, alone in the wilderness, content with wild meat and fruits.

The long absence of Daniel Boone and his companions from their homes had created doubts about their safety. Much concerned over this, Squire Boone, a brother of Daniel, with one companion, undertook the dangerous task of a search. His venture was most fortunate and timely. In the biography of himself, Daniel Boone tells the story in his own simple way:

> About this time my brother, Squire Boone, with another adventurer, was wandering through the forest in search of me, and, by accident, found our camp. Although our situation was dangerous, surrounded with hostile savages, our meeting in the wilderness made us sensible of the utmost joy and satisfaction. Sorrows and sufferings vanish at the meeting of friends. Soon after this, my companion in captivity, John Stewart, was killed by the savages. The man who came with my brother returned home by himself. We were then exposed daily to perils and death among savages and wild beasts, not a white

man in the country but ourselves. We hunted every day, and prepared a little cottage to defend us from the winter storms. On May 1, 1770, my brother returned home by himself for a new recruit of horses and ammunition, leaving me alone, without bread, salt, or sugar, and without the company of man, or even a horse or dog. Thus, through scenes of sylvan pleasures, I spent the time until July 27 following, when my brother, to my great joy, met me, according to appointment, at our old camp. Shortly after, we left this place, journeying toward the Cumberland River until March 1771, giving names to the different waters. Soon after, I returned home to my family, resolving to bring them as soon as possible to live in Kentucky, which I esteemed a second paradise, at the risk of my life and fortune.

Early in the same year that Boone was exploring Kentucky, 1769, a party of forty hunters and trappers gathered and crossed the mountains from Virginia, on a route farther west. Passing the south fork of the Cumberland River, they selected a site for a camp. Here they constructed a depot for their supplies and skins. They hunted far out to the south and west. This region they found an open prairie land. It was covered with grass and abounding with wild animals of every kind, which they hunted and trapped. As no forest existed here at the time, this country was called "The Barrens." The Native Americans were in the habit of burning the dry grass over the prairies in their hunting seasons. Thus the young plants which might have grown into trees were killed by fire. After colonial settlement, the burning ceased, and forests grew.

For two years this band of bold backwoodsmen continued to hunt and explore the country, from the headwaters of Dick's and Green Rivers to Warren County. They returned to Virginia in 1772. Their long absence gave them the name of "Long Hunters." It is a notable fact that Boone and his comrades knew nothing of the presence of this party in the wilderness.

1. What was the primary purpose of Finley's first excursion into the wilderness?

   a. to river raft
   b. to explore
   c. to hunt
   d. to survey

2. Which statement is **true**?

   a. The Boone excursion lasted for 38 days.
   b. Boone and Stewart were held captive for 38 days.
   c. It took Boone's group 38 days to reach their base camp.
   d. It took Boone's group 38 days to prepare for their excursion.

3. According to the passage, which of the following do we know to be **true** about the region explored by Boone's group?

   a. It was uninhabited.
   b. It was dangerous.
   c. It was sterile.
   d. It was fertile.

4. Which word **best** describes how Finley, Boone, and the rest of their party felt during the first months of their excursion?

   a. frightened
   b. delighted
   c. tired
   d. curious

5. Which of the following **best** describes the game found by the explorers?

   a. plentiful
   b. sparse
   c. elusive
   d. tame

6. How did Boone and Stewart escape their captors?

   a. They killed them all.
   b. They were rescued by their party.
   c. They bribed them with promises of animal skins.
   d. They snuck away in the middle of the night.

7. Which of the following occurred **first**?

   a. Boone's group built a base camp.
   b. Finley returned home from his first excursion into the wilderness.
   c. Boone's group dispersed and went home.
   d. Boone and Stewart were captured and held prisoner.

8. Why did Squire Boone first venture into the Kentucky wilderness?

   a. to follow in his big brother's footsteps.
   b. to rescue Daniel from his captors
   c. to find Daniel
   d. to hunt wild and abundant game

9. Which of the following **best** describes how the brothers must have felt upon seeing each other?

   a. They were sorrowful because John Stewart had died.
   b. They were exhausted from the numerous hardships of the wilderness.
   c. They were frustrated that it had taken so long to find each other.
   d. They were relieved to have found each other.

10. How did Daniel come to be left alone in the wilderness?

   a. His brother and his friends had been killed by Native Americans.
   b. Stewart had been killed and Squire had returned home to get more equipment.
   c. Squire returned home to be with the rest of the Boone family.
   d. Squire returned home after a terrible quarrel with Daniel.

11. Approximately how much time passed before Squire then returned to the wilderness?

   a. one month
   b. two months
   c. ten months
   d. one year

12. Which of the following is a **true** statement?

   a. Boone and the group of forty hunters and trappers never met.
   b. The group of forty hunters and trappers killed Stewart.
   c. Boone's brother was the leader of the group of forty hunters and trappers.
   d. Boone joined the group of forty hunters and trappers.

13. According to the passage, what were Daniel Boone's plans after he returned home to his family?

   a. to bring his family to Kentucky
   b. to relax at home after his struggles in the wilderness
   c. to venture even further west
   d. to start building his fortune

211

14. What initially kept the forests from growing?

    a. Settlers used all the trees to build their homes.
    b. Floods destroyed the young trees.
    c. Young trees could not take root in the poor Kentucky soil.
    d. Native Americans burned the land during hunting seasons.

15. Imagine that you are a pioneer in Kentucky in 1769. Write a journal entry about your observations.

TWO OKLAHOMA WILDLIFE REFUGES

Tishomingo National Wildlife Refuge

The 16,464-acre Tishomingo National Wildlife Refuge (NWR) is on Lake Texoma in Oklahoma. It was created for the benefit of migratory waterfowl in the Central Flyway. Most of the refuge was acquired in 1946. In its midst is the 4,500-acre Cumberland Pool.

Tishomingo NWR is a place where it's easy to imagine the past era when great herds of wild animals grazed the prairies and bird flocks darkened the skies. It's appropriate that the refuge is named for a famous Chickasaw chief.

WILDLIFE

Dense hardwood forests line the road into Tishomingo NWR. Within the shelter of southern red oak, post oak, blackjack oak, hickory, pecan, mulberry, and American elm trees live white-tailed deer, wild turkeys, armadillos, opossums, and fox squirrels. Cottontails venture from forest to fields. They have to be careful, though. They are always on the lookout for hungry hawks. From spring through early fall, leaves rustle with the activity of migratory songbirds. Warblers and vireos join year-round residents like red-headed woodpeckers.

Other habitats sheltering wildlife include wild plum thickets that give way to grasslands. Along the river bottom, you might spot raccoon tracks among the willow, cottonwood, and box elder. Late fall and winter mark the best time to see wildlife. One great spot is the observation tower that juts up east of Big Sandy Creek. Here, you can look through a mounted spotting scope. Watch flocks of waterfowl and deer herds eating crops planted just for them. Beyond the fields, look for wading birds along the shoreline and ducks in the lake. Occasionally, you'll see bald eagles perched in dead trees at the field edge. Signs help to identify birds. Jemison Lookout, near Nida Point, provides a beautiful view of the Cumberland Pool year-round.

WILDLIFE WATCHING TIPS

- Dawn and dusk are the best times to see wildlife.
- In warmer climates, little is moving on hot summer afternoons or on windy days.
- Observe from the sidelines. Leave "abandoned" young animals alone. A parent is probably close by waiting for you to leave. Don't offer snacks. Your lunch could disrupt wild digestive systems.

213

- Cars make good observation blinds. Drive slowly, stopping to scan places wildlife might hide. Use binoculars or a long lens for a closer look.

- Try sitting quietly in one good location. Let wildlife get used to your presence. Many animals that have hidden will reappear once they think you are gone. Walk quietly in designated areas, being aware of sounds and smells. Often you will hear more than you will see.

- Teach young children quiet observation. Other wildlife watchers will appreciate your consideration.

- Look for animal signs. Tracks, scat, feathers, and nests left behind often tell interesting stories.

Washita National Wildlife Refuge

The Washita National Wildlife Refuge was established in 1961. It was created primarily to provide a resting and feeding area to migrating and wintering waterfowl. The 8,200-acre refuge is on the mixed grass plains of west-central Oklahoma. It is located on Foss Reservoir. The reservoir and waterfowl refuge are ideally located. They are in a part of the great Central Flyway used by migrating birds and waterfowl to travel between Canada on the north and Mexico on the south.

This area of western Oklahoma produces a considerable amount of oil and gas. Custer County is located on top of the Anadarko Basin. It is one of the largest known reserves of natural gas in the world. There are seven active wells on the refuge.

Archaeological finds on the refuge indicate a prior civilization of nomadic hunters. Bison horns, antlers, stone scrapers and points chronicle the Native American's dependence on the wildlife resources. Pottery shards, fire rings, and pole marks have also been found on the refuge. Initial surveys indicated the existence of village and burial sites on the refuge dating back to the 1500s. The nomads tended to use the same camp site year after year as they moved through the area. Most activity occurred on the second terrace level overlooking the Washita River. The area was probably also a camp ground for General Custer's 7th Cavalry. Very little excavating has been done on the refuge. Known or suspected sites are protected from disturbance.

When this area was first settled it was a rolling prairie of bluestem, grama, and buffalo grass. The more fertile soils were transformed into cropland. After the Dust Bowl days of the 1930s, many of the old homesteads were abandoned as families moved to town. Many of the highly erodible sites have now been taken out of crop production. They have been placed back into native prairie.

1. About how much of Tishomingo National Wildlife Refuge is **not** part of Cumberland Pool?

   a. 4,500 acres
   b. 12,000 acres
   c. 16,500 acres
   d. 21,000 acres

2. Which of the following is **not** part of the dense hardwood forest?

   a. oak trees
   b. hickory trees
   c. pecan trees
   d. willow trees

3. Which of the following kinds of trees would you **not** find along the river bottom of the refuge?

   a. elm
   b. cottonwood
   c. willow
   d. box elder

4. Which animal are you most likely to find along river bottoms?

   a. deer
   b. turkey
   c. raccoons
   d. opossums

5. Which of the following eats rabbits?

   a. warblers
   b. vireos
   c. hawks
   d. woodpeckers

215

6. Which of the following animal signs is most likely to tell scientists about an animal's diet?

   a. tracks
   b. scat
   c. feathers
   d. nests

7. Why do cars make good blinds?

   a. They go slowly.
   b. They are quiet.
   c. You can stop them when you want.
   d. Animals can't see you inside them.

8. How are Tishomingo and Washita similar?

   a. They are both on mixed grass plains.
   b. They are about the same size.
   c. They are located along the great Central Flyway of birds migrating to and from Canada.
   d. They were both established in the 1950s.

9. Why haven't archaeologists been able to examine more of the ancient sites, or Custer's camp, in the Washita refuge?

   a. The natural gas wells are in the way.
   b. It is against the rules to disturb the area.
   c. It is too dangerous.
   d. It is too expensive.

10. Do you think natural gas wells belong inside a wildlife refuge? Why or
    why not?

SUTTER BUYS OUT THE RUSSIANS
by John Bidwell

John A. Sutter was born in Baden in 1803 of Swiss parents. He was proud of his connection with the only republic of consequence in Europe. He was a warm admirer of the United States. Some of his friends had persuaded him to come across the Atlantic. He first went to a friend in Indiana. He stayed awhile, helping to clear land, but it was business that he was not accustomed to. So he made his way to St. Louis. There he invested what means he had in merchandise. He went out as a New Mexican trader to Santa Fe. Having been unsuccessful at Santa Fe, he returned to St. Louis. He joined a party of trappers. He went to the Rocky Mountains. He then found his way down the Columbia River to Fort Vancouver. There he formed plans for trying to get down to the coast of California to establish a colony.

> He took a vessel that went to the Sandwich Islands. But as there was no vessel going direct from the Sandwich Islands to California, he had to take a Russian vessel by way of Sitka. In the Sandwich Islands he induced five or six natives to accompany him to start the contemplated colony. He expected to send to Europe and the United States for his colonists. When he came to the coast of California, in 1840, he had an interview with the governor, Alvarado. He obtained permission to explore the country and find a place for his colony. He came to the bay of San Francisco. He procured a small boat and explored the largest river he could find. He selected the site where the city of Sacramento now stands.

A short time before we arrived Sutter had bought out the Russian-American Fur Company at Fort Ross and Bodega on the Pacific. That company had a charter from Spain to take furs, but had no right to the land. Against the protest of the California authorities the Russians had extended their settlement southward some twenty miles farther than they had any right to. They had occupied the country to, and even beyond, the bay of Bodega.

The charter had about expired. The time came when the taking of furs was no longer profitable. The Russians were ordered to vacate and return to Sitka. They wished to sell out all their personal property and whatever remaining right they had to the land. So Sutter bought them out. He bought cattle and horses. He acquired a little vessel of about twenty-five tons burden, called a launch. The other property included forty odd pieces of old rusty cannon and one or two small brass pieces, with a quantity of old French flintlock muskets. These Sutter claimed to be among those lost by Bonaparte in 1812 in his disastrous retreat from Moscow. This ordinance Sutter conveyed up the Sacramento River on the launch to his colony.

As soon as the native Californians heard that he had bought out the Russians and was beginning to fortify himself by taking up the cannon they began to fear him. They were doubtless jealous because Americans and other foreigners had already commenced to make the place their headquarters. They foresaw that Sutter's fort would be for them, especially for Americans, what it naturally did become in fact, a place of protection and general rendezvous. So they threatened to break it up. Sutter had not yet actually received his grant. He had simply taken preliminary steps and had obtained permission to settle and proceed to colonize. These threats were made before he had begun the fort, much less built it. Sutter felt insecure. He had a good many Indians whom he had collected about him. He also had a few white men (perhaps fifteen or twenty) and some Sandwich Islanders.

When he heard of the coming of our thirty men he inferred at once that we would soon reach him and be an additional protection. With this feeling of security, even before the arrival of our party Sutter was so indiscreet as to write a letter to the governor or to some one in authority. It said that he wanted to hear no more threats of dispossession, for he was now able not only to defend himself but to go and chastise them. That letter was dispatched to the city of Mexico.

The authorities there sent a new governor in 1842. He was sent with about six hundred troops to subdue Sutter. But the new governor, Manuel Micheltorena, was an intelligent man. He knew the history of California. He was aware that nearly all of his predecessors had been expelled by insurrections of the native Californians. Sutter sent a courier to meet the governor before his arrival at Los Angeles, with a letter in French. It conveyed his greetings to the governor and expressed a most cordial welcome. In it Sutter submitted cheerfully and entirely to his authority. In this way the governor and Sutter became fast friends. Through Sutter the Americans had a friend in Governor Micheltorena.

1. When John Sutter was a youth, the only republic of consequence in Europe was

   a. Germany.
   b. Italy.
   c. England.
   d. Switzerland.

2. John Sutter's first stop in America was

    a. New Mexico.
    b. Indiana.
    c. St. Louis.
    d. Fort Vancouver.

3. John Sutter failed as a _____ in New Mexico.

    a. trapper
    b. farmer
    c. trader
    d. storekeeper

4. In Fort Vancouver, Sutter decided to farm a colony in California with the help of natives from

    a. Hawaii.
    b. Canada.
    c. Europe.
    d. Russia.

5. At the time Sutter passed through, Sitka was a colony of

    a. Hawaii.
    b. Canada.
    c. Europe.
    d. Russia.

6. Alvarado, the governor of California, was appointed by

    a. Mexico.
    b. America.
    c. Russia.
    d. England.

7. Sutter, with Alvarado's permission, chose a site on

    a. San Francisco Bay.
    b. Bodega Bay.
    c. a large river.
    d. Fort Ross.

8. Sutter bought out the Russians at Fort Ross a short time

    a. before he arrived in California.
    b. after he arrived in California.
    c. before Bidwell arrived in California.
    d. after Bidwell arrived in California.

9. The purchase Sutter made which was most worrisome to native Californians was

    a. old flintlock muskets.
    b. forty cannon pieces.
    c. a launch.
    d. cattle and horses.

10. Sutter felt safer from the threats to break up his colony after he

    a. had collected many Native Americans about him.
    b. had collected 15–20 white men.
    c. had collected some Sandwich Islanders.
    d. heard Bidwell's party of 30 men was coming.

11. Sutter's first letter

    a. never reached anyone of authority in California.
    b. never reached anyone of authority in Mexico.
    c. frightened the authorities.
    d. angered or annoyed the authorities.

12. Sutter's letter to Governor Micheltorena was probably written in French because

    a. it was the only language Sutter knew.
    b. it was the only language Micheltorena knew.
    c. it was the only language they both knew.
    d. Sutter had learned French in Switzerland.

13. How many different countries' colonies and how many different
    independent countries did Sutter visit, travel through, or live in? Be
    specific and tell when and why he was in each place.

    _____

    _____

    _____

    _____

    _____

    _____

    _____

    _____

    _____

    _____

    _____

    _____

    _____

    _____

    _____

    _____

    _____

223

THE BLACK HAWK WAR

The Black Hawk War was fought in northwest Illinois and in what is now southwest Wisconsin in 1832. It pitted a band of Sauk and Fox, led by Black Hawk, against the Illinois militia and the U.S. Army. The conflict had its roots in a controversial 1804 treaty. The Sauk and Fox had ceded fifty million acres to the United States for $2,234.50, plus a $1,000-per-year annuity. Under the terms of the treaty, the tribes could continue to live on the land until it was sold.

The Lead Rush

The discovery of lead in the Galena area during the 1820s brought many miners to the area. Nearby, at the Apple River Settlement, the miners built a cluster of cabins. In 1827, they opened the first general store. When the Sauk and Fox returned from their winter hunt early in 1829, they found settlers living in their villages. Later that year, their land was offered for sale. The Sauk and Fox were then forced to relocate on the west side of the Mississippi River.

The Fight for Land

Black Hawk was a Sauk warrior who had fought with the British against the United States in the War of 1812. He was determined to return to the land he believed belonged to his people. On April 5, 1832, he started up the Rock River with a band of five hundred warriors and about seven hundred women, children, and old men. Governor Reynolds immediately called out the militia. Black Hawk's warriors routed the militia at the Battle of Stillman's Run on May 14th. The Black Hawk War had begun.

The Black Hawk War

The settlers in the mining area were panic-stricken. Many left Galena by steamboat. At the Apple River Settlement, the miners quickly built a fort around existing cabins. They had not long to wait. On June 24th, Black Hawk and some two hundred warriors attacked the Apple River Fort. Inside, the men kept up a steady stream of fire. The women molded musket balls and loaded weapons. The battle raged for about forty-five minutes. Then Black Hawk, thinking the fort was heavily armed, abandoned the battle. As he and his warriors departed, they raided nearby cabins for supplies.

The next day, at the Second Battle of Kellogg's Grove, the arrival of U.S. Army troops forced Black Hawk to flee north to Wisconsin. Finding his band hungry and disheartened, Black Hawk decided to lead his followers west across Wisconsin and back into Iowa. Pursued by the army and the militia, Black

224

Hawk's band struggled on to the Mississippi at the mouth of the Bad Axe River. The Black Hawk War ended on August 2nd. The Indians were caught between the steamboat, *Warrior*, and the army troops. Of the one thousand two hundred who had started out with Black Hawk, only about one hundred and fifty survived. Black Hawk escaped, but was later captured. The Apple River Fort, hastily erected that May, survived its first and only attack that June Sunday. It was torn down some fifteen years later in 1847. Its lumber was used to build a barn.

The war had lasted only sixteen weeks. It ended the threat of Indian attacks in the area and opened the region to further settlement. Many notable men participated in the Black Hawk War. They included young Abraham Lincoln, Jefferson Davis, and General Winfield Scott. Abraham Lincoln and his militia company arrived at the fort the day after the battle.

Apple River Fort Today

FINDING THE FORT

In the spring of 1995, the Apple River Fort Historic Foundation set out to locate the Apple River Fort. It had been torn down in 1847. That was fifteen years after the historic attack during the Black Hawk War. Local lore said the fort had been located on a hillside not far from Main Street in Elizabeth, Illinois. Uncertain, the foundation hired an archaeologist. The initial inspection of the site turned up a variety of artifacts from the 1830s. Excavations revealed musket balls, a small cellar, and a trash pit. They also revealed the fort's footprint. It was a fifty-by-seventy-foot area. That was somewhat smaller than had originally been speculated.

BUILDING THE FORT

Rebuilding the fort's cabins began in 1996. Volunteers used the same tools and materials as those that had been used by the original settlers. Logs were tripped and shingles split by hand. A two- to three-foot trench was dug to connect the two cabins. A surrounding palisade was erected using fourteen- to fifteen-foot logs. The blockhouse was created by constructing a second story. It projected some two feet over the building's lower story. At the two corners opposite the buildings, firing stands were built. They were supplied with hand-hewn ladders.

THE INTERPRETIVE CENTER

The Interpretive Center is located a short walk from the fort. It relates the story of the Black Hawk War and the Apple River Fort. A series of illustrated panels tells the story of the Sauk and Fox people, the early miners, and the conflict between the two cultures that led to the Black Hawk War. There is a fifteen-minute video of the Black Hawk War. There are archaeology exhibits telling how the remains of the fort were located and displaying some of the artifacts uncovered at the site. Exhibits along the trail to the fort explore the role of Abraham Lincoln and other notables in the Black Hawk War, the building of the fort, and the June 24, 1832, attack by Black Hawk and his warriors.

1. The Treaty of 1804 gave the Sauk and Fox Indians all of the following **except**

   a. 50 million acres.
   b. $2,234.50.
   c. $1,000 per year.
   d. the right to live on their land until it was sold.

2. White people were first attracted to the Galena area by

   a. good hunting.
   b. a general store.
   c. free living quarters.
   d. lead.

3. The Sauk and Fox lived undisturbed on what had been their land for _____ years after the treaty.

   a. 4
   b. 23
   c. 25
   d. 28

4. Which of the following synonyms for "band," which appears in the third paragraph, could be used in its place?

   a. orchestra
   b. gather
   c. strap
   d. party

5. Black Hawk had with him a total of _____ people.

   a. 500
   b. 700
   c. 1,200
   d. 1,700

226

6. The first battle of the Black Hawk War was fought

   a. on Rock River.
   b. at Stillman's Run.
   c. at Apple River Fort.
   d. on April 5, 1832.

7. Black Hawk attacked Apple River with

   a. all of his warriors.
   b. over half of his warriors.
   c. less than half of his warriors.
   d. his old men, women, and children.

8. Who defended the fort at the Apple River?

   a. Governor Reynolds and the Illinois militia
   b. Black Hawk and his warriors
   c. miners and Black Hawk
   d. miners and women who helped them

9. Why did Black Hawk give up the attack on the Apple River Fort?

   a. He thought there were too many defenders there.
   b. He knew he was outnumbered.
   c. He was afraid to fight women.
   d. He was afraid to fight miners.

10. Which of the following statements about the Second Battle of Kellogg's Grove is **true**?

    a. It was won by the Illinois militia.
    b. It was won by Black Hawk.
    c. It was fought on June 25, 1832.
    d. It forced Black Hawk to retreat into northern Illinois.

11. Who finally defeated Black Hawk?

    a. the Illinois militia
    b. the U.S. Army and a steamboat on the Apple River
    c. the U.S. Army and a steamboat on the Bad Axe River
    d. the U.S. Army and a steamboat on the Mississippi River

12. Write a story about the Apple River Fort and the attack on Black Hawk. Make it as realistic as possible.

_____

_____

_____

_____

_____

_____

_____

_____

_____

_____

_____

_____

_____

_____

_____

_____

229

13. If you were to visit the Apple River Fort today, what would you be most interested in seeing or learning more about? Why?

STEPHEN MACK AND HONONEGAH

by Anna Elizabeth Carlson
Heritage School, Rockford
Illinois History, *December 2000*

Stephen Mack was born in Poultney, Vermont, on February 20, 1798. His father owned a fur company called Mack and Conant. Stephen Mack attended the Moors Charity School. After a few years there he joined his father's business.

While in the Green Bay area he met fur traders. They told him of the Rock River Valley's potential for trading. He traded for several years near a Potawatomi village. Today it is Grand Detour. In 1829 he married Hononegah. She was the Potawatomi chief's daughter. They married in a Native American ceremony.

Stephen Mack had the advantage of knowing the area. As settlers poured into the lands, he decided to make his claim. In 1835 he selected a section on a bluff above the Rock River. It was just below the mouth of the Pekatonica River. This was a natural crossroad. Here, he plotted his town of Pekatonica. Settlers later called it "Macktown." Mack acquired about a thousand acres. When Mack was told it was too hilly here he said, "It is far better than Milwaukee." Native Americans had used this site for ten thousand years.

Stephen Mack intentionally chose his claim for its position on the rivers. He wanted to make a river town, since travel by road was slow and difficult. At this time, Chicago and Galena were the two developed towns in northern Illinois. Lead from the mines in Galena took eleven days by wagon to reach Dixon's Ferry. Traveling by road was inefficient. For growth to occur, farmers had to be able to deliver their grain and produce to Chicago. The mines had to be able to ship their lead. Mack judged the Rock River navigable for 150 miles and the Pekatonica River for 100 miles. The state of Illinois agreed. In 1837 the Illinois General Assembly declared the Rock River navigable. It directed that $100,000 be spent for improvements.

Stephen Mack built a double cabin. In 1839 he constructed the largest frame house west of Chicago. Mack also established a store called a "mercantile." He soon founded a school. Later, Mack built a second school with a large stone fireplace and chimney. Mack paid the teacher's salary. Mack's double cabin became a tavern for travelers. Records show that people were continually arriving.

Mack was a generous man. He allowed the settlers to borrow money from him to buy their lots. Between 1836 and 1845, he sold property to H.M. Bates,

David Jewett, L.W. Osgood, Robert Gilmour, Darius Adams, Isaac Adams, and John Spafford. At the same time, he continued to purchase additional land. It is interesting to note that beside his signature for the sale of the lots was Hononegah's mark. Their joint ownership of land was unusual for the time. Stephen Mack plotted his entire property. Most early towns were never plotted this large. He felt his lots were a bargain. He created ten lots to a block instead of the usual twelve. He claimed that a corner lot by his store was worth a thousand dollars.

Pekatonica attracted numerous craftsmen, including a tailor, W.M. Halley. He sewed the latest fashions. However, the residents of Pekatonica did not need these fashions, so the Talcott family paid him to stay. John Jewett was a blacksmith. Thomas Farmer was a stone mason. Other craftsmen in Pekatonica were a saw miller, a wagon maker, a carpenter, a cabinetmaker, a boot maker, and a maker of holloware.

In 1837 Stephen Mack established a ferry. It carried people across the Rock River. Because of the ferry, the main road north passed through Pekatonica. Between 1842 and 1843, Mack built a bridge to replace the ferry, largely with his own funds. It was the first bridge across the Rock River. It had a draw of thirty-six feet to allow for steamboats. When the rival city of Rockford decided to build a bridge with state funds, Stephen Mack wrote to legislator Robert Cross. He argued that it was unjust for the state to build a bridge with public money when Illinois had refused to fund his structure.

On April 4, 1840, Mack made his first will for his nine children. Five months later, Hononegah and Stephen Mack were remarried in a Christian ceremony. This remarriage was to prevent confusion in his will.

In spite of being the first settlement in the Rock River frontier, Pekatonica failed. Its population peaked at about three hundred people. Stephen Mack placed M.E. Mack, his cousin, in charge of his store. However, the store lost two thousand dollars. It turned out that M.E. Mack was stealing money. When M.E. Mack died, Stephen Mack was responsible for his debts. Stephen Mack called in the sheriff, but nothing could be done.

In 1836 General Chiopicki—a hero of the Polish War for Independence—claimed some of Mack's land under the Polish Claim Act of 1834. This prevented secure title to property until an act of Congress in 1842.

Sadly, another cause of the town's failure was Mack's marriage to a Native American. When settlers arrived in Pekatonica and saw an Indian, they left. New settlers from the East did not want to live with Indians. William Talcott, the founder of Rockton across the Rock River from Pekatonica, had a son, Thomas, who kept a journal. In it, Thomas Talcott referred to Hononegah as "that squaw."

1. The Potawatomi village was in

    a. Poultney, Vermont.
    b. Moors Charity School.
    c. Rock River Valley.
    d. Pekatonica.

2. Stephen Mack married Hononegah in what is now

    a. Poultney, Vermont.
    b. Grand Detour, Illinois.
    c. Macktown.
    d. Pekatonica.

3. What did Stephen Mack call his village?

    a. Poultney, Vermont
    b. Grand Detour, Illinois
    c. Macktown
    d. Pekatonica

4. The village was located at the junction of the _____ and _____ Rivers.

    a. Mark . . . Conant
    b. Rock . . . Pekatonica
    c. Green Bay . . . Potawatomi
    d. Hononegah . . . Potawatomi

5. Why did Stephen Mack choose to place his town near two rivers?

    a. He liked the way the surrounding area looked.
    b. He was a farmer.
    c. He was a miller.
    d. He thought it could be a center of transportation.

6. The Illinois General Assembly agreed to pay $100,000 to

    a. improve navigation on the Rock and Pekatonica Rivers.
    b. improve navigation on the Ohio and Mississippi Rivers.
    c. build a bridge over the Rock River.
    d. provide ferry service over the Rock River.

7. Stephen Mack's double cabin became

    a. his home.
    b. a store.
    c. a school.
    d. a tavern.

8. Of the following, which did Stephen Mack **not** start or build?

    a. a ferry
    b. two schools
    c. a church
    d. a store

9. Why did Stephen Mack object to Rockford's bridge?

    a. It was in the same place as his.
    b. It used state funds and he had used his own money.
    c. It was higher than his.
    d. It was longer than his.

10. Which was **not** a reason that Macktown failed?

    a. Stephen Mack was dishonest.
    b. Stephen Mack's cousin was dishonest.
    c. For a long time it wasn't clear who owned all the land.
    d. People did not want to live near Hononegah.

11. Which of the following statements made in the passage is an opinion?

    a. It is far better than Milwaukee.
    b. This remarriage was to prevent confusion in his will.
    c. Thomas Farmer was a stone mason.
    d. Traveling by road was inefficient.

234

12. Why was Stephen Mack's relationship with Hononegah so unusual?

_____

_____

_____

_____

_____

_____

_____

_____

_____

_____

_____

_____

_____

_____

_____

_____

_____

_____

_____

_____

LA SALLE CLAIMS LOUISIANA

Robert Cavelier, Sieur de La Salle, was born in France in 1643. He received his education through Jesuit schools. He had planned to enter the priesthood. However, in an age of discovery, he set out for the as yet unexplored regions of Canada. Here he was given land on the edge of Île de Montréal. La Salle now had the status of a landowner. He had the opportunity for exploration that he craved.

La Salle set up a fur-trading outpost. He began learning more about the territories. Through trade with Indians he learned new languages and heard tales of the world beyond his post. He became convinced that a trade route to the Orient was possible through the rivers and lakes of the Western frontier.

By 1669, he had sold his land and set out to explore the Ohio region. Although originally given credit for discovering the Ohio River, historians now question the validity of this claim. La Salle found a supporter in the Count de Frontenac, the "Fighting Governor" of New France, the French possessions in Canada. Together, they sought to expand on French holdings in the territories by setting up a fort on Lake Ontario, Fort Frontenac. Now, not only would they have more power over the Iroquois Indians, but they would also control the fur trade between the Upper Lakes and the Dutch and English coastal settlements.

Not everyone was happy with these plans. The traders in Montreal were afraid of losing their livelihood. Jesuit priests were afraid of losing influence with the Native Americans. La Salle and Frontenac won out. Fort Frontenac was built near present-day Kingston.

Frontenac recommended La Salle be instated as *seigneur*. The governor noted La Salle was the man most capable of helping France fulfill its ambitious plans for exploration and discovery in the New World. King Louis XIV not only appointed him governor, but also granted La Salle a title of nobility.

New Goals

La Salle proved to be a good businessman. By 1677, he had grown bored with life at the fur-trading outpost. He went to France to ask King Louis XIV to give him official authorization to explore the western parts of New France and to build as many forts as he saw fit. This would allow La Salle to monopolize the trading in buffalo hides.

Although La Salle had the official support of France, he received no funding. Because of this, he was forced to borrow large sums of money in both Montreal and Paris. These debts would continue to mount as he pursued his exploration. Another ongoing problem concerned the Jesuits. They never supported any of La Salle's endeavors.

La Salle returned to Canada in 1678. He was accompanied by Henri de Tonty, an Italian soldier of fortune. Tonty would become La Salle's best friend and an important ally. In 1679, the *Griffon*, the first commercial sailing ship on Lake Erie, was built. La Salle hoped that profits from this venture would provide funding for an expedition into the interior via the Mississippi.

He acquired basic survival skills from the Seneca Native Americans. He learned how to live off the land. He learned how to make long journeys overland regardless of the season, subsisting only on a bag of corn and what he could trap. His journey from Niagara to Fort Frontenac in the winter won the respect of a normally cynical member of his expeditions, the friar Louis Hennepin.

La Salle's plans to ship merchandise aboard vessels such as the *Griffon* on the lakes and down the Mississippi ended when the vessel wrecked. A second setback followed in 1680. La Salle was building a second ship at Fort Crevecoeur on the Illinois River when it was destroyed and abandoned.

Louisiana Claim

La Salle finally reached the point where the Illinois River and the Mississippi joined. Instead of exploring the river, he returned to the fort, where his friend Tonty was in danger. La Salle and Tonty eventually did canoe down the Mississippi. They reached the Gulf of Mexico. On April 9, 1682, La Salle claimed the entire Mississippi basin in the name of France. He named it "Louisiana." The region he claimed contained the best farmlands in North America.

The following year La Salle built Fort St. Louis at Starved Rock on the Illinois River. Here, he established a colony of several thousand Indians. He sought assistance from Quebec to help sustain the new colony. Frontenac, however, was no longer in office. The new governor disliked La Salle. La Salle was ordered to surrender Fort St. Louis. La Salle refused to do so. He left for France to appeal to Louis XIV. The king sided with La Salle. He ordered the governor to return La Salle's property in full.

Doomed Project

La Salle formulated another ambitious project—to build forts along the mouth of the Mississippi. From there he hoped to invade and conquer Spanish provinces in Mexico. To accomplish this he would need an army of two hundred Frenchmen, fifteen thousand Native Americans and privateers. La Salle's opponents doubted the feasibility of his plan, but Louis XIV saw it as an opportunity to strike out against Spain, with whom France was at war. La Salle was given men, ships and money.

The mission was a series of failures. La Salle and the naval commander did not get along. La Salle had a strong personality, demanding the most of himself, but also of others. Often he pushed people to their limits. He became upset when they would not see a situation his way. Not a good leader, he was never on friendly terms with most of his men.

After a stop in the West Indies, one ship was captured by pirates. Sickness took its toll. Maps were difficult to follow. Because of this, La Salle missed the mouth of the Mississippi River. He landed at Matagorda Bay in Texas, nearly five hundred miles away. While attempting to negotiate the narrow passageways of the inlets, a second ship, the *Aimable*, was lost. Valuable cargo of food, medicine, supplies and trade goods for the Indians was lost with it. A third ship, the *Belle*, became stranded on a sandbar during a storm. Several men drowned as they tried to raft away from the vessel.

La Salle made several attempts to correct his navigational error, but was never able to lead his group to the Mississippi. He established Fort St. Louis in present-day Victoria County, Texas. He then attempted to lead a party overland, but was killed by his own men near present-day Navasota, Texas. Although he was praised by his close friends, Tonty and Frontenac, detractors such as Henri Joutel, one of the few survivors of La Salle's last expedition, felt his arrogance contributed to his death. A man of great vision, La Salle lacked leadership ability. The building of a French empire in the New World would be left to other men.

1. Which of the following occurred last?

    a. The *Griffon* was built.
    b. King Louis XIV authorized La Salle to explore western New France.
    c. La Salle set up a fur-trading post.
    d. Fort Frontenac was built.

2. Which of the following occurred first?

    a. The *Griffon* was built.
    b. King Louis XIV authorized La Salle to explore western New France.
    c. La Salle set up a fur-trading post.
    d. Fort Frontenac was built.

3. The relationship between Frontenac and La Salle could **best** be described as

   a. combative.
   b. dependent.
   c. calming.
   d. unsuccessful.

4. Which fort was built after 1683?

   a. Fort St. Louis at Starved Rock
   b. Fort Crevecoeur
   c. Fort St. Louis in Texas
   d. Fort Frontenac

5. Why did La Salle have to borrow "large sums of money in both Montreal and Paris"?

   a. He had run out of money after he had built so many forts.
   b. He was constantly fighting with the Jesuits.
   c. He had so much debt that no one would fund him.
   d. The French government would not fund his expeditions.

6. Which vessel was the last to go down, has since been discovered, and is being restored in Texas?

   a. *Aimable*
   b. *Belle*
   c. the ship captured by pirates
   d. *Griffon*

239

7. If La Salle had been able to find the mouth of the Mississippi without the loss of any ships, do you think he would have been able to conquer Mexico? Why or why not?

_____

_____

_____

_____

_____

_____

_____

_____

_____

_____

_____

_____

_____

_____

_____

_____

_____

_____

240

MISSION CUSTOMS AND FAMILY CUSTOMS
by Guadalupe Vallejo

It was the custom at all the Missions, during the rules of the Franciscan missionaries, to keep the young unmarried Indians separate. The young girls and the young widows at the Mission San José occupied a large adobe building. It had a yard behind it, enclosed by high adobe walls. In this yard some trees were planted. A zanja, or water ditch, supplied a large bathing pond. The women were kept busy at various occupations. They worked in the building, under the trees, or on the wide porch. They were taught spinning, knitting, the weaving of Indian baskets from grasses, willow rods and roots, and more especially plain sewing. The treatment and occupation of the unmarried women was similar at the other Missions. When heathen Indian women came in, or were brought by their friends, or by the soldiers, they were put in these houses under the charge of older women, who taught them what to do.

The women, thus separated from the men, could only be courted from without through the upper windows facing on the narrow village street. These windows were about two feet square. They were crossed by iron bars. They were perhaps three feet deep, as the adobe walls were very thick. The rules were not more strict, however, than still prevail in some of the Spanish-American countries in much higher classes, socially, than these uneducated Indians belonged to. In fact the rules were adopted by the fathers from Mexican models.

After an Indian, in his hours of freedom from toil, had declared his affection by a sufficiently long attendance upon a certain window, it was the duty of the woman to tell the father missionary and to declare her decision. If this was favorable, the young man was asked if he was willing to contract marriage with the young woman who had confessed her preference. Sometimes there were several rival suitors, but it was never known that any trouble occurred. After marriage the couple were conducted to their home. It was a hut built for them among the other Indian houses in the village near the Mission.

The Indian mothers were frequently told about the proper care of children. Cleanliness of the person was strongly inculcated. In fact, the Mission Indians, large and small, were wonderfully clean. Their faces and hair fairly shined with soap and water. In several cases where an Indian woman was so slovenly and neglectful of her infant that it died she was punished by being compelled to carry in her arms in church, and at all meals and public assemblies, a log of wood about the size of a nine-month-old child. This was a very effectual punishment, for the Indian women are naturally most affectionate creatures. In every case they soon began to suffer greatly, and others with them, so that once a whole Indian village begged the father in charge to forgive the poor woman.

The padres always had a school for the Indian boys. My mother has a novena, or "nine-days' devotion book," copied for her by one of the Indian pupils at the Mission San José early in the [nineteenth] century. The handwriting is very neat and plain, and would be a credit to any one. Many young Indians had good voices. These were selected with great care to be trained in singing for the church choir. It was thought such an honor to sing in church that, the Indian families were all very anxious to be represented. Some were taught to play on the violin and other stringed instruments.

Father Narciso Duran was the president of the Franciscans in California. When he was at the Mission San José, he had a church choir of about thirty well-trained boys to sing the mass. He was himself a cultivated musician. He had studied under some of the best masters in Spain. So sensitive was his ear that if one string was out of tune he could not continue his service. He would at once turn to the choir, call the name of the player, and the string that was out of order, and wait until the matter was corrected. There were often more than a dozen players on instruments. Every prominent Mission had fathers who paid great attention to training the Indians in music.

A Spanish lady of high social standing tells the following story, which will illustrate the honor in which the Mission fathers were held:

> Father Majin Catala, one of the missionaries early in the century, was held to possess prophetic gifts. Many of the Spanish settlers, the Castros, Peraltas, Estudillos, and others, have reason to remember his gift. When any priest issued from the sacristy to celebrate mass all hearts were stirred, but with this holy father the feeling became one of absolute awe. On more than one occasion before his sermon he asked the congregation to join him in prayers for the soul of one about to die, naming the hour. In every case this was fulfilled to the very letter. The one who died could not have known of the father's words.

> This saint spent his days in labor among the people. He was loved as well as feared. But on one occasion, in later life, when the Mission rule was broken, he offended an Indian chief. Shortly after several Indians called at his home in the night to ask him to go and see a dying woman. The father rose and dressed, but his chamber door remained fast, so that he could not open it. He was on the point of ordering them to break it open from without, when he felt a warning, to the effect that they were going to murder him. Then he said, "To-morrow I will visit your sick. You are forgiven. Go in peace." Then they fled in dismay, knowing that his person was protected by an especial providence. Soon after they confessed their plans to the father.

242

He was one of the most genial and kindly men of the missionaries. He surprised all those who had thought that every one of the fathers was severe. He saw no harm in walking out among the young people, and saying friendly things to them all. He was often known to go with young men on moonlight rides, lassoing grizzly bears, or chasing deer on the plain. His own horse, one of the best ever seen in the valley, was richly caparisoned. He wore a scarlet silk sash around his waist under the Franciscan habit. When older and graver priests reproached him, he used to say with a smile that he was only a Mexican Franciscan, and that he was brought up in a saddle. He was certainly a superb rider.

It is said of Father Amoros of San Rafael that his noon meal consisted of an ear of dry corn, roasted over the coals. This he carried in his sleeve and partook of at his leisure while overseeing the Indian laborers. Some persons who were in the habit of reaching a priest's house at noontime, so as to be asked to dinner, once called on the father. They were told that he had gone to the field with his corn in his manguilla. They rode away without seeing him. That was considered a breach of good manners. Much fun was made over their haste.

In the old days everyone seemed to live outdoors. There was much gaiety and social life, even though people were widely scattered. We traveled as much as possible on horseback. Only old people or invalids cared to use the slow cart, or carreta. Young men would ride from one ranch to another for parties. Whoever found his horse tired would let him go and catch another. In 1806 there were so many horses in the valleys about San José that seven or eight thousand were killed. Nearly as many were driven into the sea at Santa Barbara in 1801. The same thing was done at Monterey in 1810. Horses were given to the runaway sailors, and to trappers and hunters who came over the mountains.

But fast and beautiful horses were never more prized in any country than in California. Each young man had his favorites. A kind of mustang, that is now seldom or never seen on the Pacific coast, was a peculiar light cream-colored horse, with silver-white mane and tail. Such an animal, of speed and bottom, often sold for more than a horse of any other color. Other much admired colors were dapple-gray and chestnut. The fathers of the Mission sometimes rode on horseback. Generally they had a somewhat modern carriage called a volante. It was always drawn by mules. There were hundreds of mules in the Mission pastures. White was the color often preferred.

Nothing was more attractive than the wedding cavalcade on its way from the bride's house to the Mission church. The horses were more richly caparisoned than for any other ceremony. The bride's nearest relative or family representative carried her before him. She sat on the saddle with her white satin shoe in a loop of golden or silver braid. He sat on the bear-skin covered anquera behind her. The groom and his friends mingled with the bride's party. All were on the best horses that could be obtained. They rode gaily from the ranch house to the Mission. Sometimes it was fifteen or twenty miles away. In April and May, when the land was covered with wildflowers, the light-hearted troops rode along the edge of the uplands, between hill and valley, crossing the streams. Some of the young horsemen, anxious to show their skill, would perform all the feats for which the Spanish Californians were famous.

After the wedding, when they returned to lead in the feasting, the bride was carried on the horse of the groomsman. One of the customs which was always observed at the wedding was to wind a silken tasseled string or a silken sash, fringed with gold, about the necks of the bride and groom, binding them together as they knelt before the altar for the blessing of the priest. A charming custom among the middle and lower classes was the making of the satin shoes by the groom for the bride. A few weeks before the wedding he asked his betrothed for the measurement of her foot. He then made the shoes with his own hands. The groomsman brought them to her on the wedding day.

Family life among the old Spanish pioneers was an affair of dignity and ceremony, but it did not lack in affection. Children were brought up with great respect for their elders. It was the privilege of any elderly person to correct young people by words, or even by whipping them. It was never told that any one thus chastised made a complaint. Each one of the old families taught their children the history of the family, and reverence toward religion. A few books, some in manuscript, were treasured in the household, but children were not allowed to read novels until [they] were grown. They saw little of other children, except their near relatives, but they had many enjoyments unknown to children now. They grew up with remarkable strength and healthfulness.

1. The Native American women at the Franciscan missions of the old California lived in a large adobe building with

   a. no a yard behind it.
   b. no bathing facilities.
   c. with no pond.
   d. a zanja supplying water.

2. According to this passage, it is unlikely that women's occupations would have included

   a. weaving.
   b. cooking.
   c. sewing.
   d. knitting.

3. Weddings for Native Americans in the missions came after a

   a. man asked a woman.
   b. woman asked a man.
   c. woman spoke to a priest, who asked a man.
   d. man spoke to a priest, who asked a woman.

4. Which of the following were Native American boys **not** taught to do?

   a. play drums
   b. play violins
   c. play stringed instruments
   d. sing

5. What is the most likely reason why Father Narciso Duran would stop mass to address an out-of-tune string?

   a. He wanted his choir boys to perform perfectly.
   b. He did not want the musicians to embarrass themselves.
   c. Out-of-tune strings must be fixed immediately.
   d. He was a trained musician.

6. Father Majin Catala inspired fear and awe by

   a. walking out among young people and being friendly.
   b. riding out in the moonlight to lasso grizzlies.
   c. riding one of the best horses in the valley and wearing a scarlet sash.
   d. predicting the hour of several deaths and foretelling his own murder.

7. Father Majin Catala's upbringing probably explained why he was in the habit of

   a. walking out among young people and being friendly.
   b. riding out in the moonlight to lasso grizzlies.
   c. spending his days in labor among the people.
   d. predicting the hour of several deaths and foretelling his own murder.

8. Apparently there were _____ in California from 1801 to 1810.

    a. not enough mules
    b. not enough horses
    c. too many horses
    d. too many mules

9. What were horses most valued for?

    a. size
    b. pedigree
    c. rarity
    d. color

10. The _____ was a modern carriage, faster than an oxcart.

    a. volante
    b. carreta
    c. anquera
    d. mustang

11. "Caparisoned," as it appears in the tenth paragraph, probably means

    a. fed.
    b. outfitted.
    c. stabled.
    d. groomed.

12. The bride traveled to her wedding by

    a. volante.
    b. carreta.
    c. anquera.
    d. horseback.

13. One custom followed at all weddings was

    a. the making of satin shoes by the groom for the bride.
    b. binding the bride and groom together with a string or sash.
    c. the wedding party riding along the edge of the uplands.
    d. the bride riding on a bear skin anquera.

246

14. Do you think the punishment for child neglect was appropriate? Why or why not?

_____

_____

_____

_____

_____

_____

_____

_____

15. Why did Father Amoros's visitors leave without seeing him?

_____

_____

_____

_____

_____

_____

_____

_____

16. Do you think that any elderly person should be permitted to chastise an unruly child? Why or why not? What about whipping?

LIFE IN KENTUCKY, 1779-1781

The first settlements in Hardin county were made late in 1780, on the site of Elizabethtown and in its neighborhood. Stations were also built in Logan County, at Maulding's, at Russellville, and on Whippoorwill Creek. This country was then almost an unbroken prairie. In November, the Virginia Assembly divided Kentucky into three counties, Jefferson, Fayette, and Lincoln.

Of gold and silver in the country there was little. The currency in use was the paper issued by the Continental Congress as a war measure. It had now sunk in value to a very low rate, and promised to become worthless. Virginia turned to her lands to replenish her treasury, and enacted the land law of May 1779, with provisions that made her Kentucky lands available. This attracted many settlers from the old colonies. They had been driven out by the contending armies of the Revolutionary War. The tide of immigration was greater than ever known before. In the spring of 1780, three hundred large family boats arrived at Louisville. From there, trains of wagons went out to interior settlements daily. By the end of the year noted, there were six stations in Beargrass Valley, near Louisville. They had a total population of six hundred.

The winter of 1779–1780 was the severest known in our history. From November 15th until February 15th—three months—the rivers and streams were solidly frozen. Much distress and want befell the people. Many cattle perished. Great numbers of wild animals died of starvation. Bears, buffaloes, deer, wolves, beavers and wild turkeys, tamed by hunger, would come around the houses with the cows and domestic fowls for morsels of food. Supplies gave out, and the distant stations were so reduced that the pioneers had to live almost entirely on the meat of the game, which fell an easy prey, sometimes without the use of a gun. For bread, a single johnnycake would be divided into a dozen parts, and made to last two days. The price of corn was fifty dollars per bushel in December and one hundred and sixty-five in January, in Continental money.

Some idea of the intensity of the cold of that winter may be formed from the facts that Chesapeake Bay was frozen solid from its head to the mouth of the Potomac, and Bayou St. John was bridged with ice as far south as New Orleans.

Prior to 1781, the immigration of males to Kentucky was far in excess of that of females. Many men had built their cabins and laid the foundations of homes and fortunes. They needed the presence of the gentler sex to bring them the full measure of comfort and content. So manifest was this desire to add to the social element, that efforts were made to largely increase the number of women. For two or three years after 1780, large numbers of female colonists came to Kentucky. These women continued to supply the social and domestic wants of the country.

The habits and customs of the pioneers were very simple, free, and independent. They gave a charm to life not often enjoyed in the present day of fashion and form. A log cabin was their lot, and with it they were content. The young husband and wife were helpmates for each other, and lived and loved together, sharing alike their joys and burdens. What did they care if the meal was grated on a board or pounded in a mortar, so long as there was plenty of it? The men cleared the woods, planted the fields and gardens, chopped and hauled the wood, boiled down the sugar and syrup at the maple camps, and did all the rough work; the women cooked, spun and wove, milked the cows, and did the housework with cheerful content. They were free from the worries of the complex changes which came with civilization.

Skins of the deer, the bear, and the buffalo were invaluable. Deerskins were used for the hunting shirt, the leggings and the moccasins. Bear and the buffalo skins furnished both bed and covering for the night. Thongs were cut and ropes were made from hides. Gourds for dipping and drinking water, and larger ones for storing articles, were in common use. The tables and the stools sometimes were made of slabs set on wooden pins. The bed, stuffed with feathers or straw, was often laid on slabs, resting on poles supported by upright pieces at one end, and the other end set in between the logs of the cabin. The baby was not forgotten, but was rocked to sleep in a sugar-trough cradle, if nothing better was at hand. The food was rich milk and butter, the juiciest of beef and pork, and the wild meats of the buffalo, bear, deer, turkey, and smaller game. In addition to flour, cornmeal, and hominy, roasting ears, pumpkins, potatoes, and beans were plentiful. The orchards, now bearing rich fruits, supplemented the nuts of the hickory and walnut trees, the wild grapes and plums, and the luscious pawpaw, the banana of Kentucky. On such fare our forefathers feasted and were happy.

1. In November 1780, Kentucky was divided into three counties. What were the names of these counties?

   a. Hardin, Logan, and Lexington
   b. Hardin, Logan, and Elizabethtown
   c. Maulding, Russellville, and Whippoorwill
   d. Jefferson, Fayette, and Lincoln

2. What was the primary reason that Virginia reopened the land in Kentucky to settlers in 1779?

   a. Settlers had previously fled the land because of the Revolutionary War.
   b. Kentucky had become safe and secure from threat of Native American attack.
   c. Virginia desperately needed settlers to farm the land.
   d. Virginia desperately needed a financial boost.

3. Which of the following **best** describes the winter of 1779–1780?

   a. annoying
   b. expensive
   c. harsh
   d. boring

4. Prior to 1781,

   a. few women lived in Kentucky.
   b. many women lived in Kentucky.
   c. few pioneers were married.
   d. few cabins had been constructed.

5. Between 1780 and 1783,

   a. large numbers of women left Kentucky.
   b. many social events were held.
   c. the number of men in Kentucky increase dramatically.
   d. women flocked to Kentucky.

6. Which of the following statements **best** describes the livelihoods of young pioneer families in Kentucky?

   a. They made the best of what they had and dreamed of better days to come.
   b. They had everything they needed and were utterly content.
   c. They worked from morning until nightfall and dropped into bed exhausted.
   d. They raised large families and hoped that they would always be able to feed them.

7. What might have been on the dinner menu of a pioneer family?

8. How might a pioneer whose wife and family had finally joined him have fared better than one who remained alone?

LEWIS AND CLARK IN COLUMBIA COUNTY, WASHINGTON

Lewis & Clark Trail State Park is located just seven miles from Dayton, Washington. Dayton is known for being part of the "Forgotten Trail." That trail is a portion of Lewis & Clark's Corps of Discovery journey that historians often leave out.

Lewis and Clark camped just two miles outside of Dayton. Visitors can enjoy a marker there now. In the future you will be able to see a metal sculpture reenactment of their camp at that site.

Here are the journal entries from their travels through our county:

> "Neither the plains nor the borders of the rivers possess any timber. . . . "
> —October 12, 1805

> "We then entered an extensive level bottom, with about 50 acres of land, well covered with pine near the creek. . . . "
> —May 2, 1806

Columbia County, Washington, is a land of diverse environments. The Snake River flows through rugged basalt cliffs and arid plains in the north. There are the heavily timbered Blue Mountains and lush fertile Touchet Valley in the south.

Lewis and Clark and their company of explorers found completely different scenes during their two passages through the county because they followed different routes. While traveling west down the Snake River near present Little Goose Dam they encountered dangerous rapids. Their journal entry for October 12, 1805, indicates they camped across the river from present-day Texas Rapids. The evening was coming on. They wanted to pass through the boiling waters in the morning light. Just as today, they found " . . . there is not much driftwood, fuel is very scarce."

The next day the explorers awoke: "The morning was windy and dark; the rain, which began before daylight, continued till near twelve o'clock." Today the terrible rapids are under the waters of Lower Monumental Dam. A small boat launch and public park marks the spot where Lewis wrote, "We found it, as had been reported, very dangerous, about two miles in length and strewed with rocks in every direction, so as to require great dexterity to avoid running against them."

After a harrowing but safe passage through these rapids the explorers passed through a shorter one just east of the mouth of the Tucannon River. Lewis wrote, "This is called Kimooenim creek." Lewis would encounter this creek again on the return trip in May of 1806. The expedition continued down the river in their dugout canoes. They dodged large black rocks and ran more rapids.

Near present-day Lyons Ferry Marina, the explorers wrote the following:

> . . . a little below the mouth of this river [the Palouse River] is a large fishing-establishment, where are the scaffolds and timbers of several houses piled up against each other; and the meadow adjoining contains a number of holes, which seem to have been used as places of deposits for fish for a great length of time.

Today, a visitor can see the modern Lyons Ferry Fish Hatchery across the river from the marina. This area was also the ancestral home of the Palus Indians. On this day the natives were downriver fishing. Lewis & Clark missed them until they arrived at the mouth of the Snake River.

The explorers reached the Pacific Ocean approximately one month after leaving Columbia County. They spent a wet winter at Fort Clatsop.

On their return they hoped to travel all the way back to St. Louis in one season. A shortcut was needed. While at the mouth of the Walla Walla River they were told of a trail that did not follow the Snake River. It cut out nearly eighty miles. They set off cross country. Eventually they struck the Touchet River. On the afternoon of May 2, 1806, they passed through what is now Lewis & Clark Trail State Park on their way east.

They wrote, "We then entered an extensive level bottom, with about 50 acres of land, well covered with pine near the creek, and with the long-leaved pine occasionally on the sides of the hills along its banks." Travelers on Highway 12 just west of Dayton can still see the pines on the hills along the Touchet River as did Lewis & Clark.

The expedition spent the night of May 2nd a few miles southeast of Dayton on the Patit Creek. They noted:

> We killed nothing but a duck, though we saw two deer at a distance, as well as many sand-hill crows [cranes], curlews, and other birds common to the prairies and there is much sign of both beaver and otter along the creeks.

Columbia County is still home to all these animals.

254

The next morning, May 3, 1806, the explorers set out at an early hour. Still following the old Nez Perces trail that Chief Yellpt had told them about, they "crossed the high plains, which we found more fertile and less sandy than below; yet, though the grass is taller, there are very few aromatic shrubs."

After continuing for another twelve miles, they again came to the Tucannon River.

> This creek rises in the southwest [Blue] mountains, and though only twelve yards wide discharges a considerable body of water into Lewis' [Snake] river, a few miles above the narrows. Its bed is pebbled . . . in its narrow bottoms are found some cottonwood, willow and the underbrush which grows equally on the east branch of the Wollawollah [Touchet].

After lunch on the Tucannon River, the expedition climbed out of the valley. They continued northeast into present-day Garfield County. Their return journey through Columbia County took twenty-eight miles. It was done in almost exactly twenty-four hours.

You can visit the places that Lewis and Clark noted in their journals today. To reach the area where the Corps of Western Discovery camped on the night of May 2, 1806, follow US Highway 12 to Dayton. From there, turn on the Patit Creek Road located on the east end of town across from the Green Giant/Seneca cannery. Follow the road southeasterly for almost two miles and watch for the monument. Enjoy your visit to Columbia County!

1. Why were the journal entries for the Lewis and Clark time in Columbia County dated so far apart?

   a. They spent eight months in the county.
   b. They passed through the area both on their way to the Pacific and on their way home.
   c. One of the dates is a mistake.
   d. No one knows why the dates are so far apart.

2. Why do the descriptions of the county contradict each other?

   a. The county is a land of diverse environments.
   b. One entry was made in the fall; the other was made in the spring.
   c. The area had changed over the course of eight months.
   d. One of the entries is mistaken.

3. Why did the expedition cut cross country through Columbia County?

    a. They wanted to avoid the rapids.
    b. They wanted to avoid the Palus Native Americans.
    c. Chief Yellpt had told them of a shortcut.
    d. They wanted to explore new areas.

4. What can be found today in the place where the explorers found a large fishing establishment two hundred years ago?

    a. Little Goose Dam
    b. Lower Monumental Dam
    c. Lyons Ferry Fish Hatchery
    d. Lyons Ferry Marina

5. Write a newspaper article reporting on the event or eastbound visit of Lewis and Clark to Columbia County.

SUTTER'S FORT AND SAWMILL
by John Bidwell

Nearly everybody who came to California made it a point to reach Sutter's Fort. Sutter was one of the most liberal and hospitable of men. Everybody was welcome. One man or a hundred, it was all the same. He had peculiar traits; his necessities compelled him to take all he could buy, and he paid all he could pay; but he failed to keep up with his payments. And so he soon found himself immensely—almost hopelessly—involved in debt. His debt to the Russians amounted at first to something near one hundred thousand dollars. Interest increased apace. He had agreed to pay in wheat, but his crops failed. He struggled in every way, sowing large areas to wheat, increasing his cattle and horses, and trying to build a flouring mill.

He kept his launch running to and from the bay. It carried down hides, tallow, furs, wheat, etc. It returned with lumber sawed by hand in the redwood groves nearest the bay and other supplies. On an average it took a month to make a trip. The fare for each person was five dollars, including board. Sutter started many other new enterprises in order to find relief from his embarrassments; but, in spite of all he could do, these increased. Every year found him, worse and worse off; but it was partly his own fault. He employed men—not because he always needed and could profitably employ them, but because in the kindness of his heart it simply became a habit to employ everybody who wanted employment. As long as he had anything he trusted any one with everything he wanted—responsible or otherwise, acquaintances and strangers alike.

Most of the labor was done by Indians, chiefly wild ones, except a few from the Missions who spoke Spanish. The wild ones learned Spanish so far as they learned anything. That was the language of the country. Everybody had to learn something of it. The number of men employed by Sutter may be stated at from one hundred to five hundred—the latter number at harvest time. Among them were blacksmiths, carpenters, tanners, gunsmiths, vaqueros, farmers, gardeners, weavers (to weave course woolen blankets), hunters, sawyers (to saw lumber by hand, a custom known in England), sheep-herders, trappers, and, later, millwrights and a distiller.

In a word, Sutter started every business and enterprise possible. He tried to maintain a sort of military discipline. Cannon were mounted. They were pointed in every direction through embrasures in the walls and bastions. The soldiers were Indians. Every evening after coming from work they were drilled under a white officer, generally a German. They marched to the music of fife and drum. A sentry was always at the gate. Regular bells called men to and from work.

Sutter's Fort was an important point from the very beginning of the colony. The building of the fort and all subsequent immigration added to its importance. It was the first point of destination to those who came by way of Oregon or direct across the plains. The fort was begun in 1842. It was finished in 1844. There was no town till after the gold discovery in 1848. Then it became the bustling, buzzing center for merchants, traders, miners, etc. Every available room was in demand.

In 1849 Sacramento City was laid off on the river two miles west of the fort. The town grew up there at once into a city. The first town was laid off by Hastings and myself in the month of January, 1846. It was about three or four miles below the mouth of the American River. It was called Sutterville. But first the Mexican war, then the lull which always follows excitement, and then the rush and roar of the gold discovery prevented its building up till it was too late. Attempts were several times made to revive Sutterville, but Sacramento City had become too strong to be removed. Sutter always called his colony and fort "New Helvetia." The name mostly used by others, before the Mexican war, was Sutter's Fort, or Sacramento, and later Sacramento altogether.

Sutter's many enterprises continued to create a growing demand for lumber. Every year, and sometimes more than once, he sent parties into the mountains to explore for an available site to build a sawmill on the Sacramento River or some of its tributaries. From there the lumber could be rafted down to the fort. There was no want of timber or of water power in the mountains, but the canyon features of the streams rendered rafting impracticable. The year after the war (1847) Sutter's needs for lumber were even greater than ever, although his embarrassments had increased and his ability to undertake new enterprises became less and less. Yet, never discouraged, nothing daunted, another hunt must be made for a sawmill site.

James W. Marshall had gone across the plains to Oregon in 1844, and thence came to California the next year. He was a wheelwright by trade, but, being very ingenious, he could turn his hand to almost anything. So he acted as carpenter for Sutter. He also did many other things, among which I may mention making wheels for spinning wool, and looms, reeds, and shuttles for weaving yarn into coarse blankets for the Indians, who did the carding, spinning, weaving, and all other labor. In 1846 Marshall went through the war to its close as a private.

Besides his ingenuity as a mechanic, he had most singular traits. Almost everyone pronounced him half crazy or hare-brained. He was certainly eccentric, and perhaps somewhat flighty. His insanity, however, if he had any, was of a harmless kind; he was neither vicious nor quarrelsome. He had

258

great, almost overweening, confidence in his ability to do anything as a mechanic. I wrote the contract between Sutter and him to build the mill. Sutter was to furnish the means; Marshall was to build and run the mill, and have a share of the lumber for his compensation. His idea was to haul the lumber part way and raft it down the American River to Sacramento, and thence, his part of it, down the Sacramento River and through Suisun and San Pablo bays to San Francisco for a market. Marshall's mind, in some respects at least, must have been unbalanced. It is hard to conceive how any sane man could have been so wide of the mark, or how anyone could have selected such a site for a sawmill under the circumstances. Surely no other man than Marshall ever entertained so wild a scheme as that of rafting sawed lumber down the canyons of the American River. No other man than Sutter would have been so confiding and credulous as to patronize him.

1. Sutter was supposed to pay his debt to the Russians in

    a. dollars.
    b. gold.
    c. wheat.
    d. cattle and horses.

2. Sutter's principal source of income was

    a. passenger fares.
    b. lumber.
    c. sales of hides, furs, and wheat.
    d. wages.

3. Sutter's principal expense was

    a. passenger fares.
    b. wheat.
    c. lumber.
    d. wages and supplies.

4. Sutter's business strategy was to concentrate on

    a. every possible business and enterprise.
    b. gold mining.
    c. farming and ranching
    d. hunting and trapping.

5. Sutter was from Switzerland. The Swiss called Switzerland

    a. Sutter's Fort.
    b. Sacramento.
    c. Sutterville.
    d. Helvetia.

6. Sutter needed more and more lumber to

    a. construct more buildings for his enterprises.
    b. pay off his debts.
    c. build a sawmill.
    d. make wheels.

7. Bidwell was involved in

    a. laying out Sutterville.
    b. drawing up the contract between Sutter and Marshall.
    c. both of the above.
    d. neither of the above.

8. The problem with Marshall's plan was that apparently it was difficult to

    a. haul lumber to the American River.
    b. raft lumber down the American River.
    c. raft lumber down the Sacramento River.
    d. raft lumber through Suisun and San Pueblo Bays.

9. Which of the following sentences drawn from the passage tells readers from what point of view it is written?

    a. Sutter was one of the most liberal and hospitable of men.
    b. I wrote the contract between Sutter and him to build the mill.
    c. Sutter's many enterprises continued to create a growing demand for lumber.
    d. The wild ones learned Spanish so far as they learned anything.

10. Do you think John Bidwell liked working for Sutter? Why or why not?

THE CAMP JACKSON MASSACRE AND THE BATTLE OF LEXINGTON

For the five years before the Civil War, residents of Missouri and its neighbor to the west, Kansas, waged their own civil conflict. It was characterized by unrelenting and unparalleled brutality. Both sides were lined up along the border, ready to fight for race. War is about armies on the battlefield, but this was personal. More than anywhere else in the nation, the conflict raging in Missouri and Kansas was truly a civil war, whose wounds were a long time in healing.

The first formal military action in Missouri took place in 1861. It was less than a month after the Confederate bombardment of South Carolina's Fort Sumter in April. Missouri's fanatically pro-southern governor, Claiborne Fox Jackson, attempted to force secession. He planned to obtain control of the guns and ammunition stored at the U.S. Arsenal in St. Louis. He ordered the State Guard to meet at Camp Jackson, near St. Louis. Then he planned to march on the arsenal. On May 10th, the "Home Guard" of German troops led by hotheaded Captain Nathaniel Lyon of the unconditional-Union faction converged on Camp Jackson, from several directions. Lyon demanded unconditional surrender, which he received.

Lyon's force, numbering seven thousand men, marched its prisoners through the city. Hostile crowds gathered to shout insults and throw rocks. The troops fired several volleys into the crowd. Members of the crowd then drew their own weapons and returned the fire. Twenty-eight crowd members lay dead or wounded. The incident became known as the "Camp Jackson Massacre." Tensions ran high. Angry newspaper articles deplored the "massacre." Songs were even written about it. One of the songs was called "The Invasion of Camp Jackson by the Hessians." For the next month, St. Louis continued to be subject to chaos and sporadic violent outbreaks. The "massacre" was an ominous beginning to official hostilities.

Ulysses S. Grant had resigned his army commission. Reunited with his family, he began to farm on part of his father-in-law's estate south of St. Louis. Colonel Dent had given Julia the farm and four slaves. Grant's farm went under in the depression of 1857. He moved to St. Louis in search of work. Everything he tried turned out badly. Nonetheless, he freed the only slave he had ever owned in 1859. It was at a time when his fortunes were low. The Grants now had two more children, Nellie and Jesse. In desperation he finally agreed to work for his father in Illinois. However, in 1861 he happened to be back in St. Louis. Both U.S. Grant and William Tecumseh Sherman had been citizen spectators of the taking of Camp Jackson.

262

Governor Jackson made the following proclamation on June 12, 1861:

> All our efforts toward conciliation have failed. We can hope nothing from the justice or moderation of the agents of the Federal Government in this State. They are energetically hastening the execution of their bloody and revolutionary schemes for the inauguration of civil war in your midst; for the military occupation of your State by armed bands of lawless invaders; for the overthrow of your State government; and for the subversion of those liberties which that Government has always sought to protect. They intend to exert their whole power to subjugate you. . . . . Rise, then, and drive out ignominiously the invaders who have dared to desecrate the soil which your labors have made fruitful, and which is consecrated by your homes.

By the end of June, the pro-Southern governor and members of the cabinet and legislature had been driven into exile. A provisional pro-Union government had been created to rule the state. The tide turned on August 10, 1861. A Union army was defeated at the bloody Battle of Wilson's Creek near Springfield. This set the stage for a rebel offensive into the heart of the Missouri River valley. In late August, the commander of the pro-Southern state guard forces, Major General Sterling Price, set his seven thousand men in motion. Their objective was the prosperous and strongly pro-Southern Missouri River town of Lexington.

While Price was advancing on Lexington, a body of two thousand seven hundred Federals built fortifications to protect themselves. They were under the command of Colonel James A. Mulligan. They had fortified themselves inside the grounds of the Masonic College. It was on the northern end of town.

By the first day of the battle, September 18th, Price's army had swelled from ten thousand to twelve thousand men. More recruits were pouring in daily from the surrounding countryside. With the strains of "Dixie" in the air, Price's men marched through Lexington. They completely encircled the college. For the next nine hours, the huddled Unionists received a continuous bombardment of shot and shell. Meanwhile, the Southerners seized the house of Oliver Anderson. It was then serving as a Union hospital. Outraged by what he considered a breach of the etiquette of war, Colonel Mulligan ordered the house to be retaken. In a bloody counter-charge, his men stormed the house and took heavy casualties. Soon after, the house changed hands for a third time as the guardsmen drove the Yankees back to their trenches.

On the second day of the battle, the bombardment was continued. The lines around the college were drawn in and tightened. The entrapped blue coats had run out of water by then. They were suffering greatly from thirst and heat.

The siege ended on the third day in a dramatic and unusual way. The Southerners had discovered a quantity of hemp bales in a nearby warehouse.

They arranged these bales in a line on the west side of the Union entrenchments. They then began rolling the bales ever closer to the line of trenches. The panicked Federals unleashed their artillery into the moving breastwork. Their cannonballs had little effect on the dense bales.

By early afternoon, the snakelike line of bales had advanced close enough to the Union trenches for a charge. The defenders of that sector engaged in a brief but bloody hand-to-hand fight. They were driven back into their entrenchments. By now, Mulligan and most of his officers had been wounded. He realized that the time for surrender had come.

The casualty count from the Battle of Lexington was twenty-five killed and seventy-five wounded on Price's side. The Federals had thirty-two killed and one hundred and twenty wounded. Price did experience some immediate gains from the battle. He captured five artillery pieces, three thousand rifles, and seven hundred and fifty horses, all of which were of great help to his under-equipped army. Beyond that, he returned some $900,000 that the Federals had looted from the local bank. He became a hero throughout the South.

The battle, also known as the "Battle of the Hemp Bales," encouraged Southern spirits. It consolidated Confederate control in the Missouri Valley west of Arrow Rock. However, the long-term gains were less significant.

In response to the defeat at Lexington, the Union commander in Missouri, General John C. Fremont, mounted a massive force to drive Price from Missouri. In the face of this threat, Price had little choice but to retreat back to southwest Missouri. Lexington and the Missouri River Valley once again returned to Union control.

1. Armed conflict in Missouri over slavery began about
   a. 1856.
   b. 1861.
   c. 1866.
   d. 1871.

2. Military conflict in Missouri began in _____ 1861.
   a. April
   b. May
   c. June
   d. August

3. The first clash of military forces led to the defeat of the

   a. Home Guard.
   b. German troops.
   c. Hessians.
   d. State Guard.

4. The "Camp Jackson Massacre" took place in

   a. Camp Jackson.
   b. St. Louis.
   c. Springfield.
   d. Lexington.

5. The Battle of Wilson's Creek took place near

   a. Camp Jackson.
   b. St. Louis.
   c. Springfield.
   d. Lexington.

6. The Battle of Wilson's Creek took place in _____ 1861.

   a. April
   b. May
   c. June
   d. August

7. The commander of the pro-Union forces at Camp Jackson was

   a. Ulysses S. Grant.
   b. William T. Sherman.
   c. Nathaniel Lyon.
   d. Claiborne Fox Jackson.

8. The commander of the pro-Union forces at Lexington was

   a. Ulysses S. Grant.
   b. John C. Fremont.
   c. Major General Sterling Price.
   d. Colonel James A. Mulligan.

9. The _____, serving as a _____, changed hands several times.

   a. Anderson house . . . hospital
   b. Anderson house . . . Union fort
   c. Masonic College . . . Union fort
   d. Masonic College . . . hospital

10. The decisive element in the Battle of Lexington was

    a. a breach of etiquette.
    b. use of hemp bales as shields.
    c. the Federal artillery.
    d. hunger.

11. Why do you think Missourians were so divided before and during the first year of the Civil War?

_____

_____

_____

_____

_____

_____

_____

_____

_____

_____

_____

_____

HARRY TRUMAN: YEARS OF GROWTH AND CHANGE (1884–1934)

Harry Truman's life began in the small, country town of Lamar, Missouri. He was born on May 8, 1884. In 1890, his family moved one hundred and twenty miles north. Their new home was the growing community of Independence. The family bought a house at 619 South Crysler Avenue. Harry made friends, attended school, and did chores.

One reason for moving to Independence was that there Harry, his brother, and sister could attend graded schools. In Lamar there was only a one-room schoolhouse. Children of all ages and grades were mixed together.

In class, Harry studied spelling, reading, literature, language, grammar and penmanship. He also studied arithmetic, geography, history, government, drawing, music, health, and physical education. Teachers had a very important impact on young Harry Truman. He later wrote in his memoirs, "I do not remember a bad teacher in all my experiences. They were all different, of course, but they were the salt of the earth. They gave us high ideals and they hardly ever received more than $40 a month for it."

Harry was very close to his family, especially his mother. She taught him how to read and play the piano. Radio and television had not yet been invented. Harry's family sang and played the piano for entertainment. The young boy also loved to read, especially history books. His interests were so widespread that he later joked, "There were about three thousand books in the library downtown. I guess I read them all, including the encyclopedias." Harry's love of reading continued throughout his life.

In 1896, his family moved to a home on the corner of Waldo Street and River Boulevard. Here, Harry and his childhood friends enjoyed sledding in the winter and fishing in the local rivers during the summer. He remembered, "Our house became headquarters for all the boys and girls around. . . . There was a wonderful barn with stalls for horses and cows. We had a corn crib and a hayloft in which all the kids met and cooked up plans for all sorts of adventures. . . . "

Harry also kept busy with chores, and later, a job. To keep warm in the winter, wood had to be hauled in for the fireplace or stoves. Much of the family's food came from backyard gardens. Even in town, many people kept chickens and dairy cows. Of course homes did not have electricity. Some had gaslights, but most relied on candles and oil lamps. At the age of fourteen, Harry began his first paying job. It was at Clinton's drugstore on the town square. He received three dollars a week for working there before school and on the weekend.

Throughout high school Harry was an excellent student. He loved to learn, especially about history. He wanted to go to college, but his family did not have the money to send him. So, following his 1901 graduation, he held a series of jobs in town. He soon moved to Kansas City. He now made a good salary as a bank clerk. In 1906, he left this job. He moved back to Grandview, Missouri, to help on his family's farm. He had never farmed before. It was hard work for someone more used to city life.

In 1906, Harry Truman left his job in Kansas City. He moved back to Grandview, Missouri, to help on his family's farm. He had never farmed before. It was hard work for someone more used to city life.

While living on the farm, Truman continued to stay in contact with his friends and relatives. They were in Independence, where Truman had grown up. By 1910, he was dating Bess Wallace. She lived across the street from his aunt and uncle in Independence. He fell in love with Bess during grade school, but both were in their mid-twenties by the time they started courting. To visit her, Truman would sometimes travel two hours between his family's Grandview farm and Bess's home on Delaware Street in Independence.

During the couple's courtship, World War I broke out. Truman served in the Army. He received basic training in Oklahoma in the fall of 1917. He "shipped out" to Europe in March 1918. By the war's end he had been promoted to the rank of captain of his artillery unit. He was in command of almost two hundred men. Truman experienced all the hardships and terror of war. He wrote later, "As a veteran of the First World War, I have seen death on the battlefield . . . I know the strain, the mud, the misery, the utter weariness of the soldier in the field."

Truman returned home safely in the spring of 1919. He married Bess Wallace in Independence at the Trinity Episcopal Church. The couple lived with Bess's mother and younger brother in the Wallace house at 219 Delaware Street. That fall, Harry and a friend from the Army opened a men's clothing store in downtown Kansas City. Because of economic hard times, the business closed only three years later, in 1922. Although he was $20,000 in debt, Truman refused to declare bankruptcy. He repaid his creditors in full over the course of the next decade.

With the support of family and friends, Truman decided to run for political office in Jackson County. He won the position of eastern county judge in 1922.

He served for a four-year term. He lost the race for re-election. Truman ran again in 1926. He became the presiding judge of Jackson Country. Although no law degree was required for the position, Truman studied law in night school for three years. He did so out of respect for his job and the people he served. Truman worked at the courthouse just a few blocks from his Delaware Street home.

Judge Truman's job was equivalent to that of a county commissioner today. He was responsible for the county finances, its budget, and road building. He was determined to see that the voters had good roads, especially in the farming communities of eastern Jackson County. Feeling that every farm should be within two and a half miles of a paved road, Truman raised $6.5 million in tax money to build them. He also helped finance the renovation of the courthouse in Independence and a new courthouse in Kansas City by 1933. During the Great Depression, Truman administered public works projects. He created a highly recognized six-county regional plan. It became a model for future town planners.

Truman had been elected judge with the support of Thomas Pendergast's Democratic political organization in Kansas City. At times, this political machine fixed primary elections using vote fraud. Then, through bribes and other illegal methods, it often controlled the government officials it had helped to elect. Harry witnessed fellow judges taking money for their vote on certain county jobs. Although he was personally honest, he was frustrated and wondered in a private note to himself, "Am I an administrator . . . ? Or am I just a crook to compromise in order to get the job done? You judge I can't."

Truman knew corrupt practices were going on. At times he looked the other way to accomplish many of his goals, but he never personally profited from his position as judge. Harry wrote, "I'm not a partner of any of them. I'll go out poorer in every way than when I came into office." Truman neither concealed nor renounced his association with Thomas Pendergast, but conducted himself in public office with such personal integrity that he continued to be elected by his Missouri constituents after the political machine had collapsed.

Still, Harry Truman wanted to do even more for the people of Missouri, and not only those from Jackson County. In 1934, he ran for the U.S. Senate. To his delight, he was elected.

1. One reason that Harry Truman's family moved was so he could attend a

   a. one-room schoolhouse in Lamar.
   b. one-room schoolhouse in Independence.
   c. school with separate grades in Independence.
   d. school with separate grades in Lamar.

2. Harry Truman was _____ years old when his family moved.

   a. 4
   b. 6
   c. 8
   d. 10

3. Of the following, which did Harry Truman **not** study?

   a. spelling
   b. reading
   c. arithmetic
   d. science

4. Harry was apparently **not** very interested in

   a. art.
   b. music.
   c. reading.
   d. history.

5. After high school, Harry Truman first worked in

   a. Kansas City.
   b. Lamar.
   c. Independence.
   d. Grandview.

6. Harry Truman worked as a bank clerk in

   a. Kansas City.
   b. Lamar.
   c. Independence.
   d. Grandview.

7. Harry worked in a drugstore in

    a. Kansas City.
    b. Lamar.
    c. Independence.
    d. Grandview.

8. Harry Truman worked on a farm in

    a. Kansas City.
    b. Lamar.
    c. Independence.
    d. Grandview.

9. About how long after Harry Truman fell in love with Bess Wallace did he start dating her?

    a. 5 years
    b. 10 years
    c. 15 years
    d. 25 years

10. About how long after Harry Truman moved to Grandview did he start dating Bess Wallace?

    a. 4 years
    b. 6 years
    c. 10 years
    d. 25 years

11. About how long did Harry Truman work on his family's farm?

    a. 4 years
    b. 6 years
    c. 10 years
    d. 25 years

12. After World War I, Harry Truman became a "haberdasher," meaning that he

    a. got married.
    b. ran a men's clothing store.
    c. declared bankruptcy.
    d. repaid his creditors over time.

13. The same year that Truman's store failed, he

  a. won election as presiding judge of Jackson County.
  b. won election as eastern county judge.
  c. won election to the U.S. Senate.
  d. lost the race for reelection.

14. While serving as Jackson County judge, Truman

  a. completed law school.
  b. continued to run his business.
  c. lived with his mother-in-law.
  d. drove a car to work.

15. While serving as a Jackson County judge, Truman's offices were in

  a. one of the farming communities of eastern Jackson County.
  b. Grandview.
  c. Independence.
  d. Kansas City.

16. Which of the following statements is **true**?

  a. As a judge, Truman's primary responsibilities were public works, finances, and road building.
  b. As a judge, Truman's primary responsibility was fixing primary elections.
  c. As a judge, Truman's primary responsibility was trying civil cases.
  d. As a judge, Truman's primary responsibility was trying criminal cases.

17. What would you do for entertainment in Truman's day?

_____

_____

_____

_____

_____

18. How did Truman justify his association with the Pendergast machine? In your opinion, was Truman right to accept help from a corrupt political organization and look away from illegal practices?

from "SAPULPA"

The life of Sapulpa, for whom the City of Sapulpa was named, reads much like the lives of other active men, whose lives have merited the confidence, honor and respect of their fellowmen. He was born in Alabama. Both his parents were full-blood Creeks. His father was O-M-I-Y-A. His mother's name and the date of his birth are unknown. Both his parents died in Alabama when he was but two or three years old. He and his three sisters were raised by his two uncles. They were brothers of his father. His boyhood and early youth were spent on the hunting grounds of their then Indian country. It extended from Florida to Mississippi.

The encroachment of white settlers into that country brought him into conflict with the governmental authorities and the soldiers. He was, for a time, what may be termed a wild Indian. It seems that the white settlers of those days (very much like some of the white settlers of later days), would not recognize the rights of Indians to any property whatsoever. These settlers proceeded to help themselves to stock belonging to the Indians. The Indians tried to retake such of their stock as they could find. Perhaps they took other stock in place of the stock not found. The white settlers, of course, chose to treat the Indians as cattle thieves and shot some of them. This conduct on the part of the white settlers aroused young Sapulpa to action. That brought the soldiers in pursuit of him; but he was too wily and fleet of foot for the soldier boys. They never caught him.

One incident of his experience with the soldiers that he often told to his children was this: While out hunting with some other men, in Florida, they saw the soldiers with blood hounds [sic]. The pursuit was on. Young Sapulpa ran into a swamp, with the blood hounds and soldiers on his trail. Coming to a creek that ran into a lake, he saw a big alligator in the creek. If he stopped or turned back, the hounds and soldiers would get him, so he made a desperate jump over both the alligator and the creek. But the hounds and soldiers were not so fortunate. When they arrived at the creek, the alligator put up such a hard fight that they gave up the chase. And so the native of the swamps saved the native of the woods from his enemies.

The Creek Native Americans of those days often visited Ste. [sic] Augustine, Florida, where they did most of their trading. Here young Sapulpa did also go quite frequently. He met and made many friends among the white people. His last trip to Ste. Augustine was his last trip from the old hunting grounds; for at Ste. Augustine some of his white friends induced him to go with them to Charleston, South Carolina. The trip was made by boat. Sapulpa was treated to the sights of whales, etc., to be seen in the briny deep. Leaving Charleston, he continued by boat to New Orleans. He then continued on to what later became the eastern part of the Creek Nation in what is now Oklahoma. Thus he became one of its pioneers and one of the leaders of his people.

Soon after his arrival in the new country, he assumed the duties of a husband by marrying NaKitty, a Native American maiden. They moved [to] what is now Creek County. He built his home and commenced farming on Rock Creek. It was about one mile southeast of Sapulpa. Sometime later, in about 1850, he started a store at his home. He sold coffee, sugar, tobacco, dry goods, flour, spices and other articles too numerous to mention. He hauled his goods in by team and pack horses from Fort Smith and the old agency about seven or eight miles northwest of Muskogee. At the end of about two years he gave up merchandising on account of the difficulties of getting in his goods. There were no other stores in the neighborhood. The nearest stores were at the old agency, near Muskogee and at Council Hill.

There may be some old timers who remember when we had no railroads, no automobiles, no trucks, no interurban lines, no bridges over our streams—and no wagon roads fit to travel. I think that the most of you would consider the traffic in merchandise, under such conditions, as unthinkable.

Three children were born of his marriage to NaKitty—James, Hanna, and Sarah. Of these three, James and Sarah are still living. James Sapulpa lives about one mile south of Sapulpa. Sarah is now the wife of Timmie Fife. She lives within the city.

Sapulpa was married again to Cho-pok-sa. She was a sister of his first wife. They had seven children—Moses, Yarna, Samuel, William, Rhoda, Becca, and Nicey. All of these children are now dead, excepting William, who now is a farmer. He lives about two miles west of Sapulpa.

When the Civil War broke out, Sapulpa loaned $1,000 in gold to the Confederate cause. He received a note as evidence thereof, which note is still in existence and held for safe keeping. He joined the Creek Regiment of the Confederate Army. He served for three years and rose to the rank of first lieutenant. He was wounded in the battle of Elk Creek, near what is now Checotah, Oklahoma.

During the years 1871–1873, about two or three hundred Osages used to come down here and camp. They stayed about two weeks at a time and traded with the Creeks, buying corn, sweet potatoes, peas, beans, peanuts, bacon, hogs and so forth. They put up their tepees on the land where the court house now stands and extending in a southeasterly direction about one-half mile.

In 1872, Sapulpa opened another store at his home on the hill southeast of what is now Sapulpa. He bought and hauled his merchandise this time from Coffeyville, Kansas. But about a year later he closed out the business again, because of the difficulties of transportation. However, he had taken a deep interest in farming and stock raising. He now devoted his time, energy and talents to those industries with such success that, in due time, all the land within ten miles of his home was embraced in his ranch. For several years he shipped cattle and hogs to the St. Louis market.

In about 1875, Sapulpa joined the Methodist Church South. He was an active member thereof from then until the time of his death. He donated liberally with cattle, flour, coffee and sugar to feed the people at Camp Meetings, which always lasted several days.

In the early days, big game, consisting of antelopes, panthers, deer, buffalo, elk and bear was plentiful. Sapulpa indulged his passionate fondness for hunting and exercised his great skill in the hunting of such game.

In about 1884 or 1885, the Frisco railroad completed the extension from Tulsa to Sapulpa. Sapulpa was invited by the Frisco officials to ride to Sapulpa on the first passenger train from Tulsa to Sapulpa.

I am pretty reliably informed that there was one store and one blacksmith shop at the end of what is now South Maple Street for several years before the Civil War. Business was kept up there until the war broke out and that during the war all the buildings were burned.

Sapulpa was a member of the Coon Clan. His wives were members of the Fox Clan. He was a member of Osocheetown. In 1868, he was elected by his town as a member of the House of Kings. It was a position of honor and trust. He held it until the date of his death, March 17, 1887.

Sapulpa was fond of the Indian ball. He was considered the best all around ball player on the Arkansas River.

~WILLIAM A. SAPULPA,
Son of Sapulpa.
1926

1. Why do we know the name of Sapulpa's father but not that of his mother?

   a. Native American women had no names.
   b. Sapulpa was raised by his father.
   c. Sapulpa was raised by his father's brothers, who did not know or mention his mother's name.
   d. It was taboo to mention Sapulpa's mother's name.

2. After white settlers shot some Native Americans, Sapulpa was "aroused to action." This probably means that he

   a. stole some cattle and began a garden.
   b. became angry and shot some settlers.
   c. complained to the authorities.
   d. shot some cattle.

3. With whom did Sapulpa travel to Charleston, South Carolina?

   a. alligators
   b. whales
   c. a Native American friend
   d. white friends

4. How did Sapulpa travel to Oklahoma?

   a. via the Trail of Tears
   b. by boat, then over land
   c. by train
   d. on horseback

5. Who lives in the town named after her father?

   a. Sarah
   b. Hanna
   c. Rhoda
   d. Becca

6. Was Sapulpa well off? Give evidence to support your position.

_____

_____

_____

_____

_____

_____

_____

_____

_____

_____

_____

_____

7. What do you suppose would motivate a Native American to fight for the South in the Civil War?

_____

_____

_____

_____

_____

8. Were you surprised to find out who authored this passage? Why or why not?

GEORGE ROGERS CLARK INVADES ILLINOIS

To appear on the Mississippi was to run the risk of betraying the object of the expedition to the defenders of the posts. Hence, the wily commander decided to make the last stages of his advance by an overland route. At the deserted site of Fort Massac, nine miles below the mouth of the Tennessee, the little army left the Ohio. They struck off northwest on a march of one hundred and twenty miles, as the crow flies. They marched across the tangled forests and rich prairies of southern Illinois.

Six days' march brought the invaders to the Kaskaskia River. They were three miles above the principal settlement. Stealing silently along the bank of the stream on the night of the 4th of July, they crossed in boats that they seized at a farmhouse. They arrived at the palisades wholly unobserved. Half of the force was stationed in the form of a cordon, so that no one might escape. The remainder followed Clark through an unguarded gateway into the village.

According to a story still told today, the officials of the post were giving a ball that night. The entire elite—not of Kaskaskia alone but of the neighboring settlements as well—were joyously dancing in one of the larger rooms of the fort. Leaving his men some paces distant, Clark stepped to the entrance of the hall. For some time he leaned unobserved against the doorpost, grimly watching the gaiety. Suddenly, the air was rent by a war-whoop, which brought the dancers to a stop. An Indian brave, lounging in the firelight, had caught a glimpse of the tall, gaunt, buff and blue figure in the doorway and had recognized it. Women shrieked. Men cursed. The musicians left their posts. All was disorder. Advancing, Clark struck a theatrical pose. In a voice of command, he told the merrymakers to go on with their dancing, but to take note that they now danced not as subjects of King George but as Virginians. Finding that they were in no mood for further diversion, he sent them to their homes. All night they shivered with fear, daring not so much as to light a candle lest they should be set upon and murdered in their beds.

This account is wholly unsupported by contemporary testimony. It probably sprang from the imagination of some good frontier storyteller. It contains at least this much truth: that the settlement, after being thrown into a panic, was quickly and easily taken. Curiously enough, the commandant was a Frenchman, Phillipe de Rastel Rocheblave. He had thriftily entered the British service. True to the trust reposed in him, he protested and threatened, but to no avail. The garrison, now much diminished, was helpless. The populace—British, French, and Indian alike—was not disposed to court disaster by offering armed resistance.

280

On the morning after the capture, the oath of fidelity was administered. The American flag was hoisted for the first time within view of the "Father of Waters." Rocheblave dispatched word to General Carleton that he had been compelled to surrender the post to "the self-styled Colonel, Mr. Clark." Rocheblave was sent as a captive to Williamsburg. He soon broke parole and escaped. His slaves were sold for five hundred pounds. The money was distributed among the troops.

A small contingent of troops was sent to the nearby town of Cahokia. It was occupied without resistance.

The rousing of the Indians against the frontiersmen was an odious act. The people of the backcountry were not in the slightest degree responsible for the revolt against British authority in the east. They were non-combatants. No amount of success in sweeping them from their homes could affect the larger outcome. The crowning villainy of this shameful policy was the turning of the Indians loose to prey upon helpless women and children.

The responsibility for this inhumanity must be borne in some degree by the government of George III. "God and nature," wrote the Earl of Suffolk piously, "hath put into our hands the scalping-knife and tomahawk, to torture them into unconditional submission." However, the fault lay chiefly with the British officers at the western posts. Most of all, it lay with Lieutenant-Governor Hamilton at Detroit. Probably no British representative in America was on better terms with the natives. He drank with them, sang war songs with them, and received them with open arms when they came in from the forests with the scalps of white men dangling at their belts. A great council on the banks of the Detroit in June 1778 was duly opened with prayer. Hamilton then harangued the assembled Chippewa, Huron, Mohawk, and Potawatomi on their "duties" in the war. He congratulated them on the increasing numbers of their prisoners and scalps. He then urged them to redouble activity by holding out the prospect of the complete expulsion of white men from the great interior hunting grounds.

Scarcely were the deputations attending this council well on their way homewards when a courier arrived from the Illinois country. He brought startling news. The story was that a band of three hundred rebels led by one George Rogers Clark had fallen upon the Kaskaskia settlements. He had thrown the commandant into irons. He had exacted from the populace an oath of allegiance to the Continental Congress. It was reported, too, that Cahokia had been taken. It was said that, even as the messenger was leaving Kaskaskia, "Gibault, a French priest, had his horse ready saddled to go to Vincennes to receive the submission of the inhabitants in the name of the rebels."

1. Fort Massac was on the _____ River.

    a. Kaskaskia
    b. Tennessee
    c. Ohio
    d. Mississippi

2. Why did the expedition leave the Ohio River at the site of Fort Massac?

    a. There were settlements along the Mississippi that might have reported their presence to the British posts.
    b. They would have had to go up the Mississippi against the current.
    c. They would have had to go down the Mississippi with the current.
    d. The Mississippi was blocked.

3. The overland march lasted until the invaders reached the _____ River.

    a. Kaskaskia
    b. Tennessee
    c. Ohio
    d. Mississippi

4. Half of Clark's forces

    a. encircled the village.
    b. found a corridor into the village.
    c. lined up in front of the village.
    d. filed away in a line away from the village.

5. The writer

    a. doesn't believe the gate was unguarded.
    b. believes the story of Clark's entrance to the ball.
    c. isn't sure whether or not to believe the story of Clark's entrance to the ball.
    d. is pretty that sure the story of Clark's entrance to the ball is not true.

6. According to the story, the first person to recognize Clark was

    a. a tall, gaunt, buff and blue figure.
    b. an Indian brave.
    c. a woman.
    d. a musician.

7. France had become America's ally. The commander of the garrison was a Frenchman who

    a. quickly took the oath of loyalty and switched to the American side.
    b. remained loyal to Britain and a prisoner of the Americans.
    c. remained loyal to Britain, but escaped from the Americans with all his slaves.
    d. remained loyal to Britain, but escaped from the Americans with none of his slaves.

8. The "Father of Waters" refers to

    a. the Kaskaskia River.
    b. the Mississippi River.
    c. Lake Michigan.
    d. the Pacific Ocean.

9. "Odious," as it is used in paragraph 7, means

    a. clever.
    b. spiteful.
    c. bold.
    d. awful, hateful.

10. Why do you think the Native Americans agreed to assist the British?

_____

_____

_____

_____

_____

_____

_____

_____

_____

_____

_____

_____

_____

_____

_____

_____

_____

Made in United States
Orlando, FL
29 May 2024

47342476R00159